# Compensation for Personal Injury in English, German and Italian Law

Cross-border claims for personal injuries are becoming more common. Furthermore, European nationals increasingly join class actions in the USA. These tendencies have created a need to know more about the law of damages in Europe and America.

Despite the growing importance of this subject, there is a dearth of material available to practitioners to assist them in advising their clients as to the heads of damage recoverable in other countries. This book aims to fill that gap by looking at the law in England, Germany and Italy. It sets out the raw data in the wider context of tort law, then provides a closer synthesis, largely concerned with methodological issues, and draws some comparative conclusions.

BASIL MARKESINIS QC, FBA is Professor of Common and Civil Law at University College London and Jamail Regents Chair in Law at the University of Texas at Austin. He is the author or co-author of twenty-five books and over a hundred articles published in major European and US legal journals. He has received high decorations from the Presidents of France, Germany, Greece and Italy for his work on European law and European integration and is Corresponding Member of the Academies of Athens, Belgium, France and the Netherlands.

MICHAEL COESTER has been an Ordinarius Professor of Law at the University of Göttingen (1983–1994) and Munich since 1994. He was Dean of the faculty in Göttingen and has served on the Senate of the University of Munich. He has been Visiting Professor at the University of Michigan, University College London, and University of Nanjing. He has authored four books and over 130 articles published in journals of several countries, and is the co-author of two leading German commentaries on private and private international law.

GUIDO ALPA FBA is Professor of Civil Law at the University of Rome 'La Sapienza' and Professor of Anglo-American Law at the University of Genoa. He has been Vice President of the Italian Bar Council since 2001 and President of the Italian Bar Council since 2004. Professor Alpa has published books on civil law, financial markets contracts and regulation, consumer protection, tort liability and comparative law.

AUGUSTUS ULLSTEIN LL B. Q.C. is a barrister practising in London. He specialises in Personal Injuries and Product Liability cases arising from accidents occurring in England, Europe and the USA. He has given expert evidence in the USA on the English Law of damages in Personal Injury cases.

With a Foreword by the Rt Hon. the Lord Steyn.

# Compensation for Personal Injury in English, German and Italian Law

A Comparative Outline

Basil Markesinis, Michael Coester, Guido Alpa and Augustus Ullstein

CAMBRIDGE UNIVERSITY PRESS

PUBLISHED BY THE PRESS SYNDICATE OF THE UNIVERSITY OF CAMBRIDGE
The Pitt Building, Trumpington Street, Cambridge, United Kingdom

CAMBRIDGE UNIVERSITY PRESS
The Edinburgh Building, Cambridge CB2 2RU, UK
40 West 20th Street, New York, NY 10011-4211, USA
477 Williamstown Road, Port Melbourne, VIC 3207, Australia
Ruiz de Alarcón 13, 28014 Madrid, Spain
Dock House, The Waterfront, Cape Town 8001, South Africa

http://www.cambridge.org

First published 2005

Printed in the United Kingdom at the University Press, Cambridge

*Typeface* Swift 10/13 pt      *System* LATEX $2_\varepsilon$   [TB]

*A catalogue record for this book is available from the British Library*

ISBN 0 521 84613 7 hardback

# Contents

# Foreword

In 1871, when reviewing Addison's recently published *The Law of Torts*, Oliver Wendell Holmes expressed the view that 'Torts is not a proper subject for a law book' ((1871) 5 Am.LR 340). In 1881 Holmes gave the lie to this idea in his famous book *The Common Law* which contained a magisterial chapter on the theory of the law of torts. Today, tort law has a strong claim to have generated more case law and more literature than any other branch of the law.

In an age in which comparative law has come of age the development of our tort law has benefited greatly from comparative methods. It has enabled us to test our law against feasible solutions adopted in foreign legal systems. Due perhaps in large measure to the relative inaccessibility of sources in foreign languages, the comparative exercise has unfortunately in English legal practice largely concentrated on decisions in common law jurisdictions, such as Australia, Canada, New Zealand and South Africa. That our courts need not be so inhibited has been underlined, for example, by three major works, i.e. Prof. Christian von Bar, *The Common European Law of Torts*, vols. 1 and 2 (2000); Prof. Walter van Gerven (van Gerven, Lever and Larouche), *Cases, Materials and Text on National, Supranational and International Tort Law* (2000); Prof. Basil Markesinis and Prof. Hannes Unberath, *The German Law of Torts* (4th edn, 2002). All three are, of course, essential reading for practitioners. The decision of the House of Lords in *Fairchild v. Glenhaven Funeral Services* [2003] 1 AC 32, which concerned the age old tort problem of uncertainty about which employment caused a disease, has demonstrated what can be done, if the complex foreign material is 'packaged' in an attractive manner. The opinion of Lord Bingham of Cornhill (at 58 to 63 and 66) relied strongly on the rich sources of modern civilian practice and doctrine: see also the opinion of Lord Rodger of Earlsferry (at 117 to 118). Practitioners need to take account of the important lesson of *Fairchild* that Continental jurisprudence really matters.

Now there is another great step forward with the publication of this book. The subject of compensation for personal injury is of great practical importance in all civil justice systems. The book compares the solutions adopted in English, German and Italian law. The aim is essentially practical, namely to make available to judges, practitioners and academic lawyers a detailed account of the decisions of foreign courts, packaged to meet the needs of practitioners, in order to enable the comparative point of view to play a dynamic role in the development of our law.

The book has been written by distinguished lawyers who share a profound knowledge of tort law and comparative methodology. Not surprisingly, they have produced a first class book which is a notable contribution to tort law and comparative law studies. It contains much material which those in practice cannot afford to ignore. I commend it unreservedly to judges, practitioners and academic lawyers.

JOHAN STEYN
*House of Lords, June 2004*

# Preface

Biblical texts warn us that no one can serve two gods. Lawyers, no doubt, have occasionally done so; and comparative lawyers must, surely, have a dispensation to do so regularly. For the *raison d'être* of the latter is to describe and compare different systems without fear or favour, largely for the sake of the advantages and the insights that flow from any comparative exercise. We have thus tried to present in a comparative juxtaposition three major legal systems of the world and have addressed our text to two readerships which are often described as being very different – practitioners (including judges) and academics. We have done this for two reasons.

Many have written about the respective tasks of these two kinds of lawyers; and in England those who have done so have stressed how different they are. There is, of course, some truth in these assertions; but in our view these differences have also been exaggerated – at any rate whenever one is trying to make the one group work closely with the other, as we feel they must. For in such circumstances academics must try to present their theories in any way that makes them palatable to practitioners; if they do not, their dish (for which read ideas) will not be savoured.

To the extent that the book describes in *modest* detail what can be claimed in the event of personal (not fatal) injuries in the three systems compared, it tries to serve the first constituency. Two of us – Basil Markesinis and Augustus Ullstein – have encountered this need in our professional careers; and one more – Guido Alpa – also practises as an *avvocato* in Rome and Genoa and knows the needs of the profession.

If the first of our targeted groups needs 'usable' *data*, the second needs *thoughts and ideas* that can promote further reflection. Here the effort had to go into the 'packaging' of the information we assembled for this book in a way that made it look more than just a list of similar and different solutions. Here, two of us – Basil Markesinis and Michael Coester – took more time to achieve this overall result by going over the entire text several times and minimising, whenever possible, the effects of a presentation that was too slanted towards national habits and methods. A few words need to be said about the difficulties the authors encountered in carrying out this enterprise.

Since this book was written in English and primarily addresses an Anglophone readership, inevitably it had to take as its starting point the classification structure known to the common law. If, as we hope, the reader thinks that, overall, the presentation of the English, German and Italian law makes good reading, it means that we have succeeded in our 'packaging' efforts of the other two legal systems. But this was by no means an easy task, as the specialist reader of any of these systems can attest. For the truth of the matter is that the structures, divisions, concepts and notions used in this book, being of common law origin, did not always fit in easily with what exists in Germany and Italy, which is often very different to the English. Even the writing style of lawyers who come from different countries is different and here, again, we have tried to produce a work which will sit well in the library of a common lawyer. But 'different' does not mean less valid, less interesting or less attractive. This, too, is made clear in several parts of the narrative; and tribute is here paid to the two non-common lawyers who co-authored this book and so generously agreed to comply with the demands of English language and practice.

'Packaging', thus *had* to take place for, otherwise, the Continental systems discussed in this book, which have served as models for many countries, would continue to be a mystery to anyone but their own nationals and devotees. In our view, the increasingly transnational nature of personal injuries litigation cannot tolerate such parochialism. Thus, the contribution to the art of 'packaging' forms the first part of the intellectual contribution this book tries to make to the art of comparison; the synthesising conclusions form the other. Broadly speaking, the whole enterprise follows the approach advocated by one of us on many occasions, most recently in his monograph entitled *Comparative Law in the Courtroom and the Classroom: The Story of the Last Thirty Five Years* (Hart Publishing, 2003) (this will soon appear in French, German and Italian translations, an indication perhaps of the interest this method is attracting in these countries) and has tried to avoid the format of a questionnaire which jurists from different systems dutifully fill in. Such works may be useful in one sense; but from a scholarly angle they seem less appealing.

One last word is needed on 'packaging'.

A number of contemporary comparatists have objected to such efforts at 'packaging' foreign law. They say it does not work. They also argue that it 'betrays' the essential features of the foreign system, which must be seen in its wider environment. We see no betrayal whatsoever in an effort which tries to make national wisdom and experience internationally known and appreciated. And we affected no cover-up of the essential features of a particular system, as our readers will see when reading *carefully* what one could loosely describe as the components of the book which contain the information about national law. For from them one can glean additional information about history, the sources of law, the identity of the major protagonists, the abstract or concrete mould of mind of each system compared in this book, the style of judgments, as well as find out how they compensate different headings of damage. Dare we thus say it? This book, like most books which contain personal experiences of many years and not just information, should therefore be read on two levels: the obvious and the concealed.

That despite our efforts, disagreements may still persist about the method is as possible as it is likely that the information provided on each particular issue will not always be found to be as extensive in all three systems under comparison. This, for instance, becomes obvious in chapter 3 as a result of the unwillingness of Italian law to devise different rules for calculating past and future economic losses. Here, then, no amount of 'packaging' could (or should) conceal existing difference. The reader must be left free to decide if the differences are 'apparent' rather than 'real', as well as the more difficult question whether the approach of Italian law could be improved. Once again, the accusation of 'betraying' a foreign system by making it accessible to lawyers of another is, to us, ludicrous.

For us, however, making value judgments of this kind was a matter of lesser import. For, this, essentially, is an essay in comparative methodology which all of us, in our similar and different ways of 'making a living out of the law', are trying to develop in order to practise our profession. If the attempt to innovate has carried with it problems, we were willing to confront them and even risk falling into error since we know that all human action entails the risk of error. For, as the great Goethe (in *Faust*, Part I (1790; Insel edn, 1965), p. 16) put it, *Es irrt der Mensch, solang er strebt.* The alternative – inaction – was not an option.

Basil Markesinis QC, FBA (London and Texas); Guido Alpa, FBA (Rome and Genoa); Michael Coester (Munich); Augustus Ullstein QC (Temple)
*London, Genoa, Munich, 24 December 2003*

# Table of cases

## Common law cases

## German cases

*Decisions of the Federal Constitutional Court*

*Decisions of the Federal Supreme Court*

*Decisions of the Courts of Appeal and Lower Courts*

*Decisions of the Supreme Court of the German Reich*

# Italian cases

# Abbreviations

| | |
|---|---|
| AC | Law Reports, Appeal Cases (Decisions of the House of Lords and the Privy Council from 1891) |
| AcP | Archiv für die civilistische Praxis |
| AfP | Archiv für Privatrecht |
| AJ Comp. L | American Journal of Comparative Law |
| All ER | All England Law Reports |
| ALR | Australian Law Reports |
| AOK | Allgemeine Ortskrankenkasse (National Health Insurance Scheme) |
| App. Cas. | Law Reports, Appeal Cases (1875–90) |
| Arch. resp. civ. | Archivio della responsabilità civile |
| AuR | Arbeit und Recht |
| BayObLG | Bayerisches Oberstes Landesgericht |
| BB | Der Betriebsberater |
| BGB | Bürgerliches Gesetzbuch (German Civil Code) |
| BGBl. | Bundesgesetzblatt (Government Gazette) |
| BGH | Bundesgerichtshof (Germany's Federal (Supreme) Court) |
| BGH GS | Decisions of the Grosser Senat (Plenum of the Court) |
| BGHZ | Entscheidungen des Bundesgerichtshofs in Zivilsachen (Decisions of the German Supreme Court in Civil Matters) |
| BRAO | Bundesrechtsanwaltsordnung (Code of Conduct for German Attorneys) |
| BVerfG | Bundesverfassungsgericht |

| | |
|---|---|
| BVerfGE | Entscheidungen des Bundesverfassungsgerichts (Decisions of the Federal Constitutional Court) |
| BVerfGG | Bundesverfassungsgerichtsgesetz (Statute of the Constitutional Court of Germany) |
| CA | Decisions of the English Court of Appeal |
| Cass. | Cour de cassation |
| CC | Code Civil (French Civil Code) |
| Ch. | Law Reports, Chancery Division (from 1891) |
| CLJ | Cambridge Law Journal |
| CLR | Commonwealth Law Reports |
| Cod. civ roc. | Codice di procedura civile (Code of Civil Procedure) |
| Consiglio di Stato | Council of State (Supreme Administrative Court) |
| Corte di Cass. | Corte di Cassazione (Supreme Court for Civil and Criminal Matters) |
| Corte Cost. | Corte costituzionale (Constitutional Court) |
| Crit. pen. | Critica penale |
| Danno e resp. | Danno e responsabilità |
| DB | Der Betrieb (Law Review) |
| DStR | Deutsches Steuerrecht |
| EGBGB | Einführungsgesetz zum BGB (Introductory Law to the BGB) |
| ELR | European Law Reports |
| EuGRZ | Europäische Grundrechtezeitung |
| EWCA Civ | England and Wales Court of Appeal, Civil Division (online Reports of Judgments of the Court of Appeal) |
| Ex. D | Law Reports, Exchequer Division (1875–80) |
| FamRZ | Zeitschrift für das gesamte Familienrecht |
| FCR | Family Cases Reports |
| FLR | Family Law Reports |
| F. Supp. | Federal Supplement (American Law Reports) |
| F. 2d | Federal Reporter, 2nd series (American Law Reports) |
| Foro it. | Foro italiano |
| GG | Grundgesetz (Constitution of Germany) |
| Giust. civ. | Giustizia civile |
| Giust. civ. massimario | Massimario della giustizia civile |

| | |
|---|---|
| ICLQ | International and Comparative Law Quarterly |
| INAIL | Istituto Nazionale per L'Assicurazione contro gli Infortuni Sul Lavoro |
| IRLR | Irish Law Reports |
| JA | Juristische Arbeitsblätter |
| J Leg. Stud. | Journal of Legal Studies |
| JSB | Judicial Studies Board |
| JSPTL | Journal of the Society of Public Teachers of Law |
| JuS | Juristische Schulung |
| JW | Juristische Wochenschrift (from 1872 to 1939) |
| JZ | Juristenzeitung |
| KB | Law Reports, King's Bench (1901–52) |
| KG | Kammergericht (Court of Appeal of Berlin) |
| Lav. nella giur. | Il lavoro nella giurisprudenza |
| LG | Landegericht (Court of First Instance of General Jurisidiction) |
| Lloyd's Rep. | Lloyd's Law Reports |
| LQR | Law Quarterly Review |
| LR Ch. App. | Law Reports, Chancery Appeal Cases (1865–75) |
| LRCP | Law Reports, Common Pleas Cases (1865–75) |
| LR Ex. | Law Reports, Exchequer Cases (1965–75) |
| LRHL | Law Reports, English and Irish Appeals (1866–75) |
| LRQB | Law Reports, Queen's Bench (1865–75) |
| LT | Law Times Reports (1859–1947) |
| MDR | Monatsschrift für Deutsches Recht |
| Med. LR | Medical Law Reports |
| Med. R | Medizin und Recht |
| MLR | Modern Law Review |
| NJ | Neue Justiz |
| NJW | Neue Juristische Wochenschrift |
| NLJ | New Law Journal |
| Nuova giur. civ. comm. | La nuova giurisprudenza civile commentata |
| ObLG | Oberstes Landesgericht |
| OGH | Oberster Gerichtshof (Austrian Supreme Court) |
| OLG | Oberlandesgericht (German Court of Appeal) |
| OR | Swiss Code of Obligations |
| P | Law Reports, Probate Division (1891–) |

| | |
|---|---|
| PIQR | Personal Injury Quantum Reports |
| ProdHG | Produkthaftungsgesetz (Products Liability Act) |
| QB | Law Reports, Queen's Bench (1891–1900; 1952–) |
| QBD | Law Reports, Queen's Bench Division (1875–90) |
| Resp. civ. prev. | Responsabilità civile e previdenza |
| RG | Reichsgericht |
| RGBl. | Reichsgesetzblatt (Government Gazette) |
| RGSt | Amtliche Sammlung der Entscheidungen des Reichsgerichts in Strafsachen |
| RGZ | Entscheidungen des Reichsgerichts in Zivilsachen (Decisions of the German Imperial Court in Civil Matters) |
| Riv. dir. comm. | Rivista del diritto commerciale e delle obbligazioni |
| S Ct | Supreme Court |
| SLJ | Solictors' Law Journal |
| StGB | Strafgesetzbuch (German Criminal Code) |
| StVG | Strassenverkehrsgesetz (Road Traffic Act) |
| Tul. L Rev. | Tulane Law Review |
| UKHL | United Kingdom House of Lords Reports (online Reports of House of Lords' Decisions) |
| VersR | Versicherungsrecht |
| VVG | Versicherungsvertragsgesetz (Insurance Contracts Act) |
| WLR | Weekly Law Reports |
| WM | Wertpapier-Mitteilungen |
| ZPO | Zivilprozessordnung (Code of Civil Procedure) |
| ZRP | Zeitschrift für Rechtspolitik |

# 1 Introduction

## Preliminary observations

Cross-border claims for personal injuries are becoming more and more common, particularly within the European Union. Furthermore, we know from our personal experience that European nationals and/or residents increasingly join, or seek to join, class actions in the United States of America. This tendency leads to a need to know more about the law in Europe including, of course, English law. Thus, though this book is not about American law, it makes allusions to it where this is likely to be useful to both American lawyers using it and Continental European lawyers aware of the fact that they must constantly guard against the danger of thinking that they understand the law in the USA because they usually know something about English law.

Despite the growing importance of this subject, we believe that there is a dearth of material available to practitioners in any of these jurisdictions to assist them both in advising their clients as to the heads of damage recoverable in other countries and/or the level of damages which they might expect to be awarded. It is the objective of this book to fill that gap in sufficient (but not excessive) detail and we attempt this in chapters 2 to 5. If the transnational trend we alluded to above continues, we intend to flesh out our account further in a future edition.

In this work we have deliberately limited the scope to compensation for personal injury. Fatal accident damages is a very large subject in itself and would, we feel, either overburden a book of the size which we intend or compel contributors to reduce what they say on particular topics to a level which is unlikely to be really useful. Again, however, references to this branch of the law of damages do occasionally appear in our text, especially where this seemed to be required by the narrative.

To make this material more intelligible, and also satisfy our purely academic interest in developing suitable ways to present foreign law to national readers, we have included a fairly long introduction. In it, we have attempted to set our material in the wider context of tort law. We thus address eight, wider, issues in the hope that it will assimilate the foreign learning into the narrative of the text and explain to 'foreign' observers its background. This is especially necessary whenever we encounter 'peculiarities' found in one system alone. These wider issues we approach from the point of view of English, German and Italian law though we stress from the outset that here, and elsewhere in the book, *not all subdivisions and headings are entirely appropriate (or of equal importance) to the three systems under comparison.* A closer synthesis, largely concerned with methodological issues, will be attempted in chapter 6 in the form of comparative conclusions. There we shall, again, pick up on some of the themes found (mainly) in this (but also other chapters) and refer in greater detail to the structural differences which make it impossible to cover in each system, in an equal and precise manner, the various subtopics discussed in this book. This is a point of considerable importance and one which national lawyers must come to terms with early in this study of 'foreign' law.

## The problem of terms, concepts and language

### English law

With regard to damages the common law uses a multitude of terms: general and special, nominal and substantial, contemptuous and aggravated, compensatory and punitive, liquidated and unliquidated, pecuniary and non-pecuniary, past and future. These terms are not always understood in the same way even by common lawyers themselves; and, as we shall see, do not always have exact equivalents in other systems. This second consequence not only makes the comparative exposition of different laws difficult; it can also make the comparison of awards misleading since often one may not be comparing 'apples with apples' but 'apples with oranges'. The common law terms are often side-products of pleading rules and the use of juries in civil law trials (now almost extinct in the English but not the American common law) may have nothing to do with policy decisions taken at the level of substantive law. Two sets of such terms will make our point; and the picture will be further clarified in the account that will follow in chapters 2 to 4.

'Special damage' is thus what the plaintiff must prove as part of his cause of action in torts which are not torts actionable *per se*.[1] This will include quantifiable lost earnings up to the trial, damaged property (e.g., the plaintiff's damaged clothing) and other out-of-pocket expenses. As indicated, this distinction between special damages (as defined above) and general damages, which are the damages which are 'presumed to flow' from the wrong complained of (and include future lost earnings) is important for pleading purposes, but also has consequences for the purposes of calculating interest.

'Aggravated' and 'exemplary' damages form another heading which may cause some concern to civilians. What they have in common is that they represent a way of enhancing the award of the successful plaintiff. They also seem to frequent largely (but not entirely) the same areas of tortious liability such as defamation and false imprisonment. But the similarities end there. For the aggravated award augments the plaintiff's *compensatory*[2] amount by taking into account the aggravated injury caused to the plaintiff's 'feelings of dignity and pride'. On the other hand, exemplary damages require one to look at the tortious incident from the optic of the defendant who is deemed to be particularly opprobrious, thus deserving a form of (civil) punishment. Notwithstanding this attempt to maintain a clear conceptual differentiation between these two notions, the fact that they overlap may, in some specific areas of tort law, make the differences between common law and civil law less pronounced than it appears to be if compared at a purely dogmatic level.

## German law

German law does not draw the line between past and future losses, or between special and general damages, but rather between damages which

---

[1] Contemporary Continental European lawyers – and we shall henceforth refer to them as 'civilians' (and their law as civil law) to contrast them with the common lawyers and the common law – will regard a tort that does not include damage among its essential ingredients (tort actionable *per se*) as a paradox. Nonetheless, it is one which is easily explained once one realises that in the case of these torts (such as trespass to the person, land or libel) the prime aim of the law is to vindicate legal interests and not just compensate harm caused by the defendant. This is an acknowledged function of tort law in Continental legal systems, too (for Germany, e.g., see RG 15 February 1927, RGZ 116, 151, 153; BGH 25 November 1986, BGHZ 99, 133, 136). Needless to add, however, if damage has been caused, damages will follow.

[2] Not surprisingly, therefore, some judges have argued that the increased pain and suffering of the plaintiff should be reflected in his general damages: see *Kralj v. McGrath* [1986] 1 All ER 54, approved in *A.B. v. South West Water Services Ltd* [1993] QB 507.

can be compensated (and 'repaired') once and for all by a single sum of money (*restitutio in integrum*, § 249 II, 251 BGB), and continuing losses or costs of living which will accompany the victim's life for the (foreseeable) future (§§ 842, 843 BGB). If damages of the first category (e.g., the acquisition of a wheel-chair) are not yet compensated at the time of the court decision, they are 'future damages', based on § 249 II BGB. And if continuing needs of the victim (e.g., care) have been met already before the decision is rendered, they are 'past losses', but recoverable under § 843 I BGB (just like the care necessary in the future). It becomes obvious, however, that – as a matter of fact – the bulk of future damages belongs to the realm of §§ 842, 843 BGB.

*Non-pecuniary losses* are commonly referred to as '*Schmerzensgeld*', a not very precise and unofficial short-hand term for what the statute calls 'non-pecuniary damage' (§ 253 BGB). The danger of translating '*Schmerzensgeld*' as pain and suffering must thus be avoided since the German term encompasses additionally such well-known common law headings of damage as 'loss of amenity', 'disfigurement', 'loss of expectation of life' etc. But the notion has also, from early times, been taken to include the 'satisfaction' of the victim for what has been done to him;[3] and the 'deterrent function' of '*Schmerzensgeld*' has also been stressed by the BGH in mass media cases involving the invasion of the privacy of celebrities.[4] In such cases, therefore, the notion comes close to the concept of 'punitive damages'.

The concept of a '*damage per se*' (*danno biologico*) is rarely discussed in Germany, but is, in fact, not totally unknown. According to the Code, a 'damage' is to be assessed by the comparison of the situation *quo ante* and the situation after the injury. Where pecuniary damage is involved, the monetary award that will be made to the plaintiff becomes a simple matter of calculation, the point of reference being either the costs of repair (*restitutio in integrum*, § 249 BGB) or – where repair is not possible or sufficient – the economic loss of the victim (§ 251 BGB). The problem of non-pecuniary damage is, in general, solved by pursuing the ideas of 'fair compensation' and 'satisfaction' (atonement), which provide some guidelines for the pecuniary compensation of non-pecuniary losses (see p. 62). But these concepts fail to produce satisfactory results where, because of a fundamental destruction of the victim's body and personality, fair compensation is

---

[3] BGH 6 July 1955, BGHZ 18, 149, translated in Basil Markesinis and Hannes Unberath, *The German Law of Torts: A Comparative Treatise* (4th edn, Oxford 2002), p. 981 (henceforth referred to as *GLT* followed by the appropriate page number).

[4] BGH 15 November 1994, NJW 1995, 861; OLG Hamm 25 July 1996, NJW 1996, 2870; see also BVerfG 8 March 2000, NJW 2000, 2187; *GLT*, pp. 472–7; cf. p. 22 and p. 64.

not possible and the victim cannot feel any satisfaction. In cases such as these, the BGH has, not without some tergiversations, come to acknowledge that there must be another, specific type of 'damage' which is independent of pecuniary losses or the personal perception of the victim.[5] The severe physical impairment as such is the legitimating and decisive factor for the assessment of damages which is not treated as a conventional and paltry amount but, on the contrary, is treated as a substantial heading of damages.[6] It is, however, still unclear whether this will remain a narrowly construed exception in German law or the first example of an emerging new concept of a 'damage per se'.[7]

Tort law (*Deliktsrecht; Recht der unerlaubten Handlungen*) refers only to the relevant provisions of the BGB (§§ 823–853) which are based on the fault principle (notwithstanding some statutory modifications and exceptions). Apart from the BGB, however, there exist many specialised statutes which also provide for compensation for harm caused irrespective of fault e.g., in cases involving public traffic, nuclear energy, product liability etc. A general term, more appropriate for these types of harm, is '*Haftungsrecht*'.[8]

## Italian law

Italian law does not draw a clear line between past and future losses[9] or between special and general damages. The parallel thus seems to be more with German than English law. Rather, its main distinction is between damages which result from non-performance of obligations (*danno contrattuale*) and damages which result from a tort (*danno extracontrattuale*) – a distinction which, of course, is not unknown in both English and German law.

The measure of damages arising from breach of contract includes the loss sustained by the creditor (*danno emergente*) and lost profits (*lucro cessante*), insofar as they are a direct and immediate consequence of the

---

[5] 'Eine eigenständige Fallgruppe, bei der die Zerstörung der Persönlichkeit durch den Fortfall oder das Vorenthalten der Empfindungsfähigkeit geradezu im Mittelpunkt steht', BGH 13 October 1993, BGHZ 120, 1 = NJW 1993, 781, 783 = *GLT*, pp. 997–9.

[6] In the aforementioned case the amount thus awarded was DM50,000 in the form of a lump sum and a further DM500 per month for the duration of the victim/plaintiff's life.

[7] Christian von Bar, *Gemeineuropäisches Deliktsrecht* II, no. 16–22 argues in favour of the latter alternative.

[8] Adherence to this terminology is breaking down in practice.

[9] We use the term here in the English sense. In Italian law (unlike French law for example) future loss, in the sense of loss of a chance, is not compensated as such. The problems raised by these cases are dealt with as problems of causation. See, e.g., Corte di Cassazione 6 February 1998, no. 1286, Foro it., 1998, I, 1917.

performance or delay (*danno immediato e diretto*) (article 1223 Civil Code, cod. civ.). If the non-performance or delay is not caused by the fraud or malice of the debtor, compensation is limited to damages that could have been foreseen at the time the obligation arose (*danno prevedibile*, article 1225). If damages cannot be proved in an exact manner, they are equitably liquidated by the judge (*liquidazione equitativa del danno*, article 1226). At this level, then, the differences with English and German law are not significant. As this, and the next chapters, will show, however, the differences in the tort area are greater.

In tort cases special rules apply. The basic distinction between patrimonial and non-patrimonial damages, found in the other two legal systems, is also known to Italian law. The way, however, these are treated in practice has varied over the years. This will become increasingly obvious as the presentation of our materials unfolds.

Damage arising from loss of earnings is patrimonial loss and is equitably estimated by the judge according to the circumstances of the case (article 2056 cod. civ.). When a personal injury is of a permanent nature, the liquidation of the injury can, if the judge so decides, be in the form of a life annuity which takes into account the conditions of the parties and the nature of the injury (article 2057). But the injured party can demand specific redress when this is wholly or partially possible (article 2058 sect. 1) and is not excessively burdensome on the defendant (article 2058 sect. 2).[10] Unforeseen damages are also liquidated (*danno imprevedibile*) in the same way. We discuss these rules in greater detail in chapter 4.

Non-patrimonial (i.e., non-pecuniary) damage (*danno morale*) can also be awarded but only in cases provided by *the law* (article 2059 cod. civ.). The italicised words were, for a long time, interpreted narrowly to refer only to criminal law. So, if there was no violation of the criminal law, moral damages were not awarded. This approach did not meet with universal approval; but it survived more or less intact until recent times. Most recently, however, the highest courts of Italy, taking their cue from some judgments of lower courts, decided to liberalise the law. Thus, *in the context of fatal accident action*, they held that the claimants, 'relatives' of the deceased, could claim moral damages for their pain and suffering even in the absence of a crime. The first court to sanction this departure from older orthodoxy was the Supreme Court in a judgment delivered on

---

[10] In specific types of cases (not relevant to the subject matter of this book), special laws may decree that the compensation may take the form of specific redress or restoration. This, e.g., is the case where art. 18 of the Law on Environmental Damage is applicable (Law no. 349 of 8 July 1986).

31 May 2003;[11] and, a few weeks later, it was followed by the Constitutional Court in its own decision of 11 July 2003. The evaluation of the damages, expressly described as non-patrimonial but moral, would henceforth be undertaken on the basis of all the relevant circumstances including the closeness of the family relationship, the cohabitation with the primary victim, the size of the affected family, way of life, the age of the primary victim and the age of the relatives.

In the domain of personal injury (*danno alla persona*) some further comments are necessary to take into account an important innovation that took place in the 1970s.

In Italian law, health is looked at in a comprehensive manner so as to include injury to the body as well as the psychological consequences (*danno psicofisico*) which flow from such injury. This is seen as a subjective right (*diritto soggettivo*) protected by the Constitution (articles 2 and 32 Cost.). Due to a very long, complicated and controversial debate, which mainly took place in the 1970s between academic lawyers and judges, a new concept of damage to the person was created by case law. This is known under the untranslatable heading of *danno alla salute* or *danno biologico* – a notion which refers to any interference with the psycho-physical health of the claimant which is presumed to be actionable if affected adversely. This, then, is a third heading of damages which is awarded besides *danno patrimoniale* and *danno morale*.

*Danno biologico*, as described above (and discussed in greater detail in chapter 2), was originally awarded only to victims of traffic accidents. Subsequently, however, it was extended to victims of accidents at work and then, finally, it was awarded to other types of situations (e.g., damages caused by defective products, tobacco inhalation, etc.).

Apart from the general rules provided by the Civil Code, many special statutory rules govern specific circumstances or relationships. Indicatively one could mention the following: compulsory insurance for civil liability arising from the use of vehicles;[12] work-related accidents and occupational diseases;[13] rail, sea and air transport;[14] circulation of defective

---

[11] Decision no. 8828 has, thus far, only been published on the Internet, 11 July 2003, no. 233. See: www.cortecosttuzionale.it

[12] Law no. 990 of 24 December 1969, art. 18 ff.; Law no. 39 of 26 February 1977, art. 4; Law no. 57 of 5 March 2001; Law no. 273 of 12 December 2002.

[13] Law no. 144 of 17 May 1999; Legislative Decree no. 38 of 23 February 2000; Legislative Decree no. 202 of 19 April 2001.

[14] Warsaw Convention of 12 October 1929, implemented by Law no. 841 of 19 May 1932; Bern Convention of 21 February 1961 implemented by Law no. 806 of 2 March 1963.

products[15]and social security[16] law. There are nowadays also special rules which govern damage from vaccination and terrorist attacks for which no compensation is provided but only a simple indemnity. One feature of (some of) these statutes is that they may provide 'caps' to damages awarded under them. But no such capping of damages awarded under the Civil Code is possible.

## The impact of history: juries, non-juries, academic writers

### English law

The eminent Cambridge legal historian William Maitland encapsulated the theme of this subsection perfectly when he wrote that 'the forms of actions we have buried, but they rule us from their grave'.[17] The medieval writ system thus left the common law still bearing the marks of the nominate torts. The shaping of the early common law by practitioners rather than academics (as is the case with Continental European law) has also meant that English law has avoided wide formulations and generalisations such as those to be found in the modern civil codes. Finally, the adoption of the jury trial in the later Middle Ages also shaped English procedure and evidence and left an important mark on the law of damages.

It is with this last point that we are concerned here; and it is not an insignificant one either. For anything that pertained to damages was within the province of the jury and this meant two things. First, if the judges wished to exercise some kind of control over the case before it left their hands and went to the jury, they had to develop notions and devices that could help them achieve this aim. In the law of occupiers' liability, the distinction between different types of entrants, owed different types of duty, was just such an invention which came about in the late nineteenth century. More important was the subsequent 'invention' of the notion of duty of care which helps demarcate the range of relationships and interests protected by the law and which helped stop cases reaching juries (or full trial) for the better part of the twentieth century.

The second consequence of jury trial was the absence, for a very long time, of any legal rules and principles concerning the law of damages. This led to uncertainty, unpredictability and the lack of a corpus of law defining the principles of the law of damages. Growing realisation of the

---

[15] Presidential Decree no. 224 of 24 May 1988, art. 11.
[16] Law no. 222 of 12 June 1984.
[17] A.H. Chaytor and W.J. Whittaker (eds.), *The Forms of Action at Common Law* (CUP, 1963), p. 2.

need for consistency and comparability in awards thus led the Court of Appeal in *Ward* v. *James*[18] to rule that juries should no longer be used for the assessment of damages save in very exceptional cases.[19] Lord Denning MR, delivering the judgment of the full Court of Appeal, justified this as follows:

recent cases show the desirability of three things. First *accessibility*: In cases of grave injury, where the body is wrecked or the brain destroyed, it is very difficult to assess a fair compensation in money, so difficult that the award must basically be a conventional figure, derived from experience or from awards in comparable cases. Secondly, *uniformity*: There should be some measure of uniformity in awards so that similar decisions are given in similar cases; otherwise there will be great dissatisfaction in the community, and much criticism of the administration of justice. Thirdly, *predictability*: Parties should be able to predict with some measure of accuracy the sum which is likely to be awarded in a particular case, for by this means cases can be settled peaceably and not brought to court, a thing very much to the public good. None of these three is achieved when the damages are left at large to the jury.

It will be noticed that while the first two reasons given for the change are related to what could be called the 'fairness' of the awards, the last is a purely 'administrative' argument, though no less important for that. For it is this consistency which makes it possible to proceed to settlement out of court and thus expedites the administration of justice.

A second change of some importance to the law of damages came with *Jefford* v. *Gee*,[20] where it was held that judges must assess separately damages payable: (a) for accrued pecuniary loss; (b) for non-pecuniary damages; and (c) for damages for loss of future earnings. This threefold division was largely dictated by the passing of the Administration of Justice Act 1969, which made it obligatory for courts to award interest in any case

---

[18] [1966] 1 QB 273 at 299–300.

[19] There is, according to s. 69(1) of the Supreme Court Act 1981, a prima facie right to a jury trial in cases of fraud, malicious prosecution, false imprisonment and, of course, defamation. But s. 69(3) has been seen as strengthening further this presumption against jury trial since it gives a judge the right to deny a jury trial if the case will require a 'prolonged examination of documents or accounts or any scientific . . . investigation which cannot be made with a jury'; see *H* v. *Ministry of Defence* [1991] 2 QB 103. Recent decisions of the Court of Appeal to intervene in jury awards have struck a further blow to the unfettered powers which juries enjoyed in the past. See, in particular, Lord Woolf's judgment in *Thompson* v. *Commissioner of Police of the Metropolis* and *Hsu* v. *Commissioner of Police of the Metropolis* [1998] QB 498, where clear and thorough guidelines where given on the matter of jury instruction.

[20] [1970] 2 QB 130.

in which judgment[21] was given for more than £200, all or part of which consisted of damages in respect of personal injury or the death of a person. *Jefford* v. *Gee* was, therefore, the case that elaborated the principles of the award of interest, and it did so by dividing the heads of damages as above. After some hesitation, these principles were confirmed in *Pickett* v. *British Rail Engineering* Ltd[22] and the position is as follows: (a) special damages (i.e., pre-trial losses) carry interest at half the usual short-term rate; (b) for non-pecuniary damages the interest on damages is at a more modest rate – currently 2 per cent;[23] finally (c) future pecuniary losses carry no interest since they have not materialised at the time of the trial.

The final change was firmly established in *George* v. *Pinnock*,[24] where it was accepted that the parties themselves had a right to know how the judge arrived at his final figure. The older practice, therefore, of allowing an appeal only where the total figure was erroneous, was deemed to be incorrect. Nowadays, therefore, the most common ground for overturning an award is if there is an error in one of its component parts; and this, typically, consists of the trial judge having failed to consider whether there is an overlap between different headings of damages with the result that the plaintiff has been enriched.[25]

## German law

In terms of structure, the draftsmen of the BGB tried to steer a middle course between the casuistic approach of the Roman law (and English common law) on the one hand, and the vague general clauses of the French Civil Code (articles 1382, 1383). Thus, three basic tort provisions of the BGB (§§ 823 I, 823 II, 826) mirrored the status quo of the late nineteenth century, though they remained open to new developments in the future.

---

[21] This power of the court to award interest on a judgment meant that if the defendant paid his debt any time between the commencement of the proceedings and the giving of judgment he escaped having to pay interest at all. Now, however, as a result of s. 15 of and Sch. 1 to the Administration of Justice Act 1982 the courts are given power to award interest on any debt outstanding when the writ is issued.

[22] [1980] AC 136.

[23] *Birkett* v. *Hayes* [1982] 1 WLR 816; *Wright* v. *British Railways Board* [1983] 2 AC 773.

[24] [1973] 1 WLR 118.

[25] Thus, see, *Harris* v. *Harris* [1973] 1 Lloyd's Rep. 445, CA (future loss of earnings and loss of marriage prospects); *Clarke* v. *Rotax Aircraft Equipment Ltd* [1975] 1 WLR 1570 (loss of earning capacity and loss of future earnings). It is doubtful, but probably not finally settled, whether there can be an overlap between pecuniary and non-pecuniary losses. See Lord Scarman's obiter dictum in *Lim Poh Choo* v. *Camden and Islington Area Health Authority* [1980] AC 174 at 192.

Ideologically, tort law represents a more complex amalgam. Thus, while the tort law, which emerged around the turn of the eighteenth and nineteenth centuries, was strongly influenced by the ideas of the age of enlightenment and by liberal principles, the tort law of the German BGB was rather a 'latecomer' and as such already, albeit reluctantly, susceptible to the idea of social justice, the central problem of the twentieth century.

German tort law, as contained in the BGB, is based on the liberal fault principle, but also incorporates some concessions to the anti-fault school by introducing a number of cases where fault is presumed e.g., injuries caused by employees (§ 831 BGB), or children (§ 832 BGB) or even exceptions such as no-fault liability for damages caused by pets (§ 833 S. 1 BGB). Needless to say, however, the social and economic convulsions of the twentieth century led to further inroads into the hitherto dominant idea of (economic) freedom. The principle of '*casum sentit dominus*' was more and more pushed back by the social component of justice, which called for protection of the individual and for more extensive compensation wherever a loss had fallen upon a person. This tendency was backed by the Constitution of 1949 which declared the '*Sozialstaat*' as one of the fundamental characteristics of the then newly established Federal Republic. Thus, while German tort law is still basically rooted in the BGB, its legal and economic significance has changed substantially by, e.g., the widespread existence of private insurances, taken out by the potential victims or tortfeasors (including legal litigation insurances, see p. 31); by a comprehensive net of social security (see p. 35) or other mechanisms of immediate social help for injured persons (combined with the right of recourse against the tortfeasor); and by the emergence of the substantial body of statutory regulation outside of the BGB which – for specific areas – tends to push the fault principle further back and in many instances establishes strict liability.

The administration of tort law in Germany has always been in the hands of professional judges. There is no jury in civil cases. This has consequences for the amount of damages awarded to victims (see p. 17).

*Italian law*

Shadows of the past

Like the other two systems studied in this book, Italian law bears the marks (or scars) of the country's past. Three observations in particular need to be made at this stage; others will emerge as the exposition of the detailed rules unfolds.

First is the impact of Roman law. At the beginning this was, of course, understandable. In the country where Roman law was born, its claim on the present was obvious. The continued 'relevance' of the subject still remains a discussed and disputed issue, some lawyers championing its study merely for its historical interest while others argue that despite (or, perhaps, because of) its Ovidian metamorphoses, the ancient learning still has practical significance. Happily, we do not have to enter into this debate for the purposes of this book. For, at least as far as the law of damages is concerned, the link with the Roman past has long been attenuated almost to vanishing point.

The grip Roman law retained over the subject during the middle and latter part of the nineteenth century later gave way to German ideas which acquired new prominence with the enactment of the BGB. Soon, however, they, too, began to be overtaken by indigenous speculation, largely prompted by dissatisfaction with award practices which often distinguished levels of compensation on the basis of outmoded societal views. The work of Gioja[26] brought to the subject an approach that made great use of statistics and was thus too novel for his times. When notice finally

---

[26] Melchiorre Gioja's main work was *Dell'ingiuria dei danni del soddisfacimento e relative basi di stima avanti i Tribunali civili* (1821). In it he stressed that the assessment of damage to the *person* must have regard for the two 'substances' which constitute the person, i.e., his body and his mind. He thus argued that the sufferings of the mind also affect the body. The emphasis of compensation law must be on satisfaction for both affected elements; and it must be achieved not so much by focusing on the income of the injurer but on the situation of the victim. Gioja's ideas led him to criticise Justinianic law and re-evaluate medieval law which paid more attention to injured feelings resulting from physical injuries. But Gioja also had another aim. He was concerned to remove the danger of abuse of assessment of damages by having recourse to the science of statistics. The chosen criteria taken into account were thus the *age* of the victim, his life expectancy and, above all, his *working conditions*. For, whoever injures a working person prevents him or her from utilising his or her powers. The shoemaker, who makes shoes and who has been injured in the hand, must be awarded damages related to the income he would have produced if he had remained unhurt; the surgeon, rendered unfit for his profession, must be awarded damages related to the earnings he would have made from his activity. These premises enable us to elaborate an actual taxonomy of injuries. Gioja thus compiled very sophisticated tables reflecting his criteria. But, in addition to these damages, Gioja also considered it necessary to take into account some very intangible assets such as the deformation of beauty, something which he thought could have particular impact on a woman's (plaintiff's) life. For all persons who have an income greater than daily wages he thought one should also have regard to the negative effect of the injury on their social life. Additionally, the individual limbs of the body were classified and assessed on the basis of a particular 'price', which took into account their use in one's physical, working and social life. To all this, Gioja added the injury to one's feelings, which is not limited to pain, but includes the consideration of the victim in the society of his peers, including also his commercial standing.

came, it took a very Italian form; and this is the second feature of Italian law which needs to be stressed.

The close interrelationship of academic writings and judicial work is not a feature of Italian law alone. This symbiosis is a feature of the civilian tradition and contrasts deeply with the common law – especially English common law – practice of the first half of the twentieth century. But in Italy, and because of the country's rules of civil procedure,[27] the judicial acknowledgement of this academic inspiration and its subsequent embroidery by the courts is not obvious from the texts of their judgments. Thus, as will be noted in the next chapter, the judicial tergiversations – in particular over the way one should compensate non-pecuniary losses – closely follow these academic debates. The fact that this theorising will receive little attention in this book is dictated by the aims set out in its Preface. Yet it is clear that the really interested reader must, at some stage in his research, be able and willing to study this material if he is to understand better the judicial pronouncements on this subject. This adds a further layer of difficulty in the presentation of Italian law which almost makes it impenetrable to the outside observer – certainly the practitioner.

For present purposes, the last peculiarity of the Italian legal system which needs to be stressed, particularly for the English reader, is the system's geographical fragmentation and complexity. By this we mean to stress regional variations, both in the size of awards and, at times, the proclaimed way of calculating them. The extent to which these judicial variations can be linked to 'local' loyalties (e.g., legal theory developed by the local law school) adds further 'spice' to this complex mixture. But 'allegiances' (and the reciprocal obligations they generate) are a notable feature of Italian life as a whole. Here, we mention this feature only in order to stress that it is also found in the life of the law.

Italy's political fragmentation in the Middle Ages and, later, in the Renaissance and post-Renaissance years (lasting until its political unification during the middle of the nineteenth century) is, of course, well-known. Once again, one is bound to enquire if this picture is really *that* different from the picture one encounters in post-1871 Germany (or, even, the

---

[27] Article 118.3 of the Rules Concerning the Application of the Code of Civil Procedure (enacted along with the Civil Code in 1942) expressly states that: 'in ogni caso deve essere omessa ogni citazione di autori giuridici' ['in any case all citation of legal authors must be omitted']. The reasons are not that different to those once utilised in England to prohibit citing to English courts the works of living authors. But the citation of foreign judgments is not caught by the prohibition and is beginning to take hold though, admittedly, in a 'supporting' manner.

present United Kingdom). And yet, one is tempted to say that in Italy's case the difference may be quantitatively and qualitatively very pronounced indeed. For one is not only talking of substantive differences in *per capita* income – much higher in the North than in the South – but also differences of mentality, social structures and notions about family unity and mutual obligations – all of which have a bearing even on a mundane and technical subject such as the law of damages. To put it differently, the regional variations in awards can be pronounced, something which has led practitioners often to indulge in a sophisticated game of (internal) forum shopping.[28] If practising lawyers (and their clients) can gain (and have gained) from such ingenuity, academics end up paying a substantial price, at any rate whenever they are called upon to give to foreign lawyers a simple presentation of Italian law.

## Codal structures

In terms of structure the draftsmen of the *Codice civile* of 1942 had to make a considered choice between the Code of 1865 (of the then recently unified Italy), which was inspired by the French model (*Code Napoléon*) and the newer German Code (BGB) of 1900. (A third choice, never fully explored by the Italians, was of trying to adjust the French model to the German one and produce a synthesis of their own.) In the end, the decision was taken to build tort law around a general rule, a sort of 'general clause' (article 2043 cod. civ.) which states that any malicious, intentional or negligent act which causes an injury to another 'contrary to law'[29] obliges the tortfeasor to make amends.

As in the case of the French and German models, the fault principle governs the model. Nonetheless, presumptions of fault were introduced concerning the liability of parents, guardians, teachers, masters and employers, dangerous activities, things and animals in custody, collapsing buildings and the circulation of vehicles.

As to what was protected, the codal provision was vague and generous; and in practice it experienced a gradual expansion. Thus, during the first

---

[28] Cases concerning torts are, at the plaintiff's choice, heard by the judge of the place where the tort was committed (art. 20 Civil Procedure Code, cod. proc. civ.) or the place of the defendant's residual abode (the home for natural persons: art. 18 cod. proc. civ., or the place of the headquarters, for legal persons: art. 19 cod. proc. civ.). In car accident cases, plaintiffs usually decide between the two depending upon which court is likely to award higher damages in accordance with the tables concerning personal injuries applicable to their location.

[29] This requirement, a legacy of the Roman *iniuria*, brings Italian law closer to German than to the French.

decades of the Code's life, the notion of *danno ingiusto* (in the key provision of the Code: article 2043) was understood to refer only to interferences with absolute subjective rights such as property, bodily health and personality (surnames, pseudonym, image and, later in the 1960s, privacy). Since the 1970s, however, and thanks to a revolutionary decision of the Supreme Court,[30] even interference with contractual relations has been included within the protective scope of this provision, in marked contrast to the common law and German law which may afford such protection only when additional elements are satisfied. Since 1999, following a seminal decision of the Supreme Court,[31] damages arising from an illegal act of the administration have also been included within the protective ambit of this provision thus leading to a damage award. The general rules of the Civil Code have given rise to an enormous volume of decisions by Italian courts so that one can truthfully claim that contemporary Italian tort law is almost in its entirety case law.

Since the 1960s, the interpretation of the codified rules has been done against the background of the Republican Constitution. This gave birth to an entirely new framework of values (solidarity, equality and fairness) which, in turn, provided new and intriguing foundations for private law as part of the process which has elsewhere[32] been described by one of us as the 'constitutionalisation of private law'. This new framework offers the legal basis for some new policies for tort law concerning, for instance, the rational distribution of wealth, the protection of the individual, the balancing of conflicting interests, etc. Economic analyses of the law of torts and references to the wider constitutional order have thus become the main motors towards the introduction of strict liability in many instances. Employers' liability (article 2049 cod. civ.) and products liability[33] are notable examples.

## Legal machinery

In Italy as, indeed, in Germany, tort law has always been in the hands of professional judges and juries are not recognised.

Since 1995 small claims judges (so-called 'giudici di pace', who are lay judges and not employees of the state) are competent up to €2,500, and

---

[30] Corte di Cassazione 26 January 1971, decision no. 174, Foro it., 1971, I, 342.
[31] Corte di Cassazione 22 July 1999, decision no. 500, Foro it., 1999, I, 2487.
[32] Shimizu Trust, 'Comparative Law: A Subject in Search of an Audience' (1990) 53 MLR.
[33] Decree of the President of Republic no. 224 of 24 May 1988, enacting EEC Directive 85/374, art. 1.

in car accidents cases up to €15,000.[34] All other tort cases are submitted to courts dealing with civil matters, namely, the Court of First Instance (Tribunale), the Court of Appeal (Corte d'Appello) and the Corte Suprema di Cassazione – the Italian Supreme Court.

According to the figures of the Department of Justice (Ministero della Giustizia) there are, in Italy, 848 locations of giudici di pace, 164 locations of Tribunali, 26 Corti d'Appello and one Corte di Cassazione in Rome.

The total number of cases heard by these courts is very high. According to the last Report of the Department of Justice covering the period 1 July 2001 to 30 June 2002, giudici di pace heard 726,845 civil cases. The Tribunali heard 1,072,719 cases and the Corti d'Appello 7,899 cases. During this same period the Corte di Cassazione had to deal with circa 15,000 appeals.

The average length of civil proceedings (from initiating the relevant proceedings to decision) during this same period has been: 325 days for the giudici di pace; 963 days for the Tribunali; 727 days for the Corti di Appello; and almost two years for the Cassazione. So, theoretically, the amount of time needed from the issuing of the writ to the final decision of the Supreme Court could be something in the region of 2,320 days or over seven years – a record which has not escaped the censure of the European Court of Human Rights in Strasbourg.

## Levels of award: a first glance

*English law*

The level of awards is set, in practice, by guidelines issued from time to time by the Court of Appeal.[35] Judges, and the Court of Appeal, set what they regard as the appropriate bracket for each category of case. The highest possible award for quadriplegia or very severe brain damage is £205,000. Hence that figure sets the benchmark for all other awards in the various brackets below it.

Guidelines for the assessment of general damages have also been issued by the Judicial Studies Board, such guidelines being updated approximately every two years. Although cases may differ on their individual facts, judges will not go outside conventional brackets. In 1999, a Report of the Law Commission had recommended that general damages be increased by a factor between 1.5 and 2. The Court of Appeal in *Heil* v. *Rankin* declined to follow that recommendation and increased awards of £150,000 by 33 per cent, those of £110,000 by 25 per cent, those of £80,000

---

[34] Art. 7 cod. proc. civ.    [35] For example, what was said in *Heil* v. *Rankin* [2001] QB 272.

by 20 per cent and those of £40,000 by 10 per cent. The decision demonstrates the caution which has always been adopted by English judges in setting levels of general damages. In consequence, awards are very much lower than those in the United States of America where a jury, not a judge, sets the damages.

In common with Germany, awards in defamation cases (where the damages are set by the jury) have traditionally been much higher. Although juries do not give reasons for their decisions and no one is permitted to enquire into what happened in the privacy of the jury room, there is a widely held belief that the jury's intention is to punish the defendant. It has led the Court of Appeal again to issue guidelines for appropriate awards in defamation cases.

*German law*

The level of awards is influenced by the fact that there is no jury in civil proceedings in Germany. The amount of compensation is assessed by the judge who – with regard to mentality and personal income – could be compared with higher ranking civil servants. Thus, middle class values and economic perceptions determine the assessment of damages.[36] Attempts at the arbitrary redistribution of wealth, as one finds (or is said to find) in American jury awards, are totally unknown in German law and, indeed, the law of tort of Continental Europe.

Traditionally, German judges showed themselves very cautious in awarding damages, though the current tendency points to somewhat more generous awards. In the case of extremely severe injuries, the courts have awarded under the heading of '*Schmerzensgeld*' (non-pecuniary damages) up to €250,000 *along with* periodical payments of €1,000 per month or more.[37] Such amounts, though smaller (or much smaller) than awards

---

[36] As to the social background and mentality of German judges see Heldrich and Schmidtchen, *Gerechtigkeit als Beruf* (1982); Raiser, *Rechtssoziologie* (1987), p. 151.

[37] In one case, a three-year-old boy was hurt in the face by an exploding bottle of lemonade and became blind. The Court of Appeal of Frankfurt (OLG Frankfurt 21 February 1996, VersR 1996, 1509, 1510) awarded DM500,000 (c. €250,000) plus a monthly pension of DM500 (c. €250). In a decision delivered in 1993, the Court of Appeal of Düsseldorf (OLG Düsseldorf 10 February 1992, NJW-RR 1993, 156, 158) had to deal with the case of a thirty-three-year-old man who was hurt so badly in a car accident that he suffered tetraplegia; the court granted him DM450,000 (c. €225,000) and a monthly pension of DM750 (c. €375), which added up to c. DM600,000 (c. €300,000) when the annuity was capitalised. In a case of paraplegia, the Court of Appeal of Frankfurt (OLG Frankfurt 21 March 1990, NJW-RR 1990, 990) awarded DM200,000 (c. €100,000) plus a monthly pension of DM400 (c. €200). For cranio-cerebral injury resulting in an increased fluid

for pain and suffering made in the USA can, in fact, be larger than the above figures may suggest once one has taken into account the *additional* monthly amounts, especially where the victim has a long life ahead of him or her.

An interesting feature of the German compensation practice is the substantial gap between the level of awards for physical injuries on the one hand and compensation for infringements of personal rights on the other (for a drastic contrast compare OLG Hamburg NJW 1996, 2870 (awarding DM180,000 or €95,000 for a fictitious interview with Caroline of Monaco) and AG Radolfzell NJW 1996, 2874 (awarding DM5,000 or €2,600 for the rape of a woman)). This practice has been attacked with reference to the principle of equality (article 3 I Grundgesetz) but, thus far, the attack has not led to an upward adjustment of awards for non-pecuniary types of harm.[38]

The comparison of awards is facilitated by extensive private compilations of court awards in Germany.[39]

*Italian law*

In Italian law the assessment of the amount of compensation is done by the judge, usually on the basis of the findings of the technical report produced during the trial by a medical expert appointed by the court (subject to the right of the expert witnesses of the parties to contradict his findings). The liquidated amount is assessed according to 'equity evaluations'.[40] We can distinguish different kinds of methods.

'*Danno patrimoniale*' is calculated by taking account of expenses and the loss of earnings.

'*Danno morale*' – pain and suffering in the meaning explained above – is left to the 'wise'[41] discretion of the judge. In practice it does not reach half the amount awarded for '*danno biologico*'. Currently, there is some pressure

---

pressure in the head and partial tetraspasticity, the Court of Appeal of Nürnberg (OLG Nürnberg 21 June 1991, DAR 1994, 158) granted an indemnification of DM260,000 (c. €130,000). For more examples see Deutsch and Ahrens, *Deliktsrecht* (4th edn, 2002), pp. 230–1, as well as chapters 2 and 3.

[38] BVerfG 8 March 2000, NJW 2000, 2187; see p. 64.

[39] '*Schmerzensgeldtabellen*'; see, e.g., Beck's *Schmerzensgeldtabelle* (4th edn, 2001); Hacks, Ring and Böhm, *Schmerzensgeldbeträge* (17th edn, 1995); see *GLT*, pp. 919–20.

[40] The idea of 'equitable evaluation of damages' appears very frequently in Italian legal literature and it really means judicial discretion. The flexibility (and vagueness) of the notion must be noted; but it cannot be avoided.

[41] Another of those Italian expressions frequently encountered in this part of the law. The reader must note, however, how practice seems to have developed guidelines within which this 'wise' judgment is exercised.

to apply tables which will give the same result for all cases, according to the circumstances.

The most difficult problem is related to the calculation of '*danno biologico*'. Every (local) court has in its possession tables drafted with the help of statistics. In the Appendix, the reader can see the regional variations of awards for '*danno biologico*' in cases of permanent invalidity. The extent of (permanent) invalidity can, of course, vary; and it is measured by a points system fixed by the medical profession: 1 being the lowest; 100 being total i.e., permanent disability.

The amounts given per point of invalidity vary according to standard parameters (e.g., the age, sex, health, etc. of the victim). In the past, and to some degree even at present, these amounts are (to some extent) affected by fortuitous causes such as the judge's leanings, regional differences, and the like.

From a comparative point of view, what may be most interesting to stress are the regional differentiations that have resulted from this practice. Thus, a five-year-old child, for each 'point' of permanent disability, may obtain €550 from the Tribunal in Milan, €550 from the Tribunal in Rome, and €1,200 from the Tribunal in Genoa; a thirty-five-year-old adult, respectively €650, €400 and €900; an elderly person aged sixty-five, respectively €500, €250 and €450.

For ten 'points' of disability, a five-year-old child, again in the same Tribunals, may obtain respectively €15,000, €15,000, and €30,000; a thirty-five-year-old adult, respectively, €12,000, €10,000 and €23,000; an elderly person aged sixty-five, respectively €10,000, €6,500 and €11,000.

For 100 'points' of disability i.e., for total disability, the minor may obtain respectively €500,000, €650,000 and €300,000; the adult respectively €450,000, €420,000 and €230,000; the elderly person aged sixty-five respectively €370,000, €270,000 and €110,000.

As the text above shows, the value attributed to each point has varied from one regional court to another. Such variations have not been to everyone's liking – hence article 5 of Law no. 57 of 5 March 2001 fixed a uniform price for 'each point' of permanent disability. This was set at €600. This figure can be adjusted in order to take into account the rate of inflation and the cost of living and, indeed, the Ministry of Industry (Ministero delle Attività Produttive) raised this by decree on 22 July 2003 to €650. Uniform tables thus now exist for permanent disability *up to 9 points*. For higher forms of permanent disability, the value of each point remains to be fixed in a uniform i.e., nationwide manner. Until this is done, regional variations remain the rule.

## Basic principles of tort law, especially to the extent that they affect compensation practice

*English law*

From the point of view of a civilian lawyer, the notion of the common law of tort which will attract the most interest and cause the most concern is that of duty of care. As already stated, common lawyers use this notion to demarcate the range of relationships and interests which are protected by the law, whereas other systems have left this decision to the legislator who, once he has taken it, shapes court decisions of subsequent courts. The German and English attitude towards compensation for pure economic loss through tort rules is a good illustration. For both systems have, broadly speaking, taken the same stand (unlike, for instance, French, Italian, Dutch law) and have expressed this 'dislike'; the first by excluding pure economic loss (*reiner Vermögenschaden*) from the list of protected interests of § 823 I BGB and the second through the utilisation of the notion of duty of care. The policy arguments for such decisions can be found in either the preparatory works of the Code or, in the case of the common law, in its court decisions.

There exist, however, other areas of the law where the award of damages seems dubious but where the systems have handled the issue differently. Compensation for psychiatric injury (in the USA invariably referred to as emotional distress) is such an example. For the common lawyers, alternating between exclusionary and more liberal rules, the ambivalence is largely caused by the fear of unending litigation, vexatious or frivolous claims and exaggerated awards. Though these are not insubstantial worries, it can be argued that they seem larger in the common law systems, especially the USA, where trial by jury is still allowed (or has still left its mark). For judges are unlikely – or so the argument typically runs – to be swayed by emotional considerations and enlarge awards in an irrational manner, nor be bamboozled by the exaggerated presentation of medical evidence as it occurs in an adversarial system of justice. These concerns, as well as the need to keep litigation within reasonable bounds, saving public and private money, have made an Anglo-American court reluctant to make an award to such claimants. In Germany (and France and Italy) on the other hand, these fears seem to have been checked by the structural differences found in the trial systems of these countries with the result that not only do we find such headings of damage widely compensated but also find them compensated by relatively small amounts. Still, as we shall see, the essential difference between psychiatric harm which amounts to a recognisable medical illness and pure pain or grief is known to all three systems under comparison.

The same fears, but in a different area of civil liability, can also be found in English (and American) law. This is the troublesome area of state and local authority liability over a wide range of issues including potential liability for the police, prosecution services, school authorities and other social services bodies whose activities are primarily governed by a written regulatory regime. The no-duty option has, it is submitted, again prevailed widely in the common law systems; and this has largely been so because common law judges have seen themselves as protectors of the *fiscus*. The more liberal regimes found in Germany and France may, in part again, be explicable by the fact that awards made in these systems for violation of the rules of civil liability are relatively modest. Though these types of claims are not within the purview of this book the idea herewith sketched is one which the reader must constantly bear in mind. For the central theme behind it is that in the common law, what often happens at the liability stage of the enquiry is, in reality, determined by issues pertaining to damages and procedure.

The last general point worth raising at this stage is the common law's willingness to use the notions of damage and causation to limit liability and hence the possibility of awards. The bulk of these instances do not, once again, concern issues of personal injury and thus do not fall to be discussed in this book. Yet they do provide interesting insights into the methodological need to look at foreign systems and the solutions they provide to given factual situations from the angle of history, procedure and wider societal policy concerns.

For we can see how judges could lay down rules about what kind of damage was suitable, and the rules they laid down in fact differed according to the type of behaviour in question. Just as the most objectionable forms of behaviour (according to the early way of thinking, at any rate) were made actionable *per se*, we find that the less objectionable the behaviour, the stricter is the definition of the requisite damage. And for the least objectionable forms of damaging behaviour, such as the right to start legal proceedings and the right to speak, this strictness was extended from the definition of that damage to the prescription of the causal link between the behaviour and the damage. Thus, in an action for abuse of legal procedure the plaintiff fails unless *he* shows that because of the defendant's conduct he has suffered damage in the form of risk of imprisonment, risk to property, actual financial damage or inevitable loss of reputation. Other types of 'injury', like anxiety or a tarnished reputation, will not suffice. Similarly, in all cases of slander (save the four exceptional categories which are actionable *per se*), the plaintiff has to show that he suffered special damage in the sense of damage which is capable of pecuniary estimation. Indeed, the cases suggest that a tight causal link will also be required, for it will not suffice to establish that the normal consequence of the words complained of was to make others think worse of the plaintiff. It will also have to be shown that the words complained of *directly* led others to deny the plaintiff some economic benefit. Finally, in negligence the plaintiff must prove damage. Where the harm is physical injury to person or property, the courts' main preoccupation has been with issues of duty and remoteness; and where the plaintiff's hurt has occurred invisibly in the form of shock or pure financial loss, they have encountered the greatest difficulties. Yet, a few cases apart, the courts have refused to deal with these problems under the rubric of 'damage' and have tried to use the concepts of duty and remoteness with which they are familiar. This brings us back to our opening remarks about the tendency of common law judges to use remoteness or duty terminology where they are really expressing doubts as to the compensability of a particular type of damage.

## German law

When we move to German law we note that the problems discussed under this subheading become problems of 'structure' or arrangement of the kind which one has to consider in systems operating under written civil codes but do not arise in the common law systems. Thus, the principles of compensation for injuries are not peculiar to tort law but are laid down in the general provisions of the second book of the BGB, the 'law of obligations' (§§ 249–255 BGB). They thus apply to contractual as well as tortious liability. Indeed, only few provisions of tort law (§§ 842–845 BGB) spell out or modify these principles. A very practical consequence of this first point is that the researcher must be prepared to find the relevant material not merely in tort books but also in treatises of the entire law of obligations.

The starting principle is 'Naturalrestitution' – the wrongdoer has to repair the damaged good (§ 249 I BGB) or to pay the money necessary for its restoration (§ 249 II BGB).[42] This principle goes along with the principle of 'Totalreparation' – the damage has to be *fully* compensated.[43] It is no exception to this principle that the wrongdoer may only partially be liable

---

[42] As to the freedom of disposition of the victim see chapter 2.
[43] For the 'loss of chances' see p. 68.

for the damage because of contributory negligence of the victim or his failure to mitigate the damage (§ 254 I, II BGB).

Only where 'Naturalrestitution' is not possible or not sufficient, has the damage to be compensated in money (§ 251 I BGB). The wrongdoer can choose this method of compensation also in cases where a *restitutio* would be possible, but disproportionally expensive (§ 251 II 1 BGB).[44]

Even if the tortfeasor may be required to pay money under § 249 II and 251 BGB, the point of reference for the calculation is different: under the principle of 'Naturalrestitution' (§ 249 II BGB), it is the costs of the 'repair'; under § 251 BGB, it is the market value of the damaged good.

As a matter of principle, *non-pecuniary damages* do not have to be compensated, unless a statutory provision explicitly orders such compensation (§ 253 I BGB; see p. 4 and p. 60).

Only the person who is *directly* injured by the tortfeasor is entitled to damages under German law. Persons indirectly affected (ricochet victims) are generally not included in the protective scope of tort law.[45] German tort law, however, has established two exceptions to this general principle: §§ 844, 845 BGB, concerning 'relatives' who have lost statutory claims for alimony or services against the victim[46]. Another exception has been created by the courts, concerning shock injuries of persons who watch or learn of an accident in which a close relative is killed or severely injured.[47] A further, but veiled, exception may be found in the rules which deal with the compensation of the victim for costs which his relatives have incurred in order to care for him or visit him in hospital.[48]

## Italian law

As mentioned above, the basic rules governing compensation for personal injury are set out in the Italian Civil Code art. 2056. In its basic structure this system leans more towards the French and more 'generous' approach to tort law than towards either the English or the German. By this we mean basically that Italian law has not experienced the difficulties the other two systems have with pure economic loss, being content to leave its solution to the notion of causation. On the other controversial issue of tort

---

[44] This rule does not apply, however, with regard to injured animals: § 251 II 2 BGB.

[45] This rule may not be confused with the (irrelevant) distinction between direct and indirect damages. If the tortfeasor is liable for the injury of the victim, this includes direct damages (*Erstschaden*) as well as consequential damages (*Folgeschäden*) – as long as the latter can, according to the theories of causation, be attributed to the tortious act.

[46] For more details see *GLT*, pp. 925–30.   [47] See p. 81 and *GLT*, pp. 115–44.

[48] See chapter 3.

law – compensation of psychiatric injury – the approach is generous in practice even though this system, too, accepts in principle the (often vague) distinction between recognisable, psychiatric injury (which is compensated) and mere pain, grief and suffering, which are not. It is notable that in this area of the law we even find allusions to the floodgates argument which, one must admit, is not one overtly utilised by European legal systems.

Though in its structure, Italian tort law differs from both English and German tort law, its attitude towards the basic principles of law which affect the rules of compensation are similar to those found in the other two systems under comparison. Thus it, too, attributes to compensation the prime (if not exclusive) function in the reparation process, accepts the principle of full compensation (and rejects the idea of capping damages except in certain situations regulated by statute), distinguishes between pecuniary and non-pecuniary damages and, despite the fact that it recognises the possibility of paying damages in the form of annuities, on the whole opts for a lump sum method of settling the tortfeasor's debt. But it also has features of its own which will be stressed in the appropriate places in this book. Here suffice it to mention one only.

To understand better the current law of compensation in Italy one must also refer – even if very succinctly – to yet another aspect of the system. At one level this has more to do with wider economic and political considerations than with law in the strict sense. But since these wider considerations affect the size of awards, they have to be mentioned here, even at the risk of producing a crass account of a complex problem.

From an economic and social point of view, it is widely accepted that compensation for personal injuries does not only have a 'micro-economic' dimension i.e., that it affects the relationship between the wrongdoer and the injured party. On the contrary, the compensation of personal injuries has a bearing, often a considerable one, on other aspects of societal life: the system for the organisation of labour, social security, the system of prevention of accidents, and others. For present purposes, one more consequence must be noted: the compensation amounts that will become payable to successful claimants also have a bearing on the private insurance system. For that system, the forecast of the total amount due for compensation in relation to the number of expected road accidents is one of the components of the calculations required for the determination of reserves to be earmarked by insurance companies. But the consequences of accidents go further and deeper than what has been suggested thus far.

Given that car ownership is very extended in Italy and given also the fact that insurance for motor vehicles is compulsory, the cost of car insurance is one, effectively, carried by most Italian families. For this reason, motor car insurance has, nowadays, also become an item that interests the government since it has to be taken into account in determining the statistical index of the rate of inflation. The widespread claim for damages from the use of vehicles is taken as the benchmark against which all claims for personal injuries must compare, except for those cases where there are reasons to intervene with specific rules, such as for accidents in the workplace, catastrophic events, and so forth. Hence the widespread conviction that the rules pertaining to personal injuries should not be separated from the evaluation – of a macroeconomic nature – of their effects on the entire economic system and on that in which the insurance companies operate.

It is against this background that one must see the interventions made at the beginning of the twentieth century by the insurance companies to standardise, according to assessment tables, the amounts to be paid out to the victim in the event of permanent damage. The same is true for the agreements reached at the end of the twentieth century on the premiums to be charged to their insured parties. The Italian government assumed a big say in this.

In the 1990s the tide changed. Various EEC Directives[49] forced the Italian government to give up its right to fix premiums and leave their determination to market forces. Most observers had assumed and, indeed, predicted that this would lead to a decrease of premiums as a result of market pressures forcing insurance companies to become more competitive. Yet the premiums went up, not down, because the insurance companies argued that '*danno biologico*' and other kinds of rising costs could only be met by a rise in car insurance premiums. This, however, was the façade; the reality was different. For an enquiry by the Anti-Trust Authority subsequently determined that seventeen insurance companies had reached a secret agreement enabling them to increase premiums. For this, the 'guilty' insurance companies were fined €350,000,000;[50] and an appeal to the Consiglio di Stato was unsuccessful.[51] It is, therefore, understandable

---

[49] Directive 92/96/EEC (life) and Directive 92/49/EEC (non-life) respectively enacted with Legislative Decree no. 174 of 17 March 1995 and Legislative Decree no. 175 of 17 March 1995.

[50] Autorità di Garanzia della Concorrenza e del Mercato, delibera del 28 July 2000, no. 8546 in Boll. N. 30/2000.

[51] Consiglio di Stato, decision of 23 April 2002, no. 2199, see www.giustizia-amministrativa.it

why governments over the last few years have put forward rules concerning the criteria for the assessment of personal injuries, not so much with the aim of standardising compensation in the event of identical or similar injuries, but rather in an effort to contain the amount of the same, and therefore inflation.

## Size of judiciary, volume of litigation, delays and cost

*English law*

In 1999, civil procedure in England underwent a wholesale and radical reform as a result of the Report of the Woolf Committee. The avowed purpose of the reform was to make the resolution of all forms of civil dispute quicker, easier and cheaper.

In consequence, all claims for personal injuries must be started in the county court unless, at the time when the proceedings are issued, the claimant's solicitor files a certificate that the value of the claim is in excess of £50,000.

Claims with a value of up to £5,000 are allocated to the small claims track. At the hearing, the strict rules of evidence do not apply and the court need not take evidence on oath. Such claims are generally heard by a district judge.

The court may not order a party to pay the other party's costs in small claims cases except for a fixed sum which has to be paid by the claimant on commencement of a claim. The only other exception to that rule is that if one party has behaved unreasonably in the conduct of his claim he may be ordered to pay the costs of the other party.

Claims with a value of between £5,000 and £15,000 (and having no special difficulty) would be allocated to the fast track. The intention of the Civil Procedure Rules is that such cases should be completed within thirty weeks of the claim being instituted. Hearing times are not normally longer than a day; and the court may not award more than £500 by way of costs where the claim is worth more than £3,000 but not more than £10,000, or £750 where the value of the claim is in excess of £10,000.

The more complicated cases would be allocated to the multi-track. They may be tried either in the county court or the High Court. In practice it is only the very large or very complicated cases which will be heard in the High Court.

The length of time between injury and the date of trial in multi-track cases varies enormously. However, the court has powers of case management which it exercises to attempt to ensure that the case is not unduly delayed. Even in a complicated head injury case (where, for example, the claimant needs a lengthy period of rehabilitation) the court tends to set periodic case management conferences in order that it may be informed as to the progress of the claimant and ensure that the matter is brought to trial as expeditiously as is practicable.

In these types of cases the intention of the Woolf Committee to drive down the costs has not, thus far, succeeded. In a long, difficult and complicated case the costs could easily exceed £100,000 on each side.

In multi-track cases the costs are not fixed. Each party is entitled to spend as much as they think they need. However, once the case has been decided the losing party, which normally pays the costs of the winner, is entitled to have the winner's cost assessed by a specialist cost judge. He will determine what is reasonable. Normally the winner will recover about 80 per cent of the costs actually incurred from the other side.

*German law*

There are many more courts and judges in Germany than in England. More precisely, there are 708 Amtsgerichte, 116 Landgerichte, 25 Oberlandesgerichte and one Federal Supreme Court in civil matters (BGH).[52] Approximately 22,000 judges are employed by the single states of Germany or by the Federal Republic (with 110 judges at the BGH). The output of published decisions in civil matters, especially in tort law, is very high. The more important decisions of the BGH and the Oberlandesgerichte are published officially by the courts themselves (BGHZ, OLGZ), but any of these or other decisions may be published by interested law journals.

The duration of court proceedings varies considerably, the average duration for the court of first instance being six months (Amtsgericht) or 11 months (Landgericht), respectively. Proceedings before the courts of appeal take (on average) six to seven months (Landgerichte) or eight to ten months (Oberlandesgerichte). The third instance again takes up to one year (Oberlandesgericht or BGH). This means that parties to a lawsuit may have to wait for the final judgment of the BGH (or OLG) for four years or more.[53]

The costs of the proceedings depend on the value of the matter in dispute. They include the costs of the court and the lawyers' fees. If the value

---

[52] As to the jurisdiction of these courts see *GLT*, pp. 4–7.
[53] See Statistisches Bundesamt, Fachserie 10, Reihe 2: Rechtspflege: Gerichte und Staatsanwaltschaften; Statistisches Bundesamt, Arbeitsunterlagen Zivilgerichte 2000; for older figures see Schreiber, *Jura* 1991, 617–20.

of the matter is low, the costs may exceed the amount of money the parties are fighting for. (Example 1: value €600; costs of first instance €400, second instance €550, third instance €500 = costs of €1,450 altogether. Example 2: value €35,000; costs of first instance €6,500, second instance €8,500, third instance €8,000 = costs of €23,000 altogether.)[54]

*Italian law*

In Italy, the number of 'ordinary' (i.e., career, full-time) judges is approximately 8,000. To these must be added thousands of judges recruited on a temporary basis from practising lawyers to deal with 'severance' proceedings, which have formed a huge backlog, as well as thousands of giudici di pace.

Every town, regardless of size, has its court, whilst the districts of the Courts of Appeal correspond, by and large, to the regional capitals of Italy. The number of judgments dealing with tort litigation reached by the Corte di Cassazione every year represents, approximately, 10 per cent of this court's total number of decisions. Most are published in the law reviews, and in data-banks. Judgments by the Constitutional Court (Corte Costituzionale) on this subject are few, but highly relevant, as we have seen (and will note again, later on) concerning both damage *per se* and non-economic damage.

The duration of proceedings varies according to circumstances and the workload of each court. Usually, a trial judgment takes between three and four years to be delivered counting from the date when the writ was issued. An appeal takes a further two to three years, and recourse before the Corte di Cassazione will delay the final outcome by a further two years. These time periods are slightly reduced if judgment is sought from a giudici di pace.

The length of trials is one of the chronic problems of the administration of justice in Italy, so quite often victims have gone to the European Court of Human Rights in Strasbourg, and have obtained judgment against Italy for violation of fundamental rights.[55] Individuals who suffered a loss due to a violation of the European Convention on Human Rights may have their damage liquidated on an equitable basis according to Law no. 89 of 24 March 2001.

---

[54] Compare the examples given by legal cost insurers, at www.anwalt.net/kosten and http://www.autorecht24.de

[55] The last decision of the Strasbourg court condemning the length of the Italian proceedings was published on 27 March 2003: see www.dirittiuomo.it

The cost of trials is largely linked to the value of the lawsuit. The judge awards by judgment the amount of costs, which include both court fees and legal fees and expenses for the winning party. Court costs are not considered high – they vary from court to court, but do not exceed e.g., €3,000 to €5,000 for car accidents. Taxes for judicial acts and execution of judgments are, however, high. As regards lawyers' fees, these are set out by the National Bar Council and are fixed by a decree of the Ministry of Justice. They vary depending on the value of the case and the activity performed, in or outside the court.

## Who pays legal costs? Is legal aid available and, if so, to whom and on what basis? Does legal aid act as a brake on litigation? Are conditional fee agreements or contingency fees permitted?

*English law*

The general rule is that the losing party pays the costs of both sides. However, since the introduction of the Civil Procedure Rules in 1999 costs are more issue-based than before.[56] The overall winner may be deprived of his costs for an issue he has lost. In practice that will only be done where the issue on which he has lost played a major part in the case.

A defendant can protect himself by making a payment into court of the amount which he believes that the claimant will actually recover at trial. The claimant has the right to take the money so paid into court within twenty-one days of being notified of the payment in. In that event the defendant will pay all the claimant's costs. If, however, the matter proceeds to trial and the claimant recovers the same or less than the amount of the payment, he will have to pay the defendant's costs as well as his own from the date of such payment in.

In the event that the trial is split and liability is tried first, the claimant will be awarded his costs of that trial. If, when quantum is dealt with, he fails to beat a payment in then he will have to bear the costs of the second trial.

If the defendant is unable to protect himself by means of a payment into court (as, e.g., where liability is tried separately) he can protect himself by making an offer of settlement in a letter marked 'without prejudice save as to costs'. The letter cannot be referred to unless and until the question

---

[56] *A.E.I. Rediffusion Music Ltd* v. *Phonographic Performance Ltd* [1999] 1 WLR 1507 and *Firle Investments Ltd* v. *Datapoint International Ltd* [2001] EWCA Civ 1106.

of costs is adjudicated upon. Costs will then be awarded on the same basis as a payment in. So, e.g., if contributory negligence is in issue at the stage where liability is tried, the defendant may offer an apportionment of liability between him and the claimant. If the claimant does not do better at trial he will pay the defendant's costs as well as his own since the date of the offer.

Contingency fees, i.e., an arrangement whereby the lawyer is entitled to a percentage of the damages recovered, are not permitted. Solicitors and barristers are, however, allowed to enter into a conditional fee agreement. That means that if the case is lost the lawyers receive no remuneration. If they succeed they are entitled to their normal costs uplifted by a previously agreed percentage. Any uplift can be recovered from the loser provided that the costs judge is satisfied that the uplift is reasonable. The level of uplift will depend upon the degree of risk undertaken by the lawyers so that the lower the prospects of success in the case the higher the percentage uplift will be. Account is also taken of the length of time which the lawyer is likely to have to wait for his fees. The more complicated the case, the longer it is likely to take and, therefore, the greater the percentage uplift.

Litigants can protect themselves against losing cases by obtaining insurance to cover the eventuality that they will have to pay the other side's costs. In practice insurers are unlikely to provide cover unless the lawyers rate the prospects of success in the case at in excess of 50 per cent. The premium paid to the insurers is recoverable from the losing party as part of the winner's costs. Again, however, the amount must be reasonable.[57] Legal aid is no longer available for personal injury actions except in cases which are of special interest. The question of whether a case falls into that category is decided by a special committee set up by the Legal Services Commission (the body which now administers legal aid). In practice it is very difficult to persuade the committee that a case is of special interest. In general the category is reserved for high cost cases such as multiparty actions brought by those who, for instance, contend that they have been injured by a pharmaceutical product.

*German law*

## Costs and legal aid

The losing party has to pay all of the costs – this includes the costs of the court and the fees of the lawyers of both sides (§ 91 ZPO). If the lawsuit is

---

[57] *Callery* v. *Gray (Nos. 1 and 2)* [2002] UKHL 28; [2002] 1 WLR 2000; *Halloran* v. *Delaney* [2002] EWCA Civ 1258; [2003] 1 WLR 28.

successful only in part, the costs have to be split proportionally (§ 92 ZPO). These principles apply even if the case was won in two instances, but lost before the BGH, or if the applicable law has been changed while the lawsuit was pending. Each judgment of the court has to include the decision about the costs of the proceedings (§ 308 II ZPO). This system gives an injured person the chance to enforce his or her claim in court without having to pay any costs; it includes, on the other hand, the risk not only of losing the lawsuit but also of being liable for all of the costs, including the lawyers' fees, of the other side.

Legal aid is available in two situations: outside of court proceedings an indigent person may be entitled to obtain free legal advice from a lawyer, whose fee will be paid by the state (*Beratungshilfegesetz*). Legal aid in court proceedings is available according to §§ 114 to 127 a ZPO: the party (plaintiff or defendant) must be unable to pay the legal costs, and it must be likely that the applicant will be successful in the proceedings. The application for legal aid will be considered and decided by the court which will have to decide about the lawsuit. If legal aid is granted, the applicant does not have to pay court fees or his own lawyer; if he loses in the end, however, he will have to pay the costs (lawyers' fees) of his opponent according to § 91 ZPO (§ 123 ZPO).[58]

## Legal expenses insurance

Since the financial risk of court proceedings is high, many insurance companies in Germany offer insurance contracts which cover this special risk. In a given case, the insurer will check that the intended lawsuit is not frivolous, and will then take over the fees of the court and of its client's lawyer. Should the client win the case, the losing party has to pay all of his costs (§ 91 ZPO) which have been laid out by the insurer (but not the premium paid to the insurer by the client). Only if the client loses his case does the insurer have to carry the burden of costs permanently (including the costs of the other party to the lawsuit).

This branch of insurance has become very popular in Germany. It is especially designed for private citizens and is not open for commercial disputes. The insurance contract can be restricted to certain areas such as traffic accidents, family proceedings, or the like. The insurance is available for all kinds of compensation claims for personal injury.

The effects of legal expenses insurance are ambivalent. An injured person is no longer prevented from pursuing a reasonable claim for fear of litigation costs. On the other hand, the availability of insurance has led

---

[58] Compare: BVerfG 23 June 1999, NJW 1999, 3186.

to a substantial increase in court proceedings: the financial risk is taken from the insured, and since he has to pay the insurance premium anyway, he might want to amortise these payments by initiating a lawsuit from time to time.

### Contingency fees; commercial financing of litigation

Conditional fee agreements and contingency fees are forbidden under German law (§ 49 b II BRAO). The statute aims to protect the professional integrity and independence of lawyers (who are bound by statute to contribute to the administration of justice, § 2 BRAO). Very recently, however, commercial companies – sometimes branches of insurance companies – have appeared on the scene, offering to finance legal litigation and taking the risk if a lawsuit is lost. As consideration the party agrees to pay a contingency fee if his or her claim should be enforced successfully. For claims of between €50,000 and €1,000,000 this fee amounts to 20 to 30 per cent of the money the plaintiff actually receives from the defendant; the litigation costs which had been laid out by the financing company have to be paid back before the contingency fee is calculated. The plaintiff remains free to choose his legal representative, who will charge the normal legal fees (the financing company, however, pays him an additional fee as compensation for the communication with the company). The legality of such a financing system is disputed, but in general not seriously questioned.[59]

The BGH has not yet ruled on the issue. Economic evaluation shows that the financing companies, unlike the litigation costs insurers, have not yet achieved much market acceptance; but there is a growing interest in this method of reducing (and sharing) the risk of litigation costs – not only on the part of the plaintiffs, but also of the lawyers. If, however, the lawyers themselves establish such a company in order to finance the lawsuits of their clients, such behaviour is very likely to violate the above-mentioned § 49 b II BRAO.

### Italian law

In Italian law, the losing party must pay all costs, including court fees and the legal fees and expenses of the prevailing party. If the claimant has obtained only partial judgment in his favour, the award of costs may

---

[59] For an exhaustive discussion and references see Maubach, *Gewerbliche Prozessfinanzierung gegen Erfolgsbeteiligung* (2002); Dagobert Nitzsche, *Ausgewählte rechtliche und praktische Probleme der gewerblichen Prozesskostenfinanzierung unter besonderer Berücksichtigung des Insolvenzrechts* (München, 2002).

follow a different pattern, e.g., may end up being split equally between the litigating parties.

Defence free of charge was an institution entrusted to the local bar associations. They, in turn, would request their members, for reasons of solidarity and professional dignity, to take on the defence free of charge. Nowadays, however, such defence is no longer free of charge but is paid for by the state.

The matter has recently been the subject of reform, Law no. 217 of 30 July 1999 having radically changed the previous regulations.[60] To obtain legal aid the applicant must have a personal income, if single, not exceeding €9,000. For persons living as a family, the cut-off point is fixed by taking into account the income earned collectively by all the family members. Lawyers' fees are paid by the state and, in the event that the defended party prevails, court costs and legal fees are paid to the state by the losing party.

Legal expenses insurance can, nowadays, be found even in Italy but it is one branch of the insurance business which is not greatly developed; only a few insurance companies cover this type of risk. The relationship between the insured and the company is governed by the insurance policy.

In Italian law any agreement on making the payment of lawyers' fees conditional on the outcome of the case is forbidden by the Civil Code (article 2233). Lawyers are not allowed, even through third party intermediaries, to stipulate any agreement with their clients either excluding the payment of fees or connecting payment to the successful outcome of the trial. They are not even allowed to stipulate agreements concerning the disputed assets in relation to which they have been appointed to act. Violation of this prohibition is punished by treating the agreement as being null and void and by compensation being awarded for damages.

## Social security, other sources of revenue and tort law

*English law*

The Pearson Committee estimated[61] that every year in the United Kingdom some 3,000,000 people are injured and about 21,000 of them die of their injuries. Of these, only about 1,700,000 receive some financial assistance, but not all of them from the tort system. Indeed, only a very small minority,

---

[60] Royal Decree no. 3282 of 30 December 1923.
[61] Vol. i, para. 35 ff. There is no reason to believe that the overall picture has changed radically in the intervening twenty years or so.

estimated at about 215,000, about 6 per cent of the grand total, received any compensation in the form of tort damages. For the remainder, social security, occupational sick pay or private insurance represent the main if not sole sources of relief. But if tort victims represent only a small percentage of accident victims, their share of the aggregate value of compensation payments (estimated at £827 million at 1977 prices) amounted to just over £200 million, so that just over 6 per cent of the accident victims received some 25 per cent of the total compensation paid out. This category certainly includes a substantial percentage of the most serious types of injury, but even allowing for this, it is not disputed that tort victims fare rather better than the victims of other injuries. If these tort victims are allowed to pile on to their tort awards other benefits received from other systems of compensation (such as social security and private insurance), the danger is not only that they may end up by being overcompensated, but also that the overall compensation system may end up by being unduly costly and wasteful as regards some victims and rather mean to others. Unfortunately, there is no easy solution to this problem of double compensation. Professor Atiyah, who has written extensively on this subject, has summed up the problem as follows:

If there [were] any rational pattern to the various compensation systems as a whole, it might have been possible to construct a 'hierarchy' of systems under which a man should be compensated by system A, if that were possible, and if not, he should then be relegated to systems B, C and D in turn. But this is not how things have developed. In fact, each system by and large decides whether it is willing to shoulder a burden, irrespective of other compensation available, or whether it wishes to push the burden on to another system, or whether it is willing to share the burden. But the whole process is one of almost unbelievable complexity.[62]

A victim of an accident may thus find himself receiving financial assistance from a wide variety of sources. He may, for example, have been prudent enough to take out first party insurance against precisely such a possibility; or he may become entitled to an occupational pension paid by his employer; or he may benefit from the charitable disposition of his fellow human beings made either directly to him or, as is frequently the case these days, as a result of setting up some kind of 'disaster relief fund'. Finally, he may be eligible to receive one or more of a number of social security benefits from the state. Legislation governs the relationship

---

[62] Patrick Atiyah, *Accidents, Compensation and the Law* (Peter Cane (ed.) 4th edn, Butterworths, 1987), p. 390.

between tort and social security.[63] In other cases, it is up to the courts to decide whether a particular payment should be deducted from damages, starting from the general principle that the purpose of the tort rules is to compensate the plaintiff and not, directly or indirectly, to allow him to make a gain from the tort. In principle, the law can take one of three options with regard to collateral benefits:[64] *cumulation*, under which the plaintiff is allowed to retain the benefit in question while being paid damages which represent his full loss; *reduction*, under which the collateral benefit is fully offset against the damages; and *recoupment*, whereby the third party provider is given a right to recover the amount of the benefit through an action against the tortfeasor or, in some cases, the victim. At common law, the general approach is, in principle, to allow cumulation, but subject to a highly complex case law which attempts to distinguish (unconvincingly, in the eyes of many commentators) between those benefits which go to reduce the plaintiff's loss, and others which do not. The third option – recoupment – is seemingly barred at common law, but does operate in respect of certain social security benefits, under a statutory regime which is now provided for by the Social Security (Recovery of Benefits) Act 1997. In order to analyse this body of law it is therefore necessary to consider separately the common law rules and those applying to the statutory regime and this is done in chapter 5.

*German law*

A victim may be entitled to benefits from various branches of the social security system, especially from sickness insurance, workmen's compensation insurance, unemployment insurance (if he has lost his job because of the injury), or from care insurance (if he needs permanent care). Besides the benefits from social security, the victim may have taken out private accident insurance. As to the effect of such benefits on the compensation claim, see p. 143.

If the victim is an employee but unable to work because of his injuries, he is nevertheless entitled to full pay from his employer for the first six weeks of sickness. His claim against the tortfeasor is insofar *ex lege* transferred to the employer (§ 6 Entgeltfortzahlungsgesetz; see chapter 4).

---

[63] Social Security (Recovery of Benefits) Act 1997, for which see below.
[64] See Richard Lewis, 'Deducting Collateral Benefits from Damages: Principle and Policy' (1998) 18 *Legal Studies* 15 (Select Bibliography).

## Italian law

In Italian law the victim of a tort may draw money from several social security systems. These include national insurance for work-related accidents, national health insurance, unemployment benefits, and so forth. In the event of a road accident, the victim also benefits from the compulsory insurance for civil liability (if the wrongdoer is insured) and from the indemnity granted by the Insurance Companies' Guarantee Fund (in the event that the wrongdoer is not identified or is unable to pay for the damage caused). As regards the procedures for compensation, see below.

One peculiarity of the Italian Workers Compensation Act[65] should, perhaps be stressed from the outset. Compensation here follows strict rules which determine its percentage by reference to the injured employee's wages. The Corte Costituzionale, however, has had difficulty in accepting such reduced compensation with regard to the non-pecuniary part of the award that refers to the *danno biologico*.[66] An appeal to the Italian legislator to address the problem having fallen on deaf ears, the Corte has returned to the issue and has held that the evaluation of *danno biologico* should in these cases, as well, follow the general rules (discussed in chapter 2).

## Method of payment

### English law

The first thing to note is that in tort actions damages must be awarded[67] once only in respect of each cause of action and they take the form of a lump sum.[68] The English courts have no power to order the payment of damages in periodic sums unless the parties agree.[69] Accordingly, they

---

[65] Law no. 1124 of 30 June 1965.

[66] Corte Costituzionale 15 February 1991, no. 87, 1991 *Resp. civ. E prev.* 245.

[67] *Miliangos* v. *George Frank (Textiles) Ltd* [1976] AC 443 abolished the old rule that damages must be expressed in sterling. Thus, see *The Despina R.* [1979] AC 685. But the sterling rule still applies to non-pecuniary damages such as damages for pain and suffering and loss of amenity: *Hoffman* v. *Sofaer* [1982] 1 WLR 1350.

[68] This rule against successive actions has to be qualified in at least two major respects. First, it does not apply to continuing torts (e.g., continuing trespass) and secondly, it does not apply whenever two different rights have been violated: *Brunsden* v. *Humphrey* (1884) 14 QBD 141. For a more recent illustration see *Barrow* v. *Bankside Members Agency Ltd* [1996] 1 WLR 257 and note that the doctrine of *res iudicata* may be relevant in such cases.

[69] *Fournier* v. *Canadian National Railway Company* [1927] AC 167. At common law it was not clear whether the courts would have the power even if the arrangement was agreed to by the parties themselves (see *Metcalfe* v. *London Passenger Transport Board* [1938] 2 All ER 352 at 355); however, the Damages Act 1996, s. 2, now provides that '[a] court awarding

often have to include compensation for future damage that is likely to accrue, in addition to compensation for damage that has already accrued. This is easier to decide in theory than to apply in practice. The problems become apparent in personal injury cases, where the judge has to try to guess not only what would have happened to the victim if he had not been injured, but also what is now likely to happen to him as a result of the accident. This 'guessing game' is further aggravated by the fact that it takes place against a number of imponderables, some of which are related to the victim (e.g., the nature of his injury, its likely complications and pre-trial anxiety – known as 'compensation neurosis' – which can postpone complete recovery and complicate the task of assessment of the loss), while others are linked with wider economic factors (e.g., inflation, rates of taxation etc.) but may affect particularly harshly a victim who, because of the tort, may have reduced earning capacity. The great disadvantage of lump sum awards is not only that they make such estimates of future developments little more than educated guesses, but also that they are not open to subsequent correction. In *Lim* v. *Camden and Islington Area Health Authority*, Lord Scarman was frank about this danger when he said[70]:

Sooner or later... if the parties do not settle, a court (once liability is admitted or proved) has to make an award of damages. The award, which covers past, present and future injury and loss, must under our law be a lump sum assessed at the conclusion of the legal process. The award is final; it is not susceptible to review as the future unfolds, substituting fact for estimate. Knowledge of the future being denied to mankind, so much of the award as is to be attributed to future loss and suffering – in many cases the major part of the award – will almost surely be wrong. *There is really only one certainty: the future will prove the award to be either too high or too low.*

These remarks were prompted by Lord Denning MR's attempt in the Court of Appeal[71] to change or, at least, adapt the existing practice and to enable an award of damages in cases such as the one before the court to be regarded as an interim award, allowing the court to make further adjustments in the future. The idea, according to Lord Scarman, was:

an attractive, ingenious suggestion – but... unsound. For so radical a reform can be made neither by judges nor by modification of rules of court. It raises issues of social, economic and financial policy not amenable to judicial reform which will

---

damages in an action for personal injury may, with the consent of the parties, make an order under which the damages are wholly or partly to take the form of periodical payments'.
[70] [1980] AC 174 at 182–3 (emphasis added).    [71] [1979] QB 196 at 214 ff.

almost certainly prove to be controversial and can be resolved by the legislature only after full consideration of factors which cannot be brought into clear focus, or be weighed and assessed, in the course of the forensic process.[72]

The alternative to the lump sum method of payment of damages is the annuity system which is adopted (in theory, though not rigidly in practice) by a number of European systems such as, for instance, the French, the German and the Italian. Its main advantage is its ability to adapt the award downwards or upwards depending on whether the victim's condition and other circumstances become better or worse. In a number of instances – e.g., in cases of fatal accidents where the chances of remarriage of the surviving spouse have to be considered – this method of payment of the damages award helps avoid awkward or embarrassing guessing exercises. But annuities also have crucial weaknesses. For example, they require that the cases be 'kept open' and insurance companies, who meet most of the claims, understandably prefer to pay (if they have to pay) and 'close their books'. A mechanism must also be devised to allow for the adjustment of the sums paid, and this can involve costs and delays. Victims also tend to prefer to receive their compensation in one large amount even though the unexpected receipt of large sums may lead them to spend their awards in a very short time and then leave them without adequate financial resources to maintain themselves (with the danger of social security having to step in somewhere down the line). Last but by no means least, lawyers are more likely to receive their remuneration without complaint and expeditiously if the client/victim receives a large sum rather than modest, periodic payments. For a variety of practical reasons, therefore, the lump sum method of payment of the damages award may not be as bad as some of its critics believe; and for practical reasons it seems unlikely to be replaced completely.

In the future, therefore, the search for better solutions is likely to turn towards mixed systems which, as far as possible, will attempt to combine the advantages of the two extreme solutions, namely, the lump sum versus the system of annuity payments. The emerging practice of 'structured settlements', described at p. 179 addresses these problems in the case of damages for serious injuries; but three further ways of improving the position of deserving plaintiffs must also be considered here. They are (i) postponed or split trials; (ii) interim awards; and (iii) provisional damages.

---

[72] [1980] AC 174 at 183. See also Lord Steyn's highly critical comments on the present system of lump sum payments in *Wells* v. *Wells* [1999] 1 AC 345 at 384.

## Postponed or split trials

It has already been noted why the lump sum method of payment of damages raises serious difficulties in the calculation of the right level of the award, especially where the extent of the injury is not yet fully determined. One way around this difficulty is to postpone the trial or settlement of the claim until a clearer picture about the victim's position has emerged. Unfortunately, such a solution presupposes that such a delay will make the prognosis easier, which is not always the case. Moreover, this way of proceeding adds to the delays of the tort process, which has always been one of the major weaknesses of the system. Finally, such delays may trigger off in susceptible plaintiffs the so-called problem of 'compensation neurosis' and thus further delay their rehabilitation.

As a result of these limitations the different corrective device of 'split trials' was proposed by the Court of Appeal in 1974 in *Coenen* v. *Payne*.[73] This, as the name suggests, entails separating 'liability' which can be resolved (or admitted) as soon as possible after the accident (when recollections of witnesses are still (relatively) clear), from the 'quantum' of damages, which in most serious cases could be postponed until a clear prognosis could be attempted. Once again, however, there is no certainty that postponement makes prognosis easier; and, under existing law (and subject to what is said below), when the award is made it is final. In any event, this method of proceeding can only have its full effect if it is combined with the possibility of interim damages. Both these ideas, however, have met with little enthusiasm in practice and are mentioned here for the sake of completeness rather than as oft-used procedures in the compensation process.

## Interim damages

The idea of awarding interim damages is even older. It can be traced back to the Winn Committee Report of 1968 and is nowadays regulated by Order 29, Part II, rule 11 of the Rules of the Supreme Court. Such an order can be made at the discretion of the court where 'need' can be shown by the plaintiff.[74] The money is meant to cover the plaintiff's interim pecuniary losses (such as loss of earnings, medical expenses, and the like) and cannot include a percentage of his (possible) general damages. For a variety of reasons this procedure, too, seems to be underused in practice. Some of

---

[73] [1974] 1 WLR 984, now covered by the Civil Procedure Rules Part 3(2)(i).
[74] *Schott Kem Ltd* v. *Bentley* [1991] 1 QB 61.

the reasons for this seem to be purely technical;[75] and, nowadays, the operation of the Social Security (Recovery of Benefits) Act 1997 may also have an adverse effect in so far as there is the danger that the new scheme might swallow up all interim payments, especially in those cases involving smaller sums. So this device, too, has been of limited use to plaintiffs.

## Provisional damages

Provisional damages provide the third, comparatively recent, innovation that aims to improve the position of the deserving victim of personal injury. They were made possible by section 6 of the Administration of Justice Act 1982 which empowers the courts 'to make a provisional award in cases where the medical prognosis is particularly uncertain and where there is a *chance*,[76] falling short of probability, that some *serious* disease or *serious* deterioration in the plaintiff's condition will accrue at a later date'.[77]

In the debates in the House of Lords, the Lord Chancellor, Lord Hailsham, did not envisage that frequent use would be made of this provision;[78] and events have proved him right. The example he gave of a case suitable to be brought under this heading, was of a young child whose skull was fractured in an accident and who, at the trial, may appear to have made full recovery. Yet in cases of cranial injuries there is always a chance of subsequent epilepsy. Section 6 will now enable the court to award nothing in respect of the feared event but to give damages later if the feared event materialises. This procedure will avoid trying to evaluate the possibility of the feared event materialising and then awarding a smaller sum for this 'chance' that may end by being too low or too high. Unlike the Pearson proposals on this point, it is not obligatory for the court to adopt this procedure on its own; it will be for the plaintiff to claim that a provisional damages award be made; and the interests of the defendant will also have to be given due weight. The case of *Willson* v. *Ministry of Defence*[79] has, as already stated, revealed how conservative the approach of the courts has been.

The provisions of section 6 of the Administration of Justice Act 1982 were brought into force in July 1985.[80] Under the new regime, as it was

---

[75] They are discussed in the Law Commission Consultation Paper No. 125, pp. 71–2.

[76] In *Willson* v. *Ministry of Defence* [1991] 1 All ER 638 the trial judge was of the view that s. 32A of the Supreme Court Act 1981 was concerned with measurable not fanciful chances, thus further limiting the opportunity of using this procedure.

[77] It will be noticed that this section applies to contingencies due to medical reasons.

[78] Hansard (HL) 1982, 28.      [79] [1991] 1 All ER 638 at 641.

[80] Rules of the Supreme Court, Order 37, rules 7–12, now Civil Procedure Rules Part 41.

judicially explained in *Willson*'s case, three requirements will have to be fulfilled before use of this procedure can be sanctioned. First, there must be a *chance* of the feared event materialising at some later date. The chance may be slim but, as stated, it must be measurable. Secondly, there must be a serious deterioration of the claimant's physical (and, presumably, also mental) condition and not just an ordinary deterioration or progression of the injury or illness. This is a matter of fact and degree but the facts of *Willson*'s case suggest that the courts are taking a conservative (arguably overconservative) attitude towards this requirement. Finally, the judge must be persuaded that the case before him justifies the exercise of his discretion to give the claimant the right to return at a later date for more; or, on the contrary, that it is one that is best resolved by a once-and-for-all award of damages. In his decision, the judge will also, normally, specify the period within which the application for further damages must be made, though nowadays there seems to be a preference for not setting a limit at all.[81]

The condition of the tort victim may not just get worse as a result of his injuries; he may also die. If a provisional award has been made to him prior to the death, how will this affect the legal position of his dependants? The answer is now to be found in section 3 of the Damages Act 1996 which does not preclude his dependants from bringing a lost dependency claim. Wisely, however, the Act adds that any part of the provisional award that was 'intended to compensate him for pecuniary loss in a period that in the event falls after his death shall be taken into account in assessing the amount of any loss of support' suffered by the dependants.

For most commentators the regime described above seems to be unduly restrictive. Their arguments can be found in the specialised literature; and they are also conveniently summarised and discussed critically in the Law Commission Consultation Paper No. 125.[82] Here it is enough to note two of the most doubtful limitations and, also, add an observation of wider import.

First, one must recall that the feared event must be specified by the claimant's lawyers in the original action in considerable detail. As we have seen, the courts seem to take an overly narrow view on the question of whether the subsequent event is a serious deterioration or an ordinary deterioration or development of the injury or illness.

Secondly, the right to return to the court and have the award adjusted arises only once and this may cause injustice in some cases. For example, suppose that the claimant is injured in his legs and runs the risk of

---

[81] See Bragg, 'Provisional Damages' (1992) 136 SJ 654, at 655.    [82] At pp. 76–84.

subsequently developing arthritis. Since it is the disease that must be specified by the claimant's application and not the parts of his body that are susceptible to it, what will happen to the claimant who develops arthritis in one of the injured legs? It would be unfair to suggest that he would have to wait until the other leg was also affected by the disease; but it would be equally unfair to limit his subsequent increase of damages to include the arthritis in the one leg.

Finally, one may use this opportunity to pose a wider question concerning the attitudes of the (conservatively inclined) English legislators. For, having identified an area of the law that needs reform, why do they then feel such an irresistible urge to circumscribe the reforming rules to such an extent as to make them almost useless? The tendency is obvious in other parts of the law of torts;[83] and readers inclined towards speculating about more general matters might wish to ponder over this question. In the meantime, however, and as far as this particular topic is concerned, all one can say is that the institution of provisional damages is, over ten years after its introduction, still in its formative stages. One must, therefore, hope that the courts will be responsive to calls to liberalise their present position on this issue before judicial accretions (such as *Willson*)[84] make this task truly impossible.

## Structured settlements

We shall discuss this mechanism briefly in chapter 5.

### German law

As already mentioned before (see p. 3), German law distinguishes between single losses and continuing losses. The first type of loss has to be compensated by a single sum of money, while for the second type § 843 I BGB establishes the principle of periodical payments. These payments, however, may be capitalised if there is a serious reason to do that (§ 843 III BGB).

---

[83] For instance, the old s. 4 of the Defamation Act 1952 dealing with 'unintentional defamation'.

[84] A case law search has disclosed only one recent case in which *Willson* was considered and the judge in *Fashade* v. *North Middlesex Hospital NHS Trust* [2001] 4 QB 13 refused to grant provisional damages for the claimant's respiratory disability, on the ground that the risk was not 'clear and severable' as opposed to 'a continuing deterioration'. This continues to suggest a highly restrictive approach on the part of the courts to provisional damages claims, although some commentators justify this due to the need to prevent the introduction of a 'serious measure of uncertainty into the system': *Winfield and Jolowicz on Tort* (Horton Rogers (ed.), 16th edn, London, 2002), pp. 772–3.

In practical life, this statutory relation of rule and exception has been turned into its opposite.[85]

For those cases in which the extent of the damages is uncertain, German law of civil procedure offers two alternative ways of dealing with these situations, depending on the degree of uncertainty encountered. On the one hand, if it is not possible to foresee the future development of the damage caused with adequate probability,[86] German law (§ 256 ZPO) allows that a declaratory judgment be passed which states the liability of the wrongdoer for all damages incurred by the victim, without awarding a certain sum or pension. Later on, once the damage has become certain, either the parties will settle the victim's claims between themselves, or they can return to court in order to have the amount of damages judicially determined. The court will then proceed on the basis of the first judgment. On the other hand, if a pension (annuity) – this second possibility does not exist for the case of a sum having been awarded[87] – has been granted by the judge, based on his assessment of how the damage will develop, and if substantial new circumstances arise that make it necessary to change the amount of the pension awarded, such a change can be effected through new court proceedings (§ 323 ZPO). In this case, as well, the first judgment in principle has a binding effect on the parties and the new judge. Only circumstances that have arisen after the first decision has been passed justify a modification and may be taken into consideration when the amount of the pension due is reassessed.[88] For details see chapter 4, especially pp. 138–42.

Inquiries with insurance companies have shown that an equivalent to 'structured settlements' has not been developed in Germany. The two basic methods of compensation (lump sum, annuities) may be modified in a given case (annuities for five years, then lump sum for the rest of the life of the victim, or the other way round; or non-pecuniary damages payable

---

[85] *GLT*, p. 914; Esser/Weyers, *Schuldrecht* II/2 (8th edn, 2000) § 61 I 1; Küppersbusch no. 649.
[86] BGH 4 April 1952, BGHZ 5, 314, 315; mostly, this is either because it is likely that further damages will occur in the future (BGH 14 December 1995, NJW 1996, 1062, 1063; BGH 16 January 2001, NJW 2001, 1431, 1432), or because the damage can not yet be assessed (BGH 30 March 1983, NJW 1984, 1552, 1554; BGH 21 January 2000, NJW 2000, 1256, 1257).
[87] BGH 8 January 1981, NJW 1981, 818, 819 ff.
[88] BGH 21 February 2001, NJW-RR 2001, 937: this civil procedure provision is an application of '*clausula rebus sic stantibus*'; new circumstances exist in the case of newly occurred facts (BGH 18 March 1992, NJW-RR 1992, 1091, 1092), a change in legislation (BGH 28 November 1990, NJW-RR 1991, 514) or a different application of the law due to a decision taken by the Federal Constitutional Court (BGH 12 July 1990, NJW 1990, 3020, 3022).

in the form of annuities instead of a lump sum), but there is no 'third way' like the structured settlement. This might be due to different tax laws in Germany and the United Kingdom: under German tax law, it is not the method of payment which is decisive but the object of compensation. Damages for increased costs of living are not taxable but income tax has to be paid for payments which compensate the victim for lost income.[89] For more details see p. 59.

### Italian law

As regards the procedures for the actual payment of the amount of damages, we have said previously that the judge establishes whether to award a lump sum or a life annuity. In Italy, however (as, indeed, in France), the annuity option is rarely exercised. Provisional damages can also be awarded if requested by the claimant. The mechanism of structured settlements has not yet been considered in Italian law.

---

[89] BGH 25 October 1994, NJW 1995, 1238–40.

# 2  General damages: non-pecuniary losses

## English law

### Introduction

The guiding principle for the award of damages in respect of a tort is, in English law, to compensate the victim of the wrongdoing. That is as true in cases of personal injury as it is for any other tort. Punitive or exemplary damages may not be awarded for personal injury no matter how severe the injury may be nor how gross the negligence on the part of the wrongdoer. The difference here between English and American law is significant and accounts in large part for the different size of awards found in the two countries.

If, however, injury has been caused by a deliberate act, aggravated damages may be awarded. If the personal injury has been caused by a trespass to the person rather than by negligence, the court has discretion to make such an award.[1] Such cases are rare, and judges have discouraged the pleading of claims as a deliberate tort in an attempt to increase the damages.[2]

---

[1] *W* v. *Meah* [1986] 1 All ER 935 where aggravated damages were awarded in a case of rape and vicious sexual assault. The difference between aggravated and exemplary damages has always been troublesome even though the prevailing view is that they are different. The most recent (and thorough) discussion of the subject can be found in *Thompson* v. *Commissioner of Police of the Metropolis* and *Hsu* v. *Commissioner of Police of the Metropolis* [1998] QB 498 and *Kuddus* v. *Chief Constable of Leicestershire Constabulary* [2001] UKHL 29; [2001] 1 WLR 1789, yet even this reveals the closeness of the two notions. See also the Law Commission's Consultation Paper on *Aggravated, Exemplary and Restitutionary Damages* (Law Com. No. 132, 1993), which recommended the abolition of aggravated damages as a separate head of damages, and their absorption into a 'strict compensatory model' (para. 8.18); see also Law Commission Report No. 247 (1997).

[2] *Letang* v. *Cooper* [1965] 1 QB 232 but see *Kralj* v. *McGrath* [1986] 1 All ER 54. See also *Appleton* v. *Garrett* [1996] 5 PIQR P1.

45

There may also be a sound practical reason for framing claims in negligence. A claimant who pleads trespass in the form of assault or battery gives the defendant employer the opportunity to contend that he is not vicariously liable because the deliberate act was outside the scope of his employee's employment. It also gives the insurer standing behind the defendant the opportunity to avoid the policy. It is, therefore, prudent for the claimant to restrict his claim to one of negligence in order to be sure that he will be paid his compensatory damages. Furthermore, the limitation period is different. If an intentional tort is alleged, the limitation period is six years but cannot be extended under section 33 of the Limitation Act 1980.

As we shall see in chapter 4, in the case of pecuniary losses the law aims at full compensation (though whether it achieves this or not in all cases is another matter). Such full compensation, however, is not objectively possible in the case of non-pecuniary damage and the aim here is thus to achieve fair compensation or satisfaction. However, in English law, these words are not used as terms of art as they are in German law.

### Concept of general damages

General damages represent the amount recoverable by the injured person for pain and suffering, and loss of amenity. There is no separate award for each of those headings. In English law, the compensation is one sum, decided by the trial judge on the basis of all the evidence before him.

### Pain and suffering

Pain and suffering covers the nature of the accident and its immediate aftermath. The court will require evidence of precisely what happened. Was the claimant aware of what was going to happen to him and became afraid? For how long did he have to endure pain? A claimant is thus entitled to recover for his pain and suffering – the two terms have never been clearly distinguished by the courts – actual and prospective, resulting from the tortfeasor's conduct or from medical or surgical treatment made necessary as a result of the tortious conduct. No award for this type of damage is, however, made if the claimant is permanently unconscious and thus not in any pain.[3] Despite some earlier doubts it is now accepted

---

[3] *Wise* v. *Kaye* [1962] 1 QB 638. This is so even if the result of lack of consciousness or pain is due to drugs or anaesthetics: *H. West & Son Ltd* v. *Shephard* [1964] AC 326. The greater availability of pain-killing drugs may well reduce further these awards and, perhaps, lead the courts into making larger awards under the heading of loss of amenity.

that the claimant's economic and social position is irrelevant as far as this heading of damages is concerned.[4] Nor may damages for pain and suffering be awarded in a case where death occurs instantaneously.[5]

## Loss of amenity

The expression 'loss of amenity' is less easy to define. In *H. West & Son Ltd v. Shephard*[6] Lord Reid said:

There are two views about the true basis for this kind of compensation. One is that the man is simply being compensated for the loss of his leg or the impairment of his digestion. The other is that his real loss is not so much his physical injury as the loss of those opportunities to lead a full and normal life which are now denied to him by his physical condition – for the multitude of deprivations and even petty annoyances which he must tolerate.

It is important in each case to consider precisely what has been lost. All the personal circumstances of the injured individual must be taken into account. That includes age, lifestyle, hopes and expectations, and disabilities existing before the accident. Thus, a fit, athletic, active individual, who in consequence of an injury is unable to participate in sport or an outdoor lifestyle and who can no longer play with his young children in the manner that he did before the accident, has lost more than a seventy-year-old with a sedentary lifestyle who engages in gentler pursuits.

If the claimant's injuries thus deprive the claimant of the capacity to engage in sport or other pastimes, which he enjoyed before his injury, then this must be compensated. Other losses compensated under this heading include impairment of one of the five senses;[7] loss or impairment of sexual life;[8] diminution of marriage prospects (an item which is additional to the pecuniary loss that may result from such an event); destroyed holiday;[9] inability to play with one's children;[10] and many others.

Until fairly recently, it was uncertain whether this heading of damage was separate from or merely part of any award for pain and suffering. In other words, what was unclear was whether the damages are awarded in respect of the *objective loss of amenities*, or in respect of the subjective mental

---

[4] *Fletcher v. Autocar and Transporters Ltd* [1968] 2 QB 322 at 340–1 (per Diplock LJ) and 364 (per Salmon LJ).

[5] See *Hicks v. Chief Constable of South Yorkshire Police* [1992] 2 All ER 65.

[6] [1964] AC 326 at 341. See also *Lim Poh Choo v. Camden and Islington Area Health Authority* [1980] AC 174, per Lord Scarman at 183.

[7] e.g. taste and smell: *Cook v. J.L. Kier and Co.* [1970] 1 WLR 774.

[8] *Ibid.*     [9] *Ichard v. Frangoulis* [1977] 1 WLR 556.

[10] *Hoffman v. Sofaer* [1982] 1 WLR 1350.

suffering which comes with the appreciation of such loss. In *Wise* v. *Kaye*[11] the claimant was rendered immediately unconscious and remained so at the time of the trial three-and-a-half years later. Though she had suffered an almost complete loss of her faculties, she had no knowledge whatever of this loss. For Diplock LJ this was a good reason for awarding her a comparatively small sum under this heading. However, the majority of the Court of Appeal thought otherwise, and two years later in *H. West & Son Ltd* v. *Shephard*[12] the House of Lords agreed with this view. As Lord Morris put it:

the fact of unconsciousness is . . . relevant in respect of and will eliminate those heads or elements of damage which can exist only by being felt or thought or experienced. The fact of unconsciousness does not, however, eliminate the actuality of the deprivation of the ordinary experiences and amenities of life which may be the inevitable result of some physical injury.

This majority view was reaffirmed in *Lim Poh Choo* v. *Camden and Islington Area Health Authority*,[13] where Lord Scarman said that the cases draw a clear distinction between damages for pain and suffering and damages for loss of amenities. The former depend upon the claimant's personal awareness of pain, her capacity for suffering. But the latter are awarded for the fact of deprivation – a substantial loss, whether the claimant is aware of it or not. Nevertheless, his judgment leaves one with the impression that an important reason for accepting this view was his desire not to disturb what had become an established rule, since it has influenced both judicial awards and extra-judicial settlements for many years.[14]

The levels of awards for pain and suffering *and* loss of amenities have become an increasingly important issue over the past twenty years. In 1999, we noted that the highest awards for pain and suffering and loss of amenities were around the £100,000 mark.[15] Faced with similar (and, often, much larger) awards, various systems (e.g., Canada, Eire and a number

---

[11] [1962] 1 QB 638.

[12] [1964] AC 326. The vigorous dissents of Lords Reid and Devlin repay careful study.

[13] [1980] AC 174.

[14] [1980] AC 174 at 189. A second reason given was that this reform would be best effected by means of comprehensive legislation. Other jurisdictions have not adopted this rule; and the Pearson Committee recommended its abolition (Cmnd 7054–1, 1978), vol. I, para. 398. The Law Commission recently recommended that no change should be made to the position established since *H. West & Son Ltd* v. *Shephard* and confirmed in *Lim* (*Damages for Personal Injury: Non-Pecuniary Loss* (Law Com. No. 257, 1999), esp. paras 2.19 and 2.24).

[15] £95,000 was, e.g., awarded in *Brightman* v. *Johnson* (quoted by Kemp and Kemp, *The Quantum of Damages*, vol. 2, para. 1–010) whereas in *Housecroft* v. *Burnett* [1986] 1

of jurisdictions in the USA) have opted for judicially or legislatively imposed maxima for non-pecuniary losses. The idea – known as 'capping' –
has much to commend it, especially in the case of unconscious claimants
(who still receive substantial awards for loss of amenities). On the other
hand, the Law Commission has, on more than one occasion, suggested that
current levels may be insufficient.[16] Now, the Court of Appeal, in the case
of Heil v. Rankin,[17] has ruled that certain increases should be made for more
serious injuries where awards are over the £10,000 mark. The increases
to be made are not uniform, but range from around a one-third increase
for awards at the highest levels (i.e., very serious injuries e.g., quadriplegia and severe brain damage) tapering down to no increase for awards of
£10,000 and below.[18] The court examined the reasoning which the Law
Commission had used in making its 1999 proposals, expressing particular
appreciation for the role played by increased life expectancy in such as-
sessments, both in general and in terms of those suffering serious injury,

All ER 332, O'Connor LJ thought £75,000 was an appropriate guideline for the average
incident of tetraplegia.

[16] See *Personal Injury Compensation: How Much is Enough?* (Law Com. No. 225, 1994) and
*Damages for Personal Injury: Non-Pecuniary Loss* (Law Com. No. 257, 1999) for detailed
discussion, including the results of extensive surveys and consultation responses. The
1999 Report proposed that awards up to £2,000 should see no increase, awards between
£2,000 and £3,000 should be increased by up to 150 per cent of present levels and
awards over £3,000 should see at least an increase of 150 per cent (and, indeed, possibly
200 per cent) of present levels.

[17] [2001] QB 272. A five-judge Court of Appeal was convened to hear the appeal, indicating
the importance attached to the issue, and Lord Woolf MR delivered the court's
judgment.

[18] The judgment states that it 'is our view that between those awards at the highest level,
which require an upwards adjustment of one-third, and those awards where no
adjustment is required, the extent of the adjustment should taper downwards, as
illustrated by our decisions on the individual appeals which are before us'. On closer
inspection, this taper does not appear to descend evenly: *Warren v. Northern General
Hospital NHS Trust* and *Annable v. Southern Derbyshire Health Authority* (conjoined appeals
with *Heil v. Rankin*) saw the Court of Appeal increase the award from £135,000 to
£175,000 (the new figure amounting to c. 130 per cent of the old), *Ramsay v. Rivers* saw an
increase of approximately 25 per cent (£110,270 to £138,000), *Kent v. Griffiths (No. 2)* an
increase of around 20 per cent (£80,000 to £95,000), *Rees v. Mabco (102) Ltd* around
10 per cent (£45,000 to £50,000), *Schofield v. Saunders & Taylor Ltd* 10 per cent (£40,000 to
£44,000) and in *Connolly v. Tasker*, the court reassessed damages on the conventional
basis but made no increase in the level available (the sum being only £4,000 after the
Court of Appeal's amendment). In *Heil v. Rankin* itself, no order was made due to other
complications yet to be dealt with in the case, although the court stressed that it would
recommend no increase in the level of damages, since the sum fell below the £10,000
threshold laid down earlier in the judgment. Appended to the judgment is a diagram
showing the levels of increases made, which may aid the reader in placing these various
increases into context.

who may often live to a 'normal' average age in spite of their injuries. However, doubts were also expressed about placing too much reliance on evidence found in various surveys since the material collected might well be susceptible to a number of interpretations and explanations, rather than just dissatisfaction with the level of damages for pain and suffering and loss of amenities.[19] The very highest award available in England is thus £205,000 for quadriplegia. No individual, however seriously injured, can receive more under the heading of general damages.

## The 'assessment' concept of general damages

The above figures should not be taken to represent anything more than illustrations. In this subsection we wish to stress that the word '*assessment*' of damage is used advisedly. There is no mathematical or scientific calculation involved in arriving at the appropriate figure.[20] As stated, there exist tariffs which were recently reviewed by the Court of Appeal in *Heil v. Rankin*.[21]

The guidelines set a bracket for general damages for all types of injury. What they do not, and could not, do is to provide a bracket for every conceivable combination of injuries. How, therefore, does the trial judge approach his assessment? The answer is through a broad assessment of all the evidence. A useful checklist might be:

(a)  What were the circumstances of the accident?
(b)  What was the degree of pain and suffering undergone by the claimant in the accident itself?
(c)  What was the length and nature of the treatment undergone by the claimant?
(d)  What is the most serious injury suffered by the claimant?
(e)  What other injuries did the claimant suffer?
(f)  What are the residual disabilities of the claimant?
(g)  To what extent, if at all, has the claimant been unable to lead a normal life as a result of those disabilities up to the date of trial?
(h)  What is the extent to which, if at all, the claimant will be unable to lead a normal life as a result of those disabilities in the future?

The judge then has to make his assessment taking all these matters into account. As has already been said, the exercise is neither an exact science nor a mathematical calculation. The judge does not, for example, say that an individual should have £5,000 for a broken leg and £3,000 for an injury

---

[19]  See [2001] QB 272 at 302–13.    [20]  *Fuhri v. Jones*, CA, No. 199, 30 March 1979.
[21]  [2001] QB 272.

to his arm, making £8,000 in all. He will consider all the factors on the checklist and arrive at a final figure.

Despite appearing remote, judges, even in England, are human beings. It would be idle to deny that, inevitably, some claimants make a good impression upon them while others do not. Likewise, while some judges are parsimonious, others are inclined to greater generosity. Practitioners in the subject would subscribe to these views and would deny a too rigid differentiation between the judges' aloofness and the jury's proclivity towards deserving claimants. The Court of Appeal will not interfere with an award of general damages unless it is plainly outside the bracket of what is reasonable, having regard to the broad tariff in the Judicial Studies Board (JSB) guidelines. As a result, it is rarely possible in England to give an exact figure for what a particular claimant is likely to recover in any given case. The best any practitioner can do is to provide a bracket.

## Psychiatric injury

Special considerations apply to psychological injuries which, once known as 'nervous shock',[22] now tend to be bracketed under the heading of 'psychiatric injury'.

The starting point is to specify what is meant by psychiatric harm. Damages cannot be recovered for mere grief or emotional distress at an injury or death, even of a loved one: 'in English law no damages are awarded for grief or sorrow caused by a person's death'.[23] However, there is in principle a distinction between mere grief and a more serious, prolonged psychiatric condition which may be identified with the help of expert medical testimony. Medical science now recognises a condition known as 'posttraumatic stress disorder', which may occur in reaction to the violent or unexpected death of a close relative or friend.[24] In *Alcock* v. *Chief Constable of South Yorkshire Police*, relatives and friends of spectators who were crushed to death inside a football stadium as a result of police negligence brought actions for damages based on psychiatric illness suffered in reaction to the event. Some had witnessed the scene at the ground. Yet others had not seen the event but had suffered reactions from, amongst other things, fear that a close friend or relative had been killed or injured; being told that such a person had indeed been killed; and identifying the body at

---

[22] In American law they tend to be referred to as emotional distress.

[23] *Hinz* v. *Berry* [1970] 2 QB 40 at 42 (per Lord Denning MR).

[24] Older terms for similar conditions would include neurasthenia, shell shock and nostalgia: see [1992] 1 AC 310 at 317.

the temporary mortuary set up near the ground. The nature of the condition from which the claimants were suffering was described in court as follows:

It is classified as an anxiety disorder. It follows on a painful event, which is outside the normal human experience, the disorder involves preoccupation with the event – that is intrusive memories – with avoidance of reminders of the experience. At the same time there are persistent symptoms of increased arousal – these symptoms may be experienced in the form of sleep difficulty, irritability or outbursts of anger, problems with memory or concentration, startle responses, hyper vigilance and over-reaction to any reminder of the event... Many [of the claimants] described an inability or difficulty in carrying out normal life activities such as work, family responsibilities or any activity normally engaged in before the disaster... All those in whom post-traumatic stress disorder was identified appear to have undergone a personality change, the significant features of which [included] being moody, irritable, forgetful and withdrawn within themselves, [and] frequent unprovoked outbursts of anger and quarrelsome behaviour were reported.[25]

The House of Lords restricted damages to those who had been within sight or hearing of the event or its immediate aftermath. The House held that the law should not compensate shock brought about by communication by a third party. It also dismissed the claims of those who had seen the events on live television, holding that the television pictures did not depict suffering of recognisable individuals since that was excluded by the broadcasting code of ethics.

The next thing to note is that as a result of a complicated and not always rational development of the law in the last ten years or so, English courts have come to make compensation depend crucially upon whether the claimant is a primary or secondary victim of the accident.

## Primary victims

A 'primary victim' has been defined as one who suffers psychiatric injury after being directly involved in an accident and is *either* himself physically injured *or* put in fear of injury. A 'secondary victim' suffers psychiatric injury as a consequence of witnessing or being informed about an accident, which involves another. As far as primary victims are concerned, it is well established that an accident victim who is physically injured through the negligence of another may, in principle, recover damages for the psychiatric as well as the physical consequences of the accident, subject to the

---

[25] [1992] 1 AC 310 at 317.

normal rules of causation and remoteness of damage.[26] Equally, if the claimant's person is negligently endangered and he is placed in fear of an injury, which does not actually occur, the early cases[27] clearly indicate that there will be liability. These decisions were reaffirmed by the House of Lords in *Page* v. *Smith*[28] which, though the subject of some trenchant criticism,[29] remains good law.

## Secondary victims

The real difficulties begin when the claimant himself was neither physically injured nor threatened with injury. Such claimants were termed 'secondary victims' by Lord Lloyd. The victim may have suffered a psychological reaction after witnessing the scene of an accident where another is killed or injured or through fear of injury to another, which does not then materialise. Witnessing a scene may take the form of being present at the event itself, seeing it relayed on television or hearing about it on the radio, or coming onto the scene in its immediate aftermath.[30] Alternatively,

---

[26] In the unusual case of *Meah* v. *McCreamer (No. 1)* [1985] 1 All ER 367, the claimant recovered damages for the consequences of a car crash which included a personality change and his subsequent imprisonment following conviction for offences of rape and assault. See also the Australian case of *Jaensch* v. *Coffey* (1984) 155 CLR 549, discussed by F.A. Trindade, 'The Principles Governing the Recovery of Damages for Negligently Caused Nervous Shock' [1986] CLJ 476 at 477.

[27] *Bell* v. *Great Northern Railway Company of Ireland* (1890) 26 LR Ir. 428, not following *Victorian Railways Commissioners* v. *Coultas* (1888) 3 App. Cas. 222; *Dulieu* v. *White & Sons* [1901] 2 KB 669.

[28] [1996] 1 AC 155. In *Page*, the defendant, driving carelessly, caused a collision between his car and that being driven by the claimant. The latter, although receiving no physical injury at the time or later, later suffered a reaction which led to the revival of the condition ME (myalgic encephalomyelitis) which left him chronically ill and unable to work. In his leading judgment, Lord Lloyd said that in the case of a primary victim such as the claimant – i.e., one directly involved in an accident – it was not necessary to consider whether psychiatric injury had been foreseeable. It was enough that injury of some kind, either physical or psychiatric, was foreseeable. For an application of *Page*, see *Nobles* v. *Schofield*, CA, judgment of 14 May 1998, discussed by Nicholas Mullany, 'English Psychiatric Injury Law – Chronically Depressing' (1999) 115 LQR 30.

[29] See the judgment of Lord Goff of Chieveley in *White* v. *Chief Constable of South Yorkshire Police* [1999] 2 AC 455 at 473–7.

[30] *Atkinson* v. *Seghal* [2003] All ER (D) 341 (Mar) (Court of Appeal Civil Division, judgment of 21 March 2003); *North Glamorgan NHS Trust* v. *Walters* [2003] Lloyd's Rep. Med. 49. In both cases the Court of Appeal extended the meaning of 'immediate aftermath'. In the first case the appellant's daughter died in a road accident. The mother arrived at the police cordon whilst she was looking for E and was told by a police officer that E had died. About an hour and a half later, the mother visited the mortuary where she saw E's face and head which were disfigured. The Court of Appeal held that 'immediate aftermath' extended from the moment of the accident until the moment the appellant left the

the reaction may have been brought about by being informed of another's death or injury in particular circumstances. As the law presently stands, however, the victim who has seen the events on television or heard about them on the radio cannot be compensated.[31] Psychiatric injury could occur without a 'shock' of any kind being sustained, for example through the burden of caring for an injured relative. The nature of the relationship between the claimant and the person suffering the injury in question could range from that of a close family tie to the relations of friendship or employment; the claimant could be a rescuer or a mere bystander. At a further extreme, damage to property, such as a house, or to a much-loved pet, could induce a reaction of this kind. In each of these cases the psychological reaction suffered by the claimant may be entirely foreseeable. However, for secondary victims, foreseeability of psychiatric damage being inflicted on the claimant is a necessary but not sufficient condition for establishing a duty of care.[32] If, for these purposes, the law regarded psychiatric harm as equivalent to physical harm, there would be no difficulty about a duty of care arising and liability would then depend on questions of fault, causation and remoteness. Many cases might fail at these later stages, particularly on questions of causation. But the common law does not currently take this view.

The prevailing view instead is that the extent of the duty of care is limited by a number of essentially arbitrary factors. In particular, the claimant will have to show, in general, that: (a) he was not abnormally susceptible to this type of harm; (b) that his illness or condition was caused by a 'shock' of some kind; (c) that he either witnessed the event directly

---

mortuary. In *North Glamorgan NHS Trust*, the claimant was a mother of the baby son who suffered severe brain damage as a result of the hospital's negligence. Initially she was sleeping in the same room and saw him coughing blood. She was initially told that no brain damage had occurred. She followed the ambulance in which he was taken from one hospital to another. The following day she was advised that the brain was so badly damaged that he would have no quality of life. She agreed to terminate the life support and her son died in her arms. The Court of Appeal held that the whole thirty-six-hour period was one drawn out experience and that the claimant could recover damages in respect of her injuries for all the events which occurred during that period.

[31] *Alcock* v. *Chief Constable of South Yorkshire Police*, n. 25 above.

[32] In some early decisions the courts denied recovery to what would now be classified as 'secondary victims' who were not in the likely area of *physical* impact: see *Behrens* v. *Bertram Mills Circus Ltd* [1957] 2 QB 1 and *King* v. *Phillips* [1953] 1 QB 429, where the judges were divided on the reason for denying recovery. In *Bourhill* v. *Young* [1943] AC 92, Lords Wright and Porter argued for the test of foreseeability of shock or psychiatric damage, and this was accepted by the Privy Council in *The Wagon Mound (No. 1)* [1961] AC 388. These dicta should not now be read as referring to primary victims following the judgment of Lord Lloyd in *Page* v. *Smith* [1996] AC 155 (see in particular at 189).

or came upon its immediate aftermath; and (d) that his relationship with the accident victim was sufficiently 'proximate' in the sense defined by the judges. All these conditions have raised their own difficulties and the reader who wishes more details must look for them in the specialised textbooks on tort law.[33] But the claims of two further types of victims must be borne in mind to complete this summary picture of the law. What these cases have in common is that here – unlike the cases thus far considered – the claimant and defendant are known to each other in advance. Indeed, one could argue that the defendant in these cases can be regarded as having assumed a responsibility towards the claimant not carelessly to expose him to the risk of psychiatric harm. In other words, the existence of a pre-tort 'special relationship' of this kind may be the basis for a finding of a duty of care when, otherwise, the conditions for the existence of a duty would not be satisfied.

Thus, first, the responsibility owed by schools and educational authorities to children in their care or under their control seems fairly well established. This principle of the responsibility of the individual teacher to his students was accepted by the House of Lords in *X (Minors)* v. *Bedfordshire County Council*.[34] In *Phelps* v. *Hillingdon London Borough Council* the House of Lords refused to strike out an action based on the direct duty owed by a public authority with responsibility for educational services.[35] The potential for the application of this principle is apparent from a decision of the Court of Appeal, *Bradford-Smart* v. *West Sussex County Council*,[36] in which an action was brought against the defendant for not taking steps to prevent the bullying of the claimant by some of her schoolmates. The bullying took place out of school, but it was argued that the defendant should have taken steps to discipline the perpetrators. It was found, on the facts, that the school had not acted negligently, but the existence of a duty of care was recognised by the court.

The principle of assumption of responsibility may be taken further to cover cases in which the defendant can be seen as being under a duty of care to transmit distressing information to the claimant in a sensitive and careful manner. In *AB* v. *Tameside and Glossop Health Authority*[37] the defendant sent out letters warning former patients that a health worker

---

[33] For instance, Basil Markesinis and Simon Deakin, *Tort Law* (Simon Deakin, Angus Johnston and Basil Markesinis (eds), 5th edn, OUP, 2003), ch. 2.

[34] [1995] 2 AC 633 at 766 (per Lord Browne-Wilkinson).     [35] [2001] 2 AC 619.

[36] [2002] 1 FCR 425; [2002] LGR 489, CA, judgment of 23 January 2002; see also *Gower* v. *London Borough of Bromley* [1999] ELR 356; Paula Giliker, 'A 'New' Head of Damages: Damages for Mental Distress in the English Law of Torts' (2000) 20 *Legal Studies* 272.

[37] [1997] 8 Med. LR 91.

from whom they had previously received obstetric treatment had tested positive for HIV, leading to the risk that they would contract the disease. The letters were sent by standard post and no arrangements were made for counselling (although these were later put in place). Claims in respect of psychiatric injury caused by the way in which the news of the possible risk to health was transmitted were rejected by the Court of Appeal, but only after counsel for the defendants had conceded the existence of a duty of care. As Nicholas Mullany has argued, this concession seems justified: there was a pre-existing relationship and psychiatric harm was foreseeable.[38] The existence of a duty of care should not depend upon the information being false. Nevertheless, it should be borne in mind that even if a duty is established, there may be problems of causation: the claimant will have to show that the shock would not have been suffered anyway.

Secondly, the courts have had considerable difficulty in classifying the claims of employees who witness traumatic deaths or injuries of colleagues.

In *Dooley v. Cammell Laird & Co., Ltd*[39] an employee was allowed to recover for the fear that his workmates might have been injured when the crane he was operating, through no fault of his own, dropped a load into the hold of a ship. In *Alcock*,[40] on the other hand, Hidden J considered that it was the nature of the activity or the task undertaken by the employee, and not the relationship he might have with the accident victim, that determined liability. This seems to be the best approach: the liability of the employer in most cases should depend on the duty of care which he owes to employees not to expose them to undue risk of harm, either physical or psychiatric. An employee will only be able to claim as a *secondary* victim if he comes under one of the categories of protected close friends or relatives outlined in *Alcock*.[41] In *White*, confusion was caused by the failure of the courts to distinguish clearly between the two very different types of claim being made by the claimants, namely their claims as secondary victims and their claims as employees. The claim of an employee arises

---

[38] Nicholas Mullany, 'Liability for Careless Communication of Traumatic Information' (1998) 114 LQR 380. Mullany also suggests that even if there is no pre-existing relationship, a duty of care can arise from the assumption of responsibility, which is inherent in the transmission of bad news (see at 383). This would go further than the proposition outlined in the text. See also *Andrews v. Secretary of State for Health* (Queen's Bench Division, judgment of 19 June 1998), discussed by Mullany, (1999) 115 LQR 30 at 36.

[39] [1951] 1 Lloyd's Rep. 271. See also *Galt v. British Railways Board* (1983) 133 NLJ 870.

[40] [1992] 1 AC 310 at 346–7.

[41] See *MacFarlane v. EE Caledonia Ltd* [1994] 2 All ER 1 and *Robertson v. Forth Road Bridge Joint Board* [1995] IRLR 251.

from the relationship between him and his employer, under which the employer is under a duty to take reasonable care for the safety of his employee at work.[42] This claim is not, therefore, parasitic on witnessing a particular event, which causes harm to another. Indeed, for the purposes of this claim (in contrast to an employee's claim as a secondary victim) it is in principle *neither necessary nor sufficient* that the employer's negligence (or that of an employee of the employer) should have led to the accident in question. It is not necessary for the reason that case law suggests that the employer may be responsible for avoiding causing psychiatric harm to his employee in a number of situations. But nor is it sufficient, since an employer may be entitled to expect employees to withstand a certain level of exposure to stress. In particular, an employer is arguably entitled to expect that employees who are trained in rescue services will be able to withstand a greater degree of exposure to shock than ordinary members of the public. Thus, in such situations, police and fire officers may expect to have greater difficulty in showing that their employer has been *in breach* of the personal duty of care which he owes them.

This last point is highly relevant to *White* v. *Chief Constable of South Yorkshire Police*.[43] It cannot be argued that the Chief Constable was in breach of his duty as employer *simply* for exposing his officers to the harrowing scenes which they witnessed. If the disaster had occurred through the fault of a third party, it seems inconceivable that a reasonable employer would, in the circumstances, have withdrawn his officers from the scene. Does it make any difference that the employer, in *White*, was responsible for the accident occurring in the first place? At this point, difficult issues of causation arise. It is possible to argue that the claimants in *White* suffered *additional* distress and abuse from the crowd and from relatives during and after the events in the stadium because of the role of their fellow officers in causing the deaths of the victims. More generally, the accumulation of circumstances – the employer's initial responsibility for the disaster together with the highly stressful situation in which the claimants were then placed – could be seen as placing the employer in breach of his duty to have regard to their physical and psychiatric health and safety, as Lord Goff argued in his dissent.

Unfortunately, the approach taken by the majority in *White* was to question whether the employer owed his employees a duty of care at all, in the situation which arose in that case. According to Lord Steyn, the liability of

---

[42] *Wilsons & Clyde Coal Co., Ltd* v. *English* [1938] AC 57 and *Alcock* v. *Chief Constable of South Yorkshire Police*, n. 25 above.

[43] [1999] 2 AC 455.

the employer to his employees depended on general principles of tort law, which limited the degree to which psychiatric damage was compensable; there was nothing to be gained, then, from formulating the claim as one of employer's liability. If this approach is taken, then a major restriction has been placed on the extent of the employer's personal liability. Lord Hoffmann, on the other hand, seemed to accept that earlier cases, which had held that an employer could be liable for causing certain types of psychiatric harm to an employee, had been correctly decided. However, his Lordship seems to have considered that this line of authority was of no relevance in a case where the psychiatric harm in question was sustained through witnessing the death or injury of another, although why this exception should be carved out of the general law of employer's liability is not clear.

As the law currently stands, then, *White* has cast serious doubt over the principle that an employer can be liable under certain circumstances for psychiatric harm sustained by one of his employees. At the very least, it seems that in cases of nervous shock, where the harm is sustained by witnessing another's death or injury, there is little or nothing to be gained by framing the case as one of employer's liability. Potentially, *White* is a highly restrictive decision for the law of employer's liability.

## Loss of marriage prospects

Unsurprisingly, in the modern politically correct world, this is not formally recognised as a separate and distinct head of damage.[44] Various brackets for the type of injury which may adversely affect the ability of an individual to form a relationship with another person already encompass that fact as part of his or her loss of amenity.

Physical injury to sexual or reproductive organs is, however, a recognised, and separate, physical injury and features as such within the JSB guidelines.

Scarring may attract a greater award if the injured individual is a young female. That is not upon the basis of diminution of marriage prospects but rather general loss of amenity and embarrassment.[45]

## Loss of congenial employment

English law recognises, as a separate head of loss, that an individual may well, in consequence of his injuries, lose employment which he found

---

[44] *Moriarty* v. *McCarthy* [1978] 1 WLR 155.

[45] This is recognised in the JSB guidelines in relation to facial disfigurement where the introduction says, in terms, that the distinction between male and female and the subjective approach are of particular significance.

fulfilling and satisfying. A separate sum, in addition to general damages for pain and suffering, and loss of amenity, may be awarded for such loss.

It is not necessary that the employment which has been lost should be glamorous or even particularly extraordinary. In *Hale v. London Underground Ltd*,[46] Otton J said:

> There can be no doubt that there is a considerable feeling of fulfilment and satisfaction to attend a fire, to extinguish it quickly and safely, and to rescue any persons inside the building before they suffer fatal or other terrible injuries. I consider this a real loss to Mr Hale and it is not mitigated by any enjoyment from his present work.

The evidence required to establish this head of loss is, as appears from that passage, fulfilment and satisfaction in the job and an obvious commitment to it.

As with general damages, awards are not calculated on any mathematical or scientific basis. In *Hale v. London Underground Ltd* the award was £5,000. That is probably the middle of the bracket for the average case although it is capable of being considerably more in the case of a glamorous occupation. In 2001, a claimant received £7,500 for loss of congenial employment as a kick-boxer and instructor![47] A similar sum was awarded to a twenty-five-year-old woman who lost her career as a professional woman. She was said to have been an exceptionally gifted double bass player, having studied at the Royal Academy of Music under some of the foremost double bass players in the world. Had she not succeeded as a soloist, she would have obtained a post in a leading orchestra.[48] The highest award which we have been able to find, to date, is £8,750 for the loss of an executive position.[49]

As is apparent from the foregoing, the amounts under this head are not large.

## German law

### Introduction

### General principles

The German law of damages is based on the principle of putting the claimant in the position he was in before the commission of the wrong (*Naturalrestitution*). Thus, as a basic principle, damages aim at restoring the

---

[46] [1993] PIQR Q30.    [47] *Langford v. Hebran* [2001] EWCA Civ 361; [2001] PIQR Q160.
[48] *Byers v. London Borough of Brent*, QBD, judgment of 24 April 1998 (unreported).
[49] *Pratt v. Smith*, 2003 (unreported).

status quo ante. To this end, the situation of the claimant is considered hypothetically as it would have been without the conduct or event that entitles him to damages. The resulting difference is the object of the claim.

As for pecuniary headings, a claimant entitled to damages on the grounds of violation of his person or property can, by choice, demand payment of the amount of money necessary for the reparation instead of 'restitution' proper. Payment of money can also be demanded if, for certain legally defined reasons, the 'restitution' is either impossible or not feasible.

It is, however, in the nature of non-pecuniary headings that 'restitution' in the sense understood by German law (i.e., *return to the status quo ante*) cannot truly be achieved.

The loss suffered by the claimant may, however, be compensated by means of a payment of an adequate sum of money which can grant a certain amount of satisfaction. It is therefore seen in this light rather than as a straightforward indemnification of the loss. The abstract idea of an appropriate indemnification thus prevails over the notion of *restitutio in integrum*.[50]

This has led the German legislator basically to exempt, in essence, non-pecuniary headings from the system of damages and to allow compensation in the above-mentioned sense only in particular and legally defined cases. The basic regulation is found in § 253 BGB, which in its first paragraph states the basic rule, namely, the non-compensability of non-pecuniary headings of harm. Exceptions from this basic rule require explicit legislative authorisation.

By far the most important regulation of that kind is to be found in the second paragraph of § 253 BGB (formerly § 847 BGB). It grants compensation for non-pecuniary headings as a consequence of any claim on the grounds of an injury of the body, freedom, health or sexual self-determination of the claimant. Here, the technical relation of rule and exception is virtually converted into its opposite.

The legal basis for the original claim, formerly[51] playing a crucial role as non-pecuniary losses were compensable only under tort law, is now irrelevant. Any claim for damages involving a violation of any of the interests enumerated in § 253 II BGB, automatically entitles the claimant

---

[50] On this see Basil Markesinis and Hannes Unberath, *The German Law of Torts: A Comparative Treatise* (4th edn, Oxford, 2002), p. 981 (henceforth referred to as *GLT*).

[51] Before the 'Zweites Gesetz zur Änderung Schadensersatzrechtlicher Vorschriften' took effect on 1 August 2002.

to non-pecuniary damages as far as they result from the violation of the respective interest.

Other provisions, such as § 11 S. 2 StVG or § 8 S. 2 ProdHG simply extend the rule of § 253 II BGB to the area of strict liability. The extent of such a claim for compensation is, of course, subject to general and further regulations as, for example, the crucial principle of causality. Furthermore, it is defined by the idea and intention of the rule of law upon which the claim is based.

The only other statutory regulations granting compensation for non-pecuniary headings are § 651 f II BGB which compensates for spoilt holidays, and § 611 a II, III BGB which compensates for sex discrimination in employment matters.

## Interference with honour and reputation[52]

A judge-made exception to the rule in § 253 I BGB in cases of the infringement of personality rights has recently been established in an incontrovertible way by the BGH in the 'Caroline' case.[53]

Even before the above-mentioned decision, and notwithstanding § 253 I BGB, the BGH granted compensation for immaterial damages resulting from interference with honour and reputation. Thus, in the *Herrenreiter* case,[54] the claimant, a well-known industrialist, was an amateur equestrian. The manufacturer of a tonic designed to increase sexual performance used, without the claimant's consent, a picture of him taken during a tournament for the purposes of advertising its product.

The claimant claimed DM15,000 (c. €7,500) as compensation for interference with his honour and reputation on the grounds that his advertising a product was incompatible with his social status and exposed him to the opprobrium of his peers. The BGH confirmed the judgment of the trial court granting DM10,000 (c. €5,000). The compensation was justified as satisfaction for the immaterial damage done to the claimant's personality. The court assumed from article 1, 2 of the Constitution that personality itself was to be protected to a larger extent than originally intended by the legislator of the BGB. For without the entitlement to damages, the constitutional protection of human dignity (and personality) would be ineffective. Thus, § 847 BGB (the former version of § 253 II BGB) was to be applied by analogy. In a subsequent decision, the BGH preferred to base

---

[52] Detailed and comparative to English law: Funkel, *Schutz der Persönlichkeit durch Ersatz immaterieller Schäden in Geld* (München, 2001).

[53] For details on the evolution of the substantive law, see *GLT*, pp. 472 ff., 685 ff. and 923.

[54] BGH 14 February 1958, BGHZ 26, 349 ff.

the claim directly on § 823 I BGB in connection with article 1, 2 Grundge-setz (instead of on § 847).[55] Therefore, the violation of personality rights was not expressly mentioned when the legislator moved the former § 847 to § 253 II BGB in 2002; the basis for such claims has not been altered.

*Principles of fair compensation and satisfaction*[56]

### Basic principles

According to § 253 II BGB, the injured person is entitled to 'fair compen-sation by payment of money'. In its case law regarding the former § 847 BGB (now the statutory regulation preceding § 253 II BGB), the BGH has over the years developed principles for the assessment of the damages. As usual, therefore, in German law one has to consult the case law in order to add flesh to the bones of the codal structure. The basic ideas can be found in the judgment of the Great Senate of the Federal Court of 6 July 1955.[57]

In this judgment, the Great Senate analysed the idea of indemnification as expressed in § 253 II BGB and found two basic principles, thus acknowl-edging the dual function of this provision.[58] In the first place, it is aimed at granting the claimant fair compensation for the infringements caused by the act complained of. To that extent, it compensates for the loss of amenities and joy of life of the injured person as a result of the injury by making other amenities possible.[59]

This idea of fair compensation by payment of money will, however, fail in cases where the claimant is so well situated that he can afford every form of amenity even without any payment from the tortfeasor. Since neither § 253 II BGB nor the former § 847 BGB establishes exceptions for such cases, the character of the provision could not fully be explained by the concept of fair compensation. In search of further elements, the Great Senate thus stated that the provision, on a second level, also aimed at providing satisfaction for the infringement, an idea already known to Swiss law.[60]

---

[55] BGH 5 December 1995, NJW 1996, 984, 985 ('*verfassungsunmittelbarer Ersatz des immateriellen Schadens*').

[56] See also *GLT*, p. 916 ff.

[57] BGH 6 July 1955, BGHZ 18, 149–68 (the Great Senate has the sole function to decide issues disputed between the Senates of the Federal Court, § 132 Gerichtsverfassungsgesetz).

[58] BGHGS 6 July 1955, BGHZ 18, 149, 154 ff.

[59] See Hermann Lange/Gottfried Schiemann, *Schadensersatz*, § 7 V 2 with further citations.

[60] Articles 47, 49, 60 OR; BGHGS 6 July 1955, BGHZ 18, 149, 155 ff.

This second element has generated substantial criticism from the legal literature. To grant satisfaction regardless of the situation of the injured person is considered a penalty under civil law and that, in principle at least, is unknown to the German legal system. Furthermore, the German Constitution requires procedural standards for the infliction of a criminal penalty and also provides specific remedies against its wrongful imposition which German civil procedural law does not do. Some authors thus find the element of satisfaction to be unconstitutional.[61]

The Federal Court, on the other hand, denied the punitive character of the compensation.[62] While punishment serves the interests of the public, which would not be within the scope of civil law, satisfaction concerns the injured person's private interests. It is therefore entirely of a private law nature. It is for this reason that the fact that the tortfeasor has already been sentenced in a criminal trial has been held to have no effect on the measure of the damages awarded in the subsequent civil trial.[63] To an outside observer, however, this result does not appear to be equitable.

In another decision of the Federal Court,[64] the defendant bank robber had put his arm around the claimant's neck while at the same time holding an authentic-looking (but, in reality, fake) gun to her head. He threatened to shoot her if he were not given enough money. The claimant experienced great fear and, as a result, suffered sleep disorder and nightmares for a period of at least six months. Even at the time of the judgment, she complained of increased irritability with the consequence that her ability to work under pressure was lowered, something which had even forced her to give up her previous employment. Upon the defendant's appeal against the judgment of the Landgericht, the OLG lowered the amount granted as damages from DM8,000 (c. €4,000) to DM4,000 (c. €2,000) on the grounds that the element of satisfaction was of no relevance to the level of damages since the defendant had already been punished by a criminal court.

---

[61] Hermann Lange/Gottfried Schiemann, *Schadensersatz*, § 7 V 2 with further citations. Some of these objections have, of course, also been raised in the common law context by those who find punitive damages to be – to put it mildly – an anomaly. But the different 'constitutional' settings of different common law systems give differing strength to these objections.

[62] BGH 6 July 1955, BGHZ 18, 149, 155; BGH 29 November 1994, BGHZ 128, 117, 122.

[63] BGH 29 November 1994, BGHZ 128, 117, 122 ff. with further citations; BGH 16 January 1996, NJW 1996, 1591; OLG Celle 26 November 1992, VersR 1993, 976, 977; OLG Hamm 7 June 1993, NJW-RR 1994, 94; OLG Köln 14 November 1991, NJW-RR 1992, 221.

[64] BGH 29 November 1994, BGHZ 128, 117 ff.

The claimant appealed against this judgment of the Court of Appeal and the Federal Court restored the judgment of the trial court granting the claimant an amount of DM8,000 (c. €4,000). It stated that the indemnification was not to be divided into two separate amounts, one of which met the element of fair compensation while the other corresponded to the element of satisfaction. Both were rather to be taken into account as factors in the assessment of the non-pecuniary damage. Moreover, the criminal conviction had no influence on the element of satisfaction, for the latter was not aimed at the public interest in the prosecution of the criminal but served solely the interests of the injured person.

In another case,[65] the claimant claimed compensation for sexual abuse by the defendant who had already been convicted by a criminal court. The Court of Appeal again reduced the amount granted by the trial court from DM60,000 (c. €30,000) to DM25,000 (c. €12,500) on the grounds that the claimant had already obtained justice through the criminal conviction of the delinquent. Once again, the Federal Court reversed the judgment arguing that the element of satisfaction had its origins in the relation of tortfeasor and injured person and, therefore, was substantially different from the state's right to prosecute.

## Particularities in cases of interference with honour and reputation

The above principles are valid for the compensation of pain and suffering resulting from personal injury. As for interference with honour and reputation, the German courts have established an *extra legem* exception to the rule of non-compensation of non-pecuniary headings.[66] In these cases, the claim for damages is based on the idea of preventing the tortfeasor (as well as possible successors) from repeating the interference. This different basis may lead to substantially diverging results in the assessment of the damages i.e., most probably to higher amounts. The Constitutional Court (Bundesverfassungsgericht) has considered this difference compatible with the principle of equal treatment required by article 3 of the Constitution.

Thus, in one case[67] the appellants had suffered grave mental and physical injury from the death of their three children in a traffic accident. They were awarded by the civil courts a compensation for pain and suffering, with DM70,000 (c. €35,000) going to the mother, and DM40,000

---

[65] BGH 16 January 1996, NJW 1996, 1591.    [66] See p. 61.
[67] BVerfG 8 March 2000, NJW 2000, 2187.

(c. €20,000) going to the father, which was only about one-third to one-half of what they had claimed. They filed a complaint of unconstitutionality on the grounds that the principle of equal treatment (article 3 GG) was violated. They argued that in cases of interference with honour and reputation significantly higher amounts had been granted.

The Bundesverfassungsgericht did not accept the complaint. It denied a violation of article 3 GG. The principle of equal treatment could not limit the respective courts in their independence from each other and especially not hinder a diverging interpretation of a legal provision. Moreover, the different treatment was justified by special reasons. While the ruthless commercial exploitation of another person's personality could be prevented by high damages, such an effect was not possible in traffic accidents (leading to personal injuries) because the damages were in these cases generally paid by the tortfeasor's insurance company.

## Assessment of non-pecuniary damages resulting from personal injury in general[68]

### Discretion of the judge

The amount of compensation depends in the first place on the degree and the extent of the impairment to the claimant's life.[69] Additionally, all particular circumstances of a given case are to be taken into account.[70] For instance it may be relevant to ask whether the injury has caused a permanent or temporary disability to the claimant, of what kind and extent, and if and to what extent the injury has affected his ability to take part in social life.[71]

The assessment of the amount to be awarded is subject to the discretion of the judge. German procedural law provides for this possibility in § 287 ZPO. Consequently, the claimant does not have to claim a specific amount of money, but may leave this amount to the discretion of the judge. He has to indicate, however, the minimum sum he is asking for.[72]

The Federal Court can only review the way the judge has exercised his discretion. It thus verifies that the decision of the judge is not arbitrary and that all relevant circumstances were taken into account by him when

---

[68] See also *GLT*, p. 915 ff.    [69] BGH 6 July 1955, BGHZ 18, 149, 157.

[70] The BGH uses the expression of circumstances which '*dem Fall ein besonderes Gepräge geben*', roughly meaning 'leave their particular stamp on the case', see BGHGS 6 July 1955, BGHZ 18, 149, 157 ff.

[71] Hein Kötz/Gerhard Wagner, *Deliktsrecht*, no. 522.

[72] See BGH 14 January 1992, MDR 1992, 349.

reaching his decision. But, subject to the above, it cannot determine the amount of compensation itself.

Thus, in one instance,[73] the BGH reversed a judgment for misuse of discretion. The fifteen-year-old claimant had suffered severe injuries to her head (skull fracture, concussion) as well as shock. As a permanent consequence of these injuries, she lost her senses of smell and taste. Further on, a significant damage of the brain functions occurred and produced a permanent change of character, diminution of intelligence and instability of the nervous system. Even the development of epilepsy in the future could not be ruled out. A pre-existing hearing disability also deteriorated further. The claimant's earning capacity was reduced by 30 per cent.

The trial court and the Court of Appeal ordered the insurance company of the defendant to pay DM30,000 (c. €15,000) for pain and suffering and an additional pension of DM300 (c. €150) per month. The Federal Court reversed the decision to the extent that it exceeded the amount of DM20,000 (c. €10,000) for pain and suffering and remanded the case to the Court of Appeal for retrial since the BGH was not, as stated above, allowed to fix the amount itself. The Federal Court did not object to the splitting up of damages into a lump sum for the actual harm and a pension for the continuing impairments. It did, however, criticise the fact that the reduction of earning capacity and marriage prospects was taken into account in the assessment of the lump sum (and not the pension), although the reduced marriage prospects would not, given the claimant's youthful age, manifest themselves until many years later. As for the risk of epilepsy, this should not have been taken into account at this stage of the proceedings for the purposes of increasing the annuity because this could be adjusted upwards if epilepsy did indeed occur by means of a simple petition to modify the judgment.[74] Additionally, in the opinion of the Federal Court, the lump sum and annuity were disproportionate to one another. For the amount awarded for the one and a half years of past and actual suffering was five times the amount of the respective annuity for the same length of time. Given the length of the in-patient treatment of only about six weeks and the duration of the acute medical treatment of only three months, as opposed to the gravity of the continuing effects, this did not reflect an appropriate balance between the two components of the award.

Even trivial inconveniences in principle entitle to compensation for pain and suffering. However, it is at the discretion of the judge to deny damages if the injury does not exceed a degree typical to the risks of

---

[73] BGH 8 June 1976, VersR 1976, 967 ff.    [74] This is made possible by § 323 ZPO.

everyday life. If, for instance, persons living in the neighbourhood of a factory have to bear foul odours for the duration of one evening, it is not a misuse of the discretion of the judge if he refuses damages on the grounds that the infringement is insignificant.[75] In its reform of the law of damages, which became effective on 1 August 2002, the German government intended to exclude trivial damages from non-pecuniary damages altogether.[76] In the end, however, the resolution of this problem was left to the courts.[77]

### Similar cases as guidelines for the assessment

Even if the German law-maker has deliberately not stated any tariffs for compensation for pain and suffering, it is an acknowledged principle that the amounts awarded should more or less be the same if the injuries of the respective claimants are comparable. This practice is based on the principle of equal treatment and serves the purpose of legal consistency,[78] not to mention the fact that such consistency can only facilitate predictability and the reaching of extra-judicial settlements. As a result of the above, previous judgments are compiled in non-statutory tables to serve as guidelines.[79] A further consequence of this is that the more the awarded amount diverges from these standards, the more reasons the judge has to give for his decision.[80]

The Federal Court developed this general assessment concept in its judgment delivered on 8 June 1976.[81] It considered the amount awarded too high, because, after the capitalisation of the annuity, the total sum amounted to DM100,000 (c. €50,000). Such a sum had, up to that date, only been awarded for the most severe continuing effects of injuries, which had not occurred in that case. For this comparison, it referred to the *Schmerzensgeld* tables. Although the comparison was to be drawn only cautiously, it had to be taken into account that the claimant was, for example, spared disfigurement.

The reference to comparable cases is a well-established practice in all cases where *Schmerzensgeld* has to be assessed. The sterilisation of women

---

[75] BGH 14 January 1992, NJW 1992, 1043; the courts of first instance usually deny compensation for petty injuries, see Küppersbusch, *Ersatzansprüche bei Personenschäden*, no. 199.

[76] BT-Drucks. 14/7752, 16, 25.    [77] BT-Drucks. 14/7752, 31.

[78] BGH 8 June 1976, VersR 1976, 967, 968.

[79] See, e.g., Susanne Hacks, Ameli Ring and Peter Böhm, *Schmerzensgeldbeträge* (20th edn, München, 2001), p. 20.

[80] BGH 8 June 1976, VersR 1976, 967, 968.    [81] BGH 8 June 1976, VersR 1976, 967 ff.

without their consent may serve as another example. In its judgment of 1989,[82] the Court of Appeal of Düsseldorf awarded DM35,000 (c. €17,500). In its decision of 1994,[83] the same court awarded DM40,000 (c. €20,000) in reference to the first judgment; it stated that in the first judgment the damage had been alleviated by the fact that the claimant's husband was likely to be infertile. It also referred to a decision of the Court of Appeal of Stuttgart[84] in which DM60,000 (c. €30,000) were awarded to a claimant who was seven years younger.

### *Particular factors for the assessment of the compensation*

### Factors on the side of the claimant

#### *Age of the injured person*
Youthful age is commonly regarded as a factor which justifies an increase in the amount awarded.[85] In practice, however, it is doubtful whether this argument of itself weighs significantly on the minds of judges. For the decisions themselves only rarely suggest comparison has been made with a similar case involving a claimant of different age. The age of the claimant, however, was of particular importance in the above-mentioned case of the woman sterilised without her consent.[86]

In this context, claimants are considered 'young' up to about the age of thirty-three.[87] On the other hand, the courts tend to lower the awarded amount if the youthful age enables the claimant to adapt to the altered circumstances more easily.[88]

#### *Loss of marriage prospects; break-up of partnership*
It is left to the discretion of the judge to take into account the impairment of the prospects of finding a partner.[89] In the reasons given in particular cases, this issue, however, plays only a minor role. Thus, it can be doubted

---

[82]  OLG Düsseldorf 12 October 1989, VersR 1990, 852.

[83]  OLG Düsseldorf 1 December 1994, VersR 1995, 1316.

[84]  OLG Stuttgart 6 October 1988, VersR 1989, 1150.

[85]  OLG Frankfurt 21 February 1996, VersR 1996, 1509, 1510 (blindness of a seven-year-old boy); KG 16 April 1991, VersR 1992, 974 (one-sided blindness of a four-year-old girl).

[86]  OLG Düsseldorf 1 December 1994, VersR 1995, 1316; see pp. 67–8.

[87]  OLG Düsseldorf 10 February 1992, NJW-RR 1993, 156, 158 for a thirty-three-year-old; OLG Köln 20 May 1992, VersR 1992, 975, 976 for a twenty-two-year-old.

[88]  OLG Saarbrücken 16 May 1986, NJW-RR 1987, 984.

[89]  BGH 13 March 1959, NJW 1959, 1031 (syllabus only); OLG Frankfurt 11 November 1993, DAR 1994, 119; OLG Nürnberg 7 December 1993, DAR 1994, 157; OLG Oldenburg 21 January 1991, DAR 1991, 302, 303; OLG München 20 September 1988, VersR 1989, 1203; for a different view see (without explanation) OLG Hamburg 19 August 1986, VersR 1988, 720.

that it is of real significance in judicial practice. In legal literature, on the other hand, the criticism has been made that the loss of marriage prospects has been considered – predominantly but not exclusively – only in cases involving female victims.[90] Thus, only recently have the reduced prospects of men of finding a partner been taken into account as a factor to increase their compensation.[91]

A rather sophisticated practice has been established concerning the break-up of a marriage as a consequence of the injury.

Generally speaking, this risk is seen as part of the general risk of life. But it may not always be so. Thus, a decision of the Court of Appeal of Köln[92] concerned a woman injured in a bicycle accident who claimed an increased indemnification for the fact that her marriage allegedly broke up in consequence of a five weeks' stay at the hospital during which she could not care for her four children. The court denied the claim on the grounds that a direct connection between the break-up of her marriage and the harm complained of could not be proved.

Courts tend to decide otherwise if the break-up of the marriage is the result of concrete deficiencies of the victim caused by the accident, as, for example, an inability to perform sexual intercourse. Thus, in one of its decisions delivered in 1975, the Court of Appeal of Hamm[93] found that the thirty-year-old claimant was hurt on the pubic bone in a way that made sexual intercourse very painful. As a result her marriage broke up, the impaired possibility of intercourse resulting from the above-mentioned injury being one of the reasons advanced by the husband. In the light of these facts, the court accepted a causal connection between the injury and the divorce and granted the claimant an indemnification of DM35,000 (c. €17,500) plus a monthly pension of DM180 (c. €90). The Federal Court decided in a similar fashion a case where the claimant lost one of his testicles.[94] It is submitted, however, that the two factual situations do not seem to be at all similar so that, in the end, the exact facts assume particular significance.

In a case of particularly severe injuries from a car accident with substantial continuing mental and physical effects (reduced ability to walk, disfigurement because of scars, general impairment of the fine adjustment of

---

[90] Hein Kötz/Gerhard Wagner, *Deliktsrecht*, no. 525; Stuck JZ 1974, 417.
[91] OLG Frankfurt 21 February 1996, VersR 1996, 1509, 1510 on a boy who was blinded by an exploding bottle of mineral water at the age of seven; OLG Düsseldorf 10 February 1992, NJW-RR 1993, 156, 158.
[92] OLG Köln 26 April 1995, NJW-RR 1996, 986.    [93] OLG Hamm 3 July 1974, MDR 1975, 490.
[94] BGH 21 September 1982, NJW 1983, 340.

movements, memory disorder, fear of using any means of transport) the break-up of a domestic partnership may, likewise, entail the same legal consequences. But even lesser consequences – the injured person cannot dress and take part in social life according to his or her habits[95] – can justify an increase of the award.

*Impairment of professional possibilities; loss of earning capacity*
German courts are increasingly willing to increase the damages in those cases where the injured person has been forced to abandon or change his job.

In one case, the claimant, a professional chef, suffered severe injuries in a car accident, among others whiplash, a broken nose, scars and the loss of his sense of smell. The Court of Appeal of Frankfurt[96] granted a compensation of DM20,000 (c. €10,000), and placed the emphasis on the fact that as a result of the loss of his sense of smell the claimant could perform his work as a chef only with great difficulty and therefore was forced to abandon it. Additionally, however, the court took into account the impairment of appearance as well as the youthful age of the claimant.

In another case,[97] a beautician was granted DM9,000 (c. €4,500) for a scar on her face resulting from a car accident in which she was held to have been contributorily negligent to the extent of 50 per cent. It was argued that as a beautician she depended greatly on an immaculate appearance.

In the mid-1990s, the Court of Appeal of Hamm[98] awarded DM24,000 (c. €12,000) to a female certified accountant for the damage to her knee that limited her ability to move, caused when an oncoming car crashed into a petrol station. In fixing the amount, the court in the first place took into account that the claimant had to change from the profitable field service to less rewarding office work. Additionally, the general mental burden, the loss of amenity and impairment through two operations and three ancillary treatments were taken into consideration, as well as her inability to engage in sporting activities.

These considerations are even more valid when the injured person becomes disabled.

The Court of Appeal of Oldenburg[99] awarded DM100,000 (c. €50,000) as non-pecuniary damages to a twenty-six-year-old woman who had suffered

---

[95] LG Amberg 29 April 1986, NJW-RR 1986, 1357, 1359.
[96] OLG Frankfurt 25 February 1986, VersR 1987, 1140, 1141.
[97] OLG München 30 November 1984, VersR 1985, 868.
[98] OLG Hamm 15 December 1994, VersR 1996, 243, 245.
[99] OLG Oldenburg 21 January 1995, DAR 1991, 302, 303.

severe injuries to her head in a car crash. The injuries had led to a loss of the sense of smell, hearing disorder, reduced brain performance, slowed speech, hormonal malfunctions resulting in infertility, and the risk of epilepsy. The court deemed it a relevant factor that through the loss of the sense of smell the claimant could no longer be a professional chemical laboratory worker. Furthermore, the court put emphasis on her reduced marriage prospects in consequence of the infertility and the speech disorder.

The degree to which a profession is associated with particular prestige or self-satisfaction has not, thus far, influenced the assessment of the damages. In the literature, it is argued that a professional tennis player or surgeon should be entitled to higher compensation than, for instance, a factory worker.[100] This distinction is justified by reference to the basic functions of 'Schmerzensgeld' (cf. p. 62). It is argued that for a well-off person, more money is necessary to obtain a noticeable rise in amenity. These factors, however, may well be concealed under different headings of the award.

*Impairment of the possibility to engage in leisure activities or hobbies*
The amount of damages awarded to claimants is further increased if the injured person can no longer pursue a hobby as a consequence of the injury.[101]

Since an objective evaluation or even ranking of different hobbies or leisure activities does not exist, judges refrain from establishing preferences in favour of certain occupations.[102] Instead, the courts take into consideration how important the activity has been for the claimant. The objective degree of time, effort and success can only be an indicator of this subjective importance, which alone is relevant.[103] There remains, however, the questionable decision of the Court of Appeal of Köln which, in the early 1990s,[104] granted a twenty-two-year-old man who had not yet engaged in running an increased indemnification on the grounds that his injury prevented him from pursuing this sport *in the future*. The court justified its decision by arguing that the permanent impairment of the quality of life was of greater significance today than it was in former days.

---

[100] Hein Kötz/Gerhard Wagner, *Deliktsrecht*, no. 525.
[101] OLG Frankfurt 21 January 1991, VersR 1992, 621, 622; OLG Hamm 15 December 1994, VersR 1996, 243, 245; OLG Köln 16 October 1992, NJW-RR 1993, 350, 351.
[102] Critical however MünchKomm-BGB/Stein § 847 BGB no. 25.
[103] OLG Frankfurt 11 November 1993, DAR 1994, 119, 120.
[104] OLG Köln 20 May 1992, VersR 1992, 975.

*Change of personality*

If the injury affects the personality of the claimant, this may justify an increase in the amount of compensation.[105]

In a case brought before the Federal Court in 1979,[106] the fourteen-year-old claimant suffered severe injuries in a traffic accident. These led to a permanent walking impairment, scars and substantial damage to the brain. According to the decision of the Court of Appeal,[107] the brain damage resulted in a significant change of personality, evidenced in the first place by a diminished intelligence as well as emotional and sexual disorders. Whereas the claimant had successfully completed his primary school education and, by the time of the accident, had been attending a commercial school for six months, his education came to a halt after the accident. The claimant ran away from home and ended up keeping 'bad' company. This, eventually, led him to becoming a delinquent. He was convicted for his activities by a criminal court but, because of his diminished criminal responsibility, he was sent to a secure mental hospital rather than incarcerated in a prison. The Federal Court reaffirmed the judgment against the wrongdoer to pay compensation of DM70,000 (c. €35,000). The court relied heavily on the findings of the Court of Appeal according to which the mental disorder and the delinquency were connected to the accident which had resulted in his cranial injuries. The argument that the claimant may have been predisposed to such activities was ignored in view of the gravity of the accident and its consequences. Contributory negligence was also disregarded.

*Loss of senses*

As for the element of satisfaction, problems can occur if the injuries are of such a kind that the injured person loses the ability to feel satisfaction at all. It has been argued that in these cases, the compensation should be lowered as it cannot fulfil the function of granting satisfaction (see p. 62 and p. 3). This argument, however, has been rejected in later decisions.

In one case that reached the Federal Court,[108] the defendant physician had not carried out a caesarean operation during the birth of the claimant although this was medically indicated. The claimant's health was seriously damaged. Besides considerable physical impairments (such as palsy, partial diplegia, spasms etc.), substantial mental disorders ensued. The

---

[105] BGH 8 May 1979, NJW 1979, 1654; see also BGH 9 April 1991, NJW 1991, 2347, 2348.
[106] BGH 8 May 1979, NJW 1979, 1654.
[107] OLG Karlsruhe 15 December 1977, VersR 1979, 164.
[108] BGH 13 October 1992, BGHZ 120, 1 ff.

claimant did not possess the ability to speak but could only make moaning or grunting sounds thus expressing a general sense of wellbeing or discontent. Nor could she develop sophisticated feelings beyond joy, wellbeing and aversion, the latter related to the physical perception of pain or taste. Moreover, her possibilities of experiencing such feelings were restricted by anti-epileptic medication. The Landgericht awarded the claimant as compensation a lump sum of DM50,000 (c. €25,000) plus a monthly pension of DM500 (c. €250).

The Court of Appeal reversed this judgment and lowered the indemnification to a lump sum of DM30,000 (c. €15,000) and likewise reduced the monthly pension to DM250 (c. €125). In its view, account should be taken in this case of the fact that monetary compensation could not fulfil its function to satisfy the victim. She was not able to realise the connection between the injury and the payment of damages and could thus not feel satisfaction. On the other hand, it was accepted that her life could, to some extent, be eased by means of money to assist beyond the ordinary degree of care. In particular, she could enjoy the additional human attention money could provide.

The Federal Court reversed the judgment of the Court of Appeal insofar as it had reduced the damages granted by the Landgericht, and remanded the case back for the final determination of the award. It found that the Court of Appeal had misconceived the meaning of *Schmerzensgeld*. That the claimant, because of the negligence of the defendant, was deprived of the chance to develop her personality was the crucial fact which determined the seriousness of the injury. It therefore could not justify a decrease of the indemnification. A different view would misinterpret the right of personality as envisaged by articles 1 and 2 of the German Constitution. A symbolic payment was not sufficient because, by means of the indemnification, the impairment of the personality and the loss of personal quality as such were to be compensated as non-pecuniary headings.[109]

In a later case, the Federal Court confirmed this approach.[110] The defendant had left the claimant, at the time twenty-two months old, unattended for several minutes. During this time, the claimant fell into a pond. Though he narrowly avoided death by drowning, he suffered severe damage to the nervous system that destroyed most of his sensitivity. The Federal Court reversed the judgment of the Court of Appeal which

---

[109] See Deutsch, NJW 1993, 784; OLG Schleswig 24 February 1993, VersR 1994, 310 ff.; for the former jurisdiction see BGH 16 December 1975, NJW 1976, 1147; BGH 22 June 1982, NJW 1982, 2123.

[110] BGH 16 February 1993, NJW 1993, 1531.

had awarded only DM20,000 (c. €10,000) as a 'symbolic expiation' and remanded the case for rehearing.

*Unforeseeable future effects*
In many cases, the effects of the injuries cannot be completely determined at the time of the commencement of the action, nor even the trial. Some effects may only be realised in the future, so that it may not be certain to what extent, if at all, they will occur. Even so, unforeseeable future effects may justify an increase in the amount of the damages by a subsequent application to the court. Here, however, we are concerned with a different aspect of the claim: the injured person's fear and uncertainty.

In a case which reached the Court of Appeal of Hamm[111] in 1995, the claimant suffered from pneumothorax and had to undergo several operations as a result of medical malpractice on the part of the defendant. In the course of one of these operations, the right lobe of her lung had to be removed. The Landgericht and the Court of Appeal awarded DM150,000 (c. €75,000) as non-pecuniary damages. The award was influenced by the fact that the claimant had, as a result of the malpractice, been placed in a perpetual life-threatening situation. In determining the level of damages, the court also felt it had to take into account the fact that, through the loss of half her lung, the claimant's heart would be overly stressed in the long run. The damages had to be increased not only for the fear of coronary failure but also to take into account the uncertainty engendered by unforeseeable future effects.

In a similar way, the Court of Appeal of Köln[112] decided for a claimant who, as a result of medical malpractice, had to live with an oversized hip joint prosthesis for three years before a smaller one could be installed and, during this period, suffered substantial complications.

The evaluation of future effects is of great importance in cases of the negligent sterilisation of a woman without her consent.

In a decision of the Court of Appeal of Düsseldorf of 1994,[113] the claimant argued that, following a caesarean operation, she had been sterilised without her consent. The Court of Appeal ordered the surgeon in question to pay DM40,000 (c. €20,000) as compensation for pain and suffering. Although the claimant had herself considered sterilisation and already had three children (so that in fact she was not totally deprived of the joy of

---

[111] OLG Hamm 8 March 1995, VersR 1996, 892, 893.
[112] OLG Köln 16 February 1995, VersR 1996, 712, 713.
[113] OLG Düsseldorf 1 December 1994, VersR 1995, 1316, 1317.

motherhood) she was, at the time of the operation, still only twenty-seven years old and had thus been significantly restricted by the surgeon's action in her future family planning. Moreover, there was a chance that future matrimonial and family problems would arise because of the sterilisation. Similar considerations can be found in other cases.[114] In the same vein, the Court of Appeal of Saarbrücken[115] granted DM150,000 (c. €75,000) to a ten-year-old boy who had lost his genitals as a result of medical malpractice. The court based the assessment primarily on the consideration that the future mental and physical effects were not yet foreseeable.

*Relevance of pre-existing damage*
Pre-existing damage or injury may justify an increase or a reduction of the indemnification depending upon each individual case. A decrease is required if the tortfeasor proves that an impairment does not result from the injuries inflicted by him but from a preceding accident and therefore is not caused by his negligence.[116]

If the damaging event simply aggravates an existing impairment, this will also lead to a decrease in the amount of damages. Thus, in one case[117] the claimant suffered severe injuries to the spine and head in a car accident and became disabled. The injuries healed without remaining medical impairments. Yet the victim suffered pain because he lacked the mental capacity to cope with the events. The cause was the claimant's pre-morbid personality as well as eight preceding traffic accidents. The Federal Court confirmed the judgment of the Court of Appeal awarding DM50,000 (c. €25,000). But the claimant's mental condition was taken into account as a factor justifying a decrease in the amount of damages.

In some cases, however, the courts have *increased* the compensation on the grounds of pre-existing damage. Thus, in one such case the claimant requested compensation for pain and suffering from the city of Berlin because he slipped on an icy pedestrian crossing. He claimed the city had not met its obligation to clear snow from the crossing. The Kammergericht of Berlin[118] awarded DM20,000 (c. €10,000) as compensation for pain and suffering. In the reasoning of the judgment, not only the seriousness of the injuries and the duration of the treatment (of more than six months)

---

[114] OLG Düsseldorf 12 October 1989, VersR 1990, 852; OLG Stuttgart 6 October 1988, VersR 1989, 1150.

[115] OLG Saarbrücken 17 December 1974, NJW 1975, 1467.

[116] This proof indeed failed in BGH 5 November 1996, NJW 1997, 455; see also BGH 16 November 1961, NJW 1962, 243.

[117] BGH 30 April 1996, BGHZ 132, 341.      [118] KG 26 May 1989, NVwZ 1990, 406, 407.

were taken into account, but also the fact that an existing impairment of the claimant's blood circulation in his left thigh and foot deteriorated further. The court left open the question whether the partial amputation of the claimant's left foot was a necessary consequence of the fall. The acute deterioration of the claimant's pre-existing affliction was sufficient.

In another case, the claimant showed neurotic reactions as a result of being involved in a car accident. She suffered from hypochondriac self-consciousness which the court considered pathological. The undisputed cause for this was a latent disposition from which she suffered. The Court of Appeal of Frankfurt[119] decided that the law of damages could not treat a psychologically or physically predisposed person in a worse way than a sane person.[120] Although the accident was in a sense only a random occasion for the neurosis, this aspect had little or no weight in view of the severity of the accident. The Court of Appeal thus awarded the claimant DM50,000 (c. €25,000) in compensation.

Most decisions, however, which have taken into account an existing predisposition are characterised by a careful weighing of all aspects of the particular case. A definite qualification of predisposition as a factor which increases or decreases the amount of damages is therefore not possible. Some decisions underscore this point.

In one decision handed down in 1981, the Federal Court[121] had to deal with a claimant who had been bitten by the defendant's German Shepherd when he entered a tavern. Because of a pre-existing severe war wound, the dog's bite led to further severe injuries which made necessary two operations, three months of treatment, psychiatric therapy and caused disability. The Federal Court confirmed the judgment awarding only DM35,000 (c. €17,500), instead of the claimed DM60,000 (c. €30,000), as compensation for pain and suffering. The court pointed out that the injury had only aggravated a pre-existing damage. On the other hand, one had to take into account that the claimant had already been seriously affected by his war injuries.

In another case,[122] a physician had badly performed an operation on the nasal septum. As a result of this malpractice the claimant lost her sense of smell. The OLG awarded DM7,000 (c. €3,500) as compensation for pain and suffering. In reaching this figure, the court had to balance two competing factors. On the one hand, the claimant's sense of smell was

[119] OLG Frankfurt 10 February 1994, VersR 1995, 796, 797.
[120] Similarly, OLG Frankfurt 26 October 1994, VersR 1996, 864.
[121] BGH 22 September 1981, NJW 1982, 168, 169.
[122] OLG Köln 17 February 1993, NJW-RR 1993, 919, 920.

already deficient and this called for a decrease of damages. On the other hand, it was to be taken into account that the loss of the sense of smell was especially grave, since next to amenity, the claimant lost a warning function which the sense of smell could perform e.g., in the event of fire.

In 1991, the Court of Appeal of Munich[123] was confronted with a claim by a twenty-one-year-old claimant who had been involved in a traffic accident. The court regarded as negligible the pre-existence of a mental impairment, which had been severely aggravated by the accident. While the claimant before the accident had an IQ of about 50 to 70, and had thus been forced to attend a special school and had planned to become a carpenter, he had, after the accident, an IQ of about 20 to 50. This rendered any form of schooling or apprenticeship impossible. The court condemned the tortfeasor to pay damages in the form of a lump sum of DM60,000 (c. €30,000), plus a monthly pension of DM400 (€200), which would total about DM140,000 (c. €70,000) if the pension were to be capitalised.

*Social background*
In the calculation of damages, the claimant's social background is principally irrelevant. An older decision of the Reichsgericht,[124] claiming that an impairment of the appearance was especially grave when the damaged person belonged to the educated classes, can no longer be seen as acceptable, especially given the provisions and spirit of the German Constitution of 1949. Judges are thus not allowed to pursue values particular to their own social background.[125] As for the reproach of some authors that the differences in the compensation for interference with honour and reputation have, in fact, caused social injustice, see p. 64.

*Early death of the injured person*[126]
If an injury results in the early death of the claimant, this fact can be taken into account as a *decreasing* factor in the assessment. The claim passes on to the heirs of the victim though, at this stage, it no longer seeks to provide compensation for pain and suffering but only to meet the need for satisfaction.

The Federal Court has not, however, established strict criteria on how soon death has to occur to justify an *increase* of the indemnification.

---

[123] OLG München 24 July 1990, DAR 1991, 301 ff.
[124] RG 24 April 1911, RGZ 76, 174, 176.
[125] Hein Kötz/Gerhard Wagner, *Deliktsrecht*, no. 525; Christian v. Bar NJW 1980, 1724.
[126] See also p. 4.

In one case,[127] the heirs claimed indemnification in lieu of their parents who died in a car accident caused by the negligence of the defendant. The father was conscious for thirty-five minutes before he slipped into a coma. During that time, he felt pain and was worried about his wife. He died after ten days without regaining consciousness. The claimants' mother lost consciousness immediately after the accident and died within an hour. The Court of Appeal awarded an indemnification of DM28,000 (c. €14,000) for the father and DM3,000 (c. €1,500) for the mother. The Federal Court turned down the claimants' appeal. The indemnification was to be lowered if the injured person died soon after the harmful event and in consequence of the injury. As far as the father was concerned, one would have to accept that he had been conscious for only thirty-five minutes after the accident. Only within this period of time could a non-pecuniary damage occur and compensation be ordered.[128] As for the mother, the Federal Court argued that, in view of her unconsciousness, it was doubtful if immaterial damage had occurred at all. In contrast to another similar case,[129] she only had to remain unconscious for one hour, so that an affliction was not ascertainable: § 847 (the former equivalent of § 253 II BGB) was not intended to provide indemnification for the shortening of life.

In fact, in this case the line had to be drawn between the killing of a person (in which case no non-pecuniary headings of damages are owed to this person) and the injury of a person which leads to his death. The Federal Court tried to distinguish between a prolonged process of dying (no *Schmerzensgeld*) and cases in which the injury preceding the death had its own weight and could be viewed as impairment distinguishable from the ensuing death. In such a case it would be appropriate to award non-pecuniary damages.

*Relevance of psychological consequences*
Psychological effects are to be taken into account in the assessment of damages in the same way as physical injuries. Thus, in one case before the Federal Court[130] the claimant's physical injuries caused by a traffic accident had healed without lasting effects. The claimant, however, suffered

---

[127] BGH 12 May 1998, VersR 1998, 1034 ff.

[128] Other than in cases where the indemnification is granted for the lack of perception (see p. 72; BGH 13 October 1992, BGHZ 120, 1 ff.), the claimant here had not fallen into coma as a result of the injuries but had been put in this condition in the course of the medical treatment.

[129] BGH 13 October 1992, BGHZ 120, 1 ff.     [130] BGH 9 April 1991, VersR 1991, 704.

psychological consequences that were not organic in origin, such as change of character, loss of mental capacity, speech disorder, paralysis and diminution of the sexual urge. The Federal Court confirmed the award of damages on the grounds that they all formed recognisable physiological and psychological harm.

## Factors on the side of the tortfeasor

### Degree of fault

On the side of the tortfeasor, the first relevant factor is the degree of his fault. German courts take the view that an increase in the amount of damages seems particularly indicated if the wrongdoer is also convicted in a criminal procedure because of the act that had caused the injury. Thus, in one case,[131] the defendant was convicted for bank robbery. The Federal Court justified an increase of the damages with the consideration that in the case of intentional torts, a special relationship between tortfeasor and victim had been created that had to be taken into account regarding the element of satisfaction.

In one case (at least), the degree of fault was deemed to be an essential element.[132] Thus, the amount of damages was increased because the tortfeasor had intentionally stuck a knife in the claimant's back with the intention of killing him. But negligence, too, can justify an increase in the amount of damages. An example of this can be found in a decision of the Federal Court of 1993[133] in which the gross negligence of the defendant justified an increase of the compensation.[134]

On the other hand, if it can be shown that the tortfeasor intended to do the victim a favour but, nonetheless, injured him negligently, the level of damages may be reduced.[135]

### Fortune

In German law, the pecuniary situation of the tortfeasor may be taken into account when fixing the level of the award. Thus, a wealthier tortfeasor may be liable to pay a higher indemnification.[136] A tortfeasor without means must neither be ruined by the award of damages nor, on the other

---

[131] BGH 29 November 1994, BGHZ 128, 117, 120 ff.
[132] BGH 7 February 1995, NJW 1995, 1438.    [133] BGH 16 February 1993, NJW 1993, 1531.
[134] Further cases: BGH 6 July 1955, BGHZ GS 18, 149, 157 ff.; OLG Nürnberg 25 April 1997, VersR 1998, 731, 732; OLG Frankfurt 11 November 1993, DAR 1994, 119, 120.
[135] BGH 6 July 1955, BGHZ 18, 149, 158 ff.
[136] Even persons not responsible under tort law (children, insane persons) may be liable for damages in those circumstances, § 829 BGB.

hand, can compensation be totally denied in such a case.[137] But a defendant is not considered to be without means when he has taken out an insurance which covers the damage. The Federal Court has argued that the claim against the insurance company is to be seen as a part of the tortfeasor's fortune (see p. 189).

*Torts by relatives*

In principle, the above-mentioned rules also apply to claims against relatives. The fact that the parties are related to each other is, however, used as an argument to decrease the damages.

In one case,[138] the claimant was severely injured in a car accident while on the highway. The accident was caused partly by her husband, who was driving the couple's car, and partly by the driver of a military vehicle. The wife claimed compensation from the state, which, however, invoked the privilege of § 839 I 2 BGB and argued that the wife had a claim for damages against her husband which had precedence over the claim against the state. The BGH took the view that it was not against the nature of marriage to allow a claim for damages by one spouse against the other to proceed. The matrimonial bond was only to be taken into account when fixing the size of the award. For the amount had to be of a size that the respective spouse could afford without endangering the family's financial basis. Damages that resulted in a shortfall of reasonable maintenance would be inadequate.

Also, several Courts of Appeal approved a reduction of the indemnification between relatives. So, the Court of Appeal of Hamm[139] awarded a son, who suffered quadriplegia from a car accident caused by his father, an indemnification of DM250,000 (c. €125,000). It was taken into account that his father had cared for the claimant since the accident and had thus given him satisfaction. The element of satisfaction was therefore irrelevant in the assessment of the compensation. The same consideration can be found in a decision of the Court of Appeal of Schleswig,[140] where the wrongdoer/husband was made to pay to his wife DM280,000 (c. €140,000) for the quadriplegia he had caused her. The Court of Appeal of Munich, however, rejected a reduction of the compensation in similar cases where the claim was directed against an insurance company. The principles for the assessment of the compensation between relatives were said not to be applicable in these situations.[141]

---

[137] BGH 6 July 1955, BGHZ 18, 149, 162 ff.    [138] BGH 18 June 1973, BGHZ 61, 101.
[139] OLG Hamm 17 December 1997, VersR 1998, 1392.
[140] OLG Schleswig 9 January 1991, NJW-RR 1992, 95 ff.
[141] OLG München 8 July 1988, VersR 1989, 1056.

Where a third party is responsible for the damage along with the relative, their liability is treated as a joint obligation. If the relative's liability is excluded as, for example, according to § 1359 or § 1664 BGB, the third party alone is liable.[142]

*Delay of payment of the damages*
The damages for pain and suffering may be increased if the tortfeasor deliberately delays the settlement of the matter, for instance by engaging in frivolous litigation.[143] One has to be careful, however, not to regard any differing statement of facts as a frivolous protraction, even if it later proves to be false.[144] The tortfeasor is held responsible also for dilatory tactics of his insurance company. Thus, in one case,[145] the claimant was sterilised without her consent. The court awarded an increased compensation explicitly because the defendant physician had refused to accept his wrongdoing until the very end of the trial.

In an especially drastic case, the Court of Appeal of Frankfurt[146] doubled the claim for compensation for pain and suffering caused by medical malpractice from DM10,000 (c. €5,000) to DM20,000 (c. €10,000) because the physician refused to accept his liability although the malpractice was undisputed. The court considered it particularly important that the defendant refused to render any form of payment even after the Landgericht had awarded DM10,000 (c. €5,000).

*Compensation for the death of close relatives*[147]
The injured person's relatives cannot in principle claim compensation for their mental suffering caused by the death of their relative; neither does that fact have an increasing effect on the compensation of the victim.

Notwithstanding, the related third party may, through the physical injury of the relative, experience psychological pain and suffering tothe

---

[142] BGH 1 March 1998, BGHZ 103, 338 ff.; further quotations MünchKomm-BGB/Stein § 847 BGB no. 44. This is the kind of situation which the English High Court had to address in *Greatorex* v. *Greatorex* [2000] 1 WLR 1970, discussed by B. Markesinis in 'Foreign Law Inspiring National Law: Lessons from *Greatorex* v. *Greatorex*' (2002) 61 CLJ 386.

[143] BGH 9 May 1989, WM 1989, 1481, 1482 (obiter dictum); BGH 2 December 1966, VersR 1967, 256, 257; OLG Düsseldorf 1 December 1994, VersR 1995, 1316, 1317; OLG Frankfurt 22 September 1993, DAR 1994, 21, 22; OLG Nürnberg 25 April 1997, VersR 1998, 731, 732; OLG Celle 9 November 1967, NJW 1968, 1677.

[144] LG Hechingen 9 January 1981, VersR 1982, 253, critical Riecker VersR 1982, 254.

[145] OLG Düsseldorf 1 December 1994, VersR 1995, 1316, 1317.

[146] OLG Frankfurt 7 January 1999, NJW 1999, 2447.

[147] For fuller details see *GLT*, pp. 115–44.

extent that an impairment of his health is caused. In this case, the relative is himself entitled to a claim for damages (§ 823 I BGB) and thus also to compensation for non-pecuniary damages.[148]

Because German civil law principally denies compensation for injuries to third parties, the standards for such claims are very high.[149] It is necessary for the psychological impairment to have relevant medical effects and require medical treatment. The impairment of health has to exceed a degree which could normally be expected if a relative is injured.[150] This is only the case when traumatic disorders with psycho-pathological failures of some duration occur.[151] It is not sufficient if the victim's wife's alcohol addiction worsens in consequence of the husband's injury.[152] Although there is no rule that the legal interests or rights enumerated in § 823 I BGB have to be violated directly,[153] it has to be considered in these cases whether the causal nexus can still be regarded as adequate and whether the indirect violation could have been foreseen.[154]

The mental stability of the claimant, however, is of no relevance.[155] Furthermore, only close relatives, fiancés and partners of an amatory relationship are entitled to this claim.[156]

Finally, the injury of the related person has to be especially grave and beyond the general risks of life. This is only the case with death or severe personal injuries. The more severe the injury, the less relevant is the presence of the claimant at the place and time of the accident.[157]

## Italian law

### Introduction

In Italian tort law, as in its German and common law counterparts, the guiding principle for the award of damages is the compensation of the victim of the wrongdoing. But like the other two systems, with which it is compared in this book, Italian law is fully conscious of the fact that

[148] BGH 11 May 1971, BGHZ 56, 163; BGHZ 93, 351; OLG Freiburg 30 June 1953, JZ 1953, 704.
[149] Erwin Deutsch, *Unerlaubte Handlungen*, no. 472.
[150] Soergel and Zeuner § 823 BGB no. 27; BGH 5 February 1985, BGHZ 93, 351, 354 ff.; BGH 11 May 1971, BGHZ 56, 163.
[151] BGH 4 April 1989, NJW 1989, 2317, 2318; OLG Nürnberg 31 January 1984, NJW 1998, 2292, 2294.
[152] BGH 31 January 1984, NJW 1984, 1405.    [153] *GLT*, p. 137.    [154] *GLT*, pp. 126, 137.
[155] BGH 11 May 1971, BHGZ 56, 163, 165.
[156] OLG Stuttgart 21 July 1988, NJW-RR 1989, 477 ff.; LG Tübingen 29 November 1967, NJW 1968, 1187; LG Frankfurt 28 March 1969, NJW 1969, 2286. See *GLT*, p. 139.
[157] BGH 5 February 1985, BGHZ 93, 351, 354 ff.

it is easier to compensate damage to property (the amount there being calculated by reference to the market value of the damaged thing) than it is to put a monetary figure on personal injuries. For the same reason, it is easier to compensate the innocent contractual party for interference with his contractual relations than to calculate the harm to the body or fix the right amount to take care of the *danno morale* (pain and suffering) in the sense explained above in chapter 1 (and below). Personal injuries thus call for special treatment. All systems under comparison agree with this; but they differ in significant ways in matters of important detail. In particular, what stands out in the eyes of a non-Italian lawyer is the degree of fluidity that exists in Italian law. The absence of headings of damage, comparable to those used by English lawyers, also makes comparisons difficult. The reader must constantly bear this caveat in mind; and he must also be prepared to explore the possibility of certain headings of damage being taken care of obliquely by some of the more broad headings recognised by Italian law (such as that of *danno biologico*).

As already indicated in chapter 1, Italian law accepts three broad headings of damage. *Danno patrimoniale*, which comes close to the common law notion of pecuniary loss, is the subject of the next chapters. It tends to affect a person's wealth, assets or income. *Danno biologico* and *danno morale* are the main topics of the present one; and in Italian law they are collectively referred to as *danno non-patrimoniale*. What the items covered by this heading have in common is their inability to be assessed financially in an objective manner. Punitive or exemplary damages are never awarded in Italian law, no matter how severe the injury may be nor how reprehensible the *mens rea* of the wrongdoer (even though, as we shall note below, compensation is not the only recognised aim of tort law and 'punitive elements' may be concealed in some types of award). To be sure, under the influence of American law, some academics have proposed that punitive damages should also become part of Italian law; but to date these proposals have not gained wider acceptance.

## Principle of full compensation

According to the German *Differenztheorie* the injured party has the right to be put in the same situation in which he or she was before the accident, without any extra profit. This is the starting point; but in personal injury cases full compensation is achieved in an approximate manner by awarding damages related to health, pain and suffering and loss of earnings. The compensation for impaired health and pain and suffering are not affected by the earnings of the victim. Loss of earnings is taken into account only in the liquidation of the *danno patrimoniale* (future loss).

*Danno biologico* is liquidated *per se* according to tables which differ from court to court (see Appendix.)

*Danno morale* is liquidated by taking into account the circumstances of the case, though the total sum tends, in practice, to reach about half the amount (or less) awarded for *danno biologico*.[158]

*Danno patrimoniale* varies according to the category of the victim: employees are compensated according to the social security system, all the other victims according to the evidence they can produce showing their loss.

In a tort action, the victim shoulders the burden of proof. The quantification of the injury is calculated by the judge taking into account the views of an expert witness (invariably a medical doctor) appointed by the court. He, in turn, takes into account the estimates and opinions of the expert witnesses appointed by the parties (claimant and defendant).

## Danno biologico

In very general terms *danno biologico* means the interference with the health of a person considered in and of itself as a legal interest worthy of evaluation and, if affected, compensation. That the deprivation of health or the loss of a limb should be compensated as such seems obvious enough to us looking at Italian law from the perspective of late twentieth century and twenty-first century law. But things were not always so in Italy since, during the nineteenth century and the first half of the twentieth, the compensation of any interference with the health of a person was linked to the earning capacity and social status of the victim.[159] This meant, for instance, that poor people or old people could be considered as being 'people without any value'[160] and thus left without compensation, assuming, of course, they had the means and the courage to chance litigation.

---

[158] In a few court districts – for instance Genova – the courts have themselves prepared tables which set out the amount of moral damages that could be awarded (depending on a variety of factors indicated in the tables e.g., degree of relationship, duration of pain and suffering etc.). In the majority of regions, however, the evaluation of the amount is left to the discretion of the judge though, as stated, the total amount tends to be approximately one-half of the amount awarded for *danno biologico*.

[159] In Italian law, as well, prior to the introduction of the *danno biologico*, various attempts were made to provide some compensation for these items of loss. But the way this was brought about was oblique and the result, on the whole, unsatisfactory, given the fact that the lower sections of society still ended up undercompensated for certain types of harm.

[160] See, e.g., Tribunale di Firenze, 6 January 1967, 1969 Arch. Resp. civ. 130.

The compensation thus given to the victim under this new heading of damage (*danno biologico*) covers all the different kinds of damage which English law would compensate under such headings as 'loss of amenities of life', damage to the aesthetic appearance of the victim, damage to the working capacity in general, etc.

This new way of looking at things was strengthened by the Constitutional Court and the principles it developed during the early years of its existence. Health was thus seen as an essential value constituting the object of a fundamental right of the person. Such a right required full and exhaustive protection both in the public sphere as well as in the realm of private relationships. Its object is the general and common claim of individuals to such conditions of life, environment and work that do not jeopardise this fundamental right. Such protection implies a claim, including preventive measures, if this right is affected but also the obligation not to prejudice or endanger other people's health through one's own behaviour. In the event of conflict between the right to health, protected by the Constitution, and other behaviour, free but not directly covered by the Constitution, the first must necessarily prevail.[161]

According to the law currently in force,[162] such an approach implies that *danno biologico* is to be compensated within parameters which do not take into account the income-producing capacity of the injured party. The injury is, therefore, considered *per se*, as the fact causing damage to the legally (and constitutionally) protected interest of health. So the expression *danno biologico* is, in essence, identified with the expression (considered more correct by most commentators) 'damage to health' (*danno alla salute*). Health is included among the interests protected by the law and is recognised by article 32 of the Constitution. It is an absolute right, and as such it is fundamental, inalienable and indispensable.[163]

Case law still acknowledges a variety of indemnifiable headings of damages. Decisions have thus compensated interference with peaceful family life,[164] damage from demotion in one's employment,[165] damage from 'harassment',[166] damage due to loss of kinship and of enjoyment of the

---

[161] Judgment of 20 December 1996, no. 399, Cons. Stato, 1996, II, 2090; Foro it. 1997, I, 3123.

[162] Contained in art. 13 of Legislative Decree no. 38 of 23 February 2000, repeated in art. 5, para. 3 of Law no. 57 of 5 March 2001, and unchanged in the subsequent amendment by Law no. 273 of 12 December 2002.

[163] Civil Cass., labour section, 10 March 1990, no. 1954, Crit. Pen., 1995, 50.

[164] Court of Milan, 18 February 1988, Resp. civ. prev. 1988, 454.

[165] Court of Milan, 26 June 1999, Lav. nella giur., 1999, 1075.

[166] Court of Milan, 21 April 1998, Dir. lav. 1998, 957.

relative, also sometimes referred to as hedonistic damage,[167] and so on. The creation of these heads of damages is due to a kind of moral evaluation of the case. If the judge thinks that damages which are recovered by the victim should be higher than those calculated according to the ordinary methods, the way of solving the case is to create a new head of damages. An accident causes disadvantages to the parents and relatives of the victim – their life is overturned – so the judge creates the head of 'violation of peaceful family life'. If the situation of the employee is difficult because he or she is not satisfied with the work requested by the employer, or is harassed by the employer, the judge creates the head of 'demotion' and of 'harassment', etc. It is by no means certain that this catalogue of headings is closed. So now *danno biologico* is becoming and should be seen as the receptacle into which all different aspects of personal injury go, apart from *danno morale* and *danno patrimoniale*.

*Danno biologico* covers two kinds of non-pecuniary harm: *temporary disability* and *permanent disability*, depending on whether the injury has caused alterations to the psycho-physical wellbeing of the victim that will disappear after some time, or will remain for life.

On the basis of these assumptions, it becomes completely idle to discuss the nature of *danno biologico* and decide whether it belongs to the 'moral' field or to the economic field. Any attempt to follow rigidly the common law distinction between pecuniary and non-pecuniary losses would, likewise, be of little use. The attempt to present different legal systems in *exact* logical juxtaposition can only go so far and no further. *Danno biologico* may thus be considered a *tertium genus*, or a special aspect of 'moral damages' and must be examined on its own terms. In other words, the area of *danno biologico* also includes damages to social life, consisting of the impossibility or difficulty for an individual who has suffered physical impairment to reinstate himself or herself in social relationships and to keep such relationships at a normal level.[168] The damage to social life is now considered as an aspect of *danno biologico*, and it can even consist of the temporary suspension or reduction of normal life opportunities.[169]

### Statutory rules about danno biologico

The considerable uncertainty prevailing in the law of compensation for personal injury, combined with economic (mainly insurance) reasons alluded to above in chapter 1, forced the legislator to intervene repeatedly in

---

[167] Court of Milan, 1 April 1999.    [168] Cass. 24 April 2001, no. 6023.
[169] Cass. 27 November 2001, no. 15034.

order to introduce legal regulations that could, once and for all, settle the issues raised by the assessment of personal injuries. Though this attempt has been patchy in approach and limited in its effect, it has opened up a new stage in the history of personal injuries. One notable side effect was also the fact that the discussion about compensation for personal injuries was moved from the judges to the Italian Parliament.

At first instance, the provisions introduced concerned only minor injuries (9 per cent permanent incapacity or less). They further envisaged tables which should be prepared in the future by the Department of Industry with the co-operation of the Department of Health and the Department of Justice.[170] Moreover, article 5, paragraph 2 of Law no. 57 of 5 March 2001 did not deal with *danno biologico* in general, but only with injuries arising from road accidents.[171] Finally, article 5, paragraph 3 consecrated into statutory law the rule established by the courts (and mentioned above) that *danno biologico* 'should be compensated without taking into account the income-producing capacity of the injured party'.[172]

Soon after the passing of this statute and without prejudice to the *provisional* regulation of the liquidation of *danno biologico*, the legislator intervened again with the passing of Law no. 273 of 12 December 2002. This introduced additional assessment criteria aiming to cap these levels of award. Such intervention had two objectives. First, was the wish to act as a curb against inflation. The second was to complete the parameters given to judges by the first statute. More precisely, given the widespread feeling that the first statute fixed the amounts in a rigid manner, the new enactment chose to give judges the right to provide (limited) additional amounts when the personal conditions seemed to justify them. The desire to allow judicial discretion is praiseworthy. Yet, it also creates the risk of regional or other inequalities and thus returns to the status quo ante which the new statutes had aimed to terminate.

## Methods for the liquidation of danno biologico

When the official tables envisaged by the above-mentioned statutes are published *for all degrees* of permanent invalidity, the method of calculating the levels of damages for *danno biologico* will be clear and uniform over the whole of the country. Predicting a date when this process will be

---

[170] Law no. 57 of 5 March 2001, art. 5, paras 1–6.

[171] The principles of the law and the tables now in force (reproduced in the Appendix) are, however, now applied to other types of accidents.

[172] We omit here as not relevant to our main purpose the challenge that was made to the Constitutional Court concerning the constitutionality of this new statute.

completed is hazardous; but the fact that it will happen in the foreseeable future does not seem to be in doubt. Given this prediction, we feel it is not necessary to describe in any detail the current and varied ways used by the different regional courts to carry out this task. Here, then, suffice it to mention the barest outline of the procedure.

In order to liquidate damage to health, the judge must use 'ample equitable powers'. However, the discretional assessment inherent in the equitable method cannot turn into an arbitrary quantification. The Court of Cassation has, therefore, specified that trial courts must adequately justify the logical reasoning through which they have come to fix the amount of compensation, for the victim cannot be enriched at the expense of the tortfeasor. The judge must therefore indicate in his judgment the elements he deemed useful in order to reach his decision concerning the final assessment of compensation under this heading.[173]

According to the Court of Cassation the general limits to be observed by the judge when using his equitable powers are essentially two: first, the resort to an elastic criterion, allowing him to appreciate all the circumstances of the case; secondly, the justification of the use of such criteria must have regard to logic, consistency and the completeness of the statement of reasons. In practice, it is possible to resort to tables, mathematical or statistical formulae, provided that they reflect these criteria. The judge is therefore free to use formulae that are commonly accepted in practice, or are even provided for in special laws concerning particular types of accidents. The tables are prepared by medical examiners, trade associations and sometimes by the courts themselves.

As stated, it would be unnecessary to describe here the various methods of evaluation devised by various regional courts such as Genoa, Pisa, Milan and Rome, though one mentions this phenomenon in order to provide yet another specific illustration of the regionalism of Italian law noted in chapter 1. However, we feel it might be useful to draw the attention of the reader to two guidelines.

The first is found in a decision of the Supreme Court which stated that:

According to the constant trend of this Court, on the matter of liquidation of *danno biologico*, which is essentially an equitable one, the trial court may even resort to predetermined and standardised criteria, provided it does so flexibly, thus defining a general rule fitted for the particular case. The criterion that assumes as a parameter the average 'point' of disability, calculated on the average of court precedents, is a valid one: therefore the ruling that resorts to such method is not

---

[173] Cass. Se. Lav., 23 February 2000, no. 2037, Giust. civ., 2000, I, 1655.

in itself censurable under the profile of legitimacy, provided that it is supported by suitable grounds with regard to adjustment of the average value of the 'point' to the peculiarities of the case.

The second guideline can be found in article 4 of Law no. 39 of 26 February 1977, governing compulsory insurance for civil liability arising from the circulation of motor vehicles. This article contains provisions that apply in the event of personal injury when the impact of temporary or permanent disability on earned income, however qualified, is to be considered for the purposes of compensation. The indicated criteria concern income from employment and self-employed income. In all other cases 'the income to be considered for the purposes of compensation cannot in any case be lower than three times the yearly amount of the non-contributory pension' (article 4, para. 3).

## Life and death

The deprivation of *life* is not included in the heading of damage to health and, therefore, in the award for *danno biologico*. True, the injury to health results in a worsening (temporary or possibly permanent) of the quality of life and of the conditions in which the victim is forced to live after the accident, but health is a value different from life. Death is not the maximum possible damage to the psycho-physical health of the victim, but affects a different value, the loss of which terminates any right of the deceased subject to compensation for the accident.[174]

The injury to the legally protected interest of life is punished under criminal law and has legal consequences under civil law. For the surviving relatives the civil law consequence is the award of non-economic damages for the loss of the deceased.[175] If, in addition, they suffered economic loss as a result of being economically dependent on the deceased, they will be compensated for this as well, but in their own right, not *iure alieno* or *iure successionis*. What common lawyers refer to as Fatal Accidents Act actions are not within the scope of this book so little more will be said about this topic.

The different treatment – from the civil point of view – of the two cases is not surprising. Such different treatment is justified by two reasons. Damage compensation has no function of punishment in itself, but the function of reinstating and repairing damages actually suffered. Damage compensation cannot apply when the person who is the owner of the

---

[174] Cass. 20 January 1999, no. 491, Giust. civ. Massimario, 1999, 115.
[175] Cass. 2 April 2001, no. 4783, Danno e resp., 2001, 820.

right, and who should enjoy it by nature, has ceased to exist, as with death the legally protected interest inherent in the individual is extinguished. Furthermore, compensation for the right to health implies compensation for all the negative effects to which the surviving person is exposed. If death is immediate, or occurs within a negligible time lapse after the accident, any physical and mental suffering cease at the same time.[176] As the Court of Cassation correctly pointed out:

> [it cannot] . . . be considered absurd from the point of view of legal logic, that in terms of the amount of compensation, 'death' can cost less to the wrongdoer than a modest injury with permanent effects. If this occurs, it is simply the result of the different entity of the harm caused in the one and the other case, and therefore of the different legal positions of the individual affected by the tort . . . The diversity of situations, therefore, derives from the diversity of the damage to the personal or economic sphere that can be restored as 'unjust damages' caused by the tort and not by possible anomalies revealing any irrationality in the discipline of the damaging effects of the tort.[177]

### Psychiatric injury

As in England and Germany, 'psychiatric' harm (in the English sense of a recognisable illness) is compensable in Italian law under the heading of *danno biologico*. The more difficult problems arise in marginal (extreme) cases of pain or shock, usually referred to in Italian law as 'psychological damage'. The difficulties here are broadly similar to those encountered in the common law; and some Italian authors even invoke the 'floodgates' argument.

This kind of damage may be 'marginal' but it can affect the victim and his or her relatives.[178] The prevailing view is that this being pure grief, pain, etc., it is not included in *danno biologico* because it does not affect the body. Because it also tends to be very difficult to ascertain, its effects are usually not acknowledged. The possibility that some of this psychological reaction may be real and closely linked to chemical reactions of the brain does not appear to have received much attention by Italian courts which, in their decisions, tend to resemble the more conservative positions taken by the common law. But some courts have shown greater sensitivity to claims of this kind.

---

[176] Cass. 20 January 1999, no. 491, Giust. civ. Massimario, 1999, 115.
[177] Cass. 28 November 1995, no. 12299, Foro it., 1996, I, 3120.
[178] More generally see Emanuela Navarretta, *Diritti inviolabili e risarcimento del danno* (Giappichelli, Torino, 1996).

The Court of Milan, for instance, in its judgment of 2 September 1993,[179] held that this kind of award could be given to the parents who, due to their daughter's death, had incurred an injury to health consisting of an alteration of their mental equilibrium. This result divided legal writers. Some argued that psychological damage had equal dignity in respect of the injury caused to physical integrity;[180] others proposed to consider this kind of damage as 'ricochet damage', according to the well-known formula created by French case law.[181] Yet others rejected the inclusion of psychological damage in the sphere of non-economic damage or in any case in the area of application of article 2059 of the Civil Code.[182]

In practice, sometimes these kinds of damages are awarded to relatives of the victim in cases of extremely serious, but not fatal, injuries.[183]

In its judgment of 1994, referred to above, the Constitutional Court admitted compensation for 'pure' psychological damage only if based on the fault of the tortfeasor. Such compensation, however, is excluded in cases of causal i.e., strict, liability.

### Danno morale (pain and suffering)

Besides *danno biologico*, the victim and his or her relatives can be awarded another kind of compensation called *danno morale*. *Danno morale* is an ancient formula, which refers to the pain and suffering connected with an injury. It is something that concerns the moral sphere of the individual, and is usually considered as being in existence even if in reality there is no evidence that it has occurred. The relatives for whom it is usually claimed include sons, daughters, fathers, mothers, wives or husbands.

As to the individual himself, it relates to pain and suffering connected with personal injuries (light or great), defamation, the violation of privacy, the abuse of one's name, the appropriation of one's image, and so on. As already stated, the Civil Code has a provision (article 2059) concerning this kind of damage, which is called 'non-patrimonial'. The legal literature, however, refers to it as *danno morale* (damage to the moral sphere, pain and suffering).

---

[179] In Nuovagiur. civ. comm., 1993, I, 680.

[180] Paolo Cendon, *Il prezzo della follia* (Il Mulino, Bologna, 1984); Giuseppe D'Amico, *Il danno da emozioni* (Giuffré, Milan, 1992).

[181] Raffaella De Matteis, 'Il c.d. "danno biologico da morte" come lesione di un diritto riflesso,' *Nuova giur. civ. comm*, 1994, I, 682.

[182] Giulio Ponzanelli, 'La Corte costituzionale e il danno da morte', as an annotation to the decision under examination, Foro it., 1994, I, 3303.

[183] Giovanna Visintini, *I fatti illeciti, I, Ingiustizia del danno. Imputabilità* (Padova, 1987), p. 87 ff.; Guido Alpa, *La responsabilità civile* (Milano, 1999), p. 654 ff.

The said provision stipulates that this kind of damage can only be awarded in cases 'provided by law'. A strict interpretation of that formula takes the view that 'law' means 'criminal law'. It has thus led to the view that this kind of damages should be awarded only where a criminal offence has been committed. This position is taken by most authors and judges. Inevitably, however, such an approach has also had its critics, mainly on the grounds that it runs counter to the Constitution. According to this school of thought, *danno morale* should be awarded in any case, not only in criminal offences. This dispute has been a long one.

The question whether, besides pecuniary losses, harm pertaining to the sphere of feelings should also be compensated, arose in a number of cases during the late nineteenth century. At this (early) stage in the (modern) Italian law of damages, the courts showed a real inclination to favour the victims. The reason was the belief that so-called 'moral' sufferings were seen as being more serious than physical ones. Attributing to them a monetary value was thus seen as compensation taking the form of satisfaction for the injured party.[184] The cases in which this happened were those which amounted to both torts and crimes, especially where the victim's death followed the unlawful act. But non-pecuniary (or 'moral') damage was also compensated in the event of conduct which amounted to a serious interference with the plaintiff's honour or reputation.

The measure of the damages awarded was assessed equitably and was calculated by taking into account the extent of the abuse and of the consequences to the victim/plaintiff.[185] Judges of the time were particularly sensitive to the economic and social status of the victim and the persons to whom compensation was granted. Allusion to such criteria was made in various forms. The Court of Cassation of Turin, e.g., specified that 'when liquidating non-pecuniary damage caused to children by their father's death, the judge is to take into account the extent of the adversity, the conditions of age and education of the claiming persons, and the fortunes of the same'.[186] Another court, when calculating the amount of compensation, deemed it relevant to take into account the 'quality of the persons' and 'the circumstances of the whole family'.[187]

The 'social conditions of the person killed'[188] were also seen as a relevant factor. Others taken into account when fixing the amount of

---

[184]  e.g., App. Bologna, 11 October 1889, Riv. giur. bol. 1889, 309.

[185]  App. Bologna, 4 February 1889, Riv. giur. bol., 1889, 38.

[186]  22 November 1913, Giur. tor., 1914, 33.

[187]  App. Firenze, 13 September 1905, Monitore tribunali, 1906, 215.

[188]  App. Trani, 13 June 1898, Riv. giur. Trani, 1898, 747; App. Bologna, 14 February 1902, Mon. trib., 1902, 750.

compensation included the (killed) father's true affection for his children or, in the reverse case of the child being killed, the fact that the immediate victim was the only child of the suing survivor. The intensity of the claimant's grief and the premature and violent loss suffered by the father were also given some weight in the appraisal process.[189] The circumstances clearly varied from case to case; and judges could pay such attention to them as they thought fit.[190]

In the case of interference with honour and reputation, the distinction between non-pecuniary damage (consisting of hurt feelings for the insult) and the economic consequences of libellous or slanderous statements was not always made clear. Sometimes when compensation was decreed, reference was made to loss of custom deriving from the injurious statement. Thus, in a case regarding a libelled lawyer, the Court of Cassation of Palermo argued that not only should it take into account the loss of custom flowing from his defamation, but also the contempt, low regard and grief experienced by the defamed person.[191] And there were decisions following the principle according to which non-pecuniary damage could be – additionally – compensated insofar as it related to the material damage flowing from the injury.[192]

Who was entitled to such compensation? The distinction that slowly emerged from the case law of the period was rather clear. In the event of the death of the victim, non-pecuniary damage was given to the relatives in accordance with the variable criteria indicated above. In the event of injury to honour and reputation, the compensation was given to the victim himself, whether he was an individual or, even, a legal entity.[193]

At the time, attitudes towards non-pecuniary damage followed the ups and downs of particular decisions found in the case law. Thus, around the 1920s, the rulings of some Courts of Appeal expressed the opinion that non-pecuniary damage could be compensated regardless of any repercussion on the wealth of the injured party (the subject being the grief and anguish, or pain and suffering, which then had to be quantified as *pure non-pecuniary damage*).[194] Among academic writers such decisions provoked both approval[195] and criticism,[196] leading to lively debates but

---

[189] App. Torino, 3 November 1885, Giur. tor., 1886, 104.
[190] App. Bologna, 14 February 1902, n. 188 above.    [191] 4 June 1898, Foro sic., 1898, 486.
[192] App. Catania, 2 April 1900, Giur. cat., 1900, 48.
[193] App. Parma, 14 June 1910, Giur. tor., 1910, 1054.
[194] App. Milan, 11 May 1920; 15 December 1920; 21 January 1921, Riv. dir. comm, 1921, II, 448.
[195] e.g. Biagio Brugi, Riv. dir. comm., 1921, II, 448.
[196] Pacchioni, ivi, 1922, II, 178 ff. notes on Court of Appeal of Rome, 23 July 1921.

also helping to perpetuate variations – regional and in magnitude – of awards.

Since its appearance in the Civil Code (1942) under article 2059, this rule has been applied to civil cases. The victim of a crime can claim damages either in the criminal courts or in the civil courts: the choice is his.

The question of constitutionality of this restrictive approach was, recently, referred to the Constitutional Court by the Court of Rome.[197] On the basis of an elegant argumentative structure, dating back to well before the nineteenth century, the order demonstrates how the legal conscience has always been sympathetic towards the idea of compensation for non-pecuniary damage, inseparable from the protection of the fundamental rights of individuals. The drafter of the order – who is also one of the most learned experts in this matter[198] – argues that a provision like the one under examination contrasts with the constitutional provision, since it differentiates in an entirely irrational manner the treatment of those who are struck by a non-pecuniary damage caused by an *ascertained* crime (and who therefore receive satisfaction) from those who are struck by non-pecuniary damage when the crime is only *assumed* (so that the injured persons are not protected). The growing conviction nowadays is thus that article 2059 of the Civil Code should be abrogated. As already stated in chapter 1, the latest decision of the Constitutional Court opted for a wide interpretation of the wording of the Code allowing the recovery of moral damages even in the absence of a crime. Incidentally, in the context of fatal accident claims (not discussed in this work) the result is that Italian law has moved closer to the position adopted by French law than the one found in England where *solatium* is compensated only within the narrow ambit of the English statutory regime.

As *danno morale* is awarded in every case of injury to health or violation of other personal rights (honour, defamation, name, image, privacy) there are no doubts about its liquidation even if the victim was unconscious, drunk, drugged and thus unable to appreciate the loss. The judge does not decide if the victim really suffered from the tort.

### Quantification of danno morale

Compensation for this heading of damage is based on equitable criteria. The calculation of the amount is left to the 'wise' appreciation of the judge.[199]

---

[197] By order 20 June 2002, Foro it., 2002, I, 2882.
[198] Marco Rossetti, *Il danno da lesione della salute* (Cedam, Padova, 2001).
[199] Cass. 4 April 1982, no. 4815, Giur. it. Mass., 1982.

The law excludes *a priori* the possibility of producing specific evidence with regard to *danno morale*. This involves a free judgment which, as stated, is entrusted to the judge. This approach is favoured by those who believe that everyone enjoys life in a different way.[200] It is, however, criticised by those who note that in this manner judicial awards are so different from one another (as well as being very 'casual' in their assessment) that they increase unfairness in the treatment of the injured parties.[201] All agree, however, that there has to be a link between the objective extent of damage, particularly if prolonged in time, and its monetary compensation.[202]

In attempting the evaluation the courts tend to refer to many elements. These include the following: (a) the seriousness of the crime:[203] the more intense, the greater the participation of the wrongdoer in the commission of the tort; (b) the intensity of the anguish, which means that one must take into account the duration of the pain, suffering or grief,[204] as well as the age and sex of the injured party; (c) the sensitivity of the injured party: the Court of Cassation also takes into account the intellectual and moral state of the victim – the higher this is, in the judges' opinion, the greater the sorrow[205] – and the economic and social conditions of the parties. These guidelines, however, many of which would cause much concern to common lawyers and German lawyers, appear to have been superseded in some recent decisions on the grounds that they conflict with human feeling and with the principle of equality.[206] The ties of marriage or kinship and the presence or absence of cohabitation (for legitimate relatives) remain, however, important factors,[207] in the latter case because common law spouses are still denied compensation by the large majority of judges.

Notwithstanding the above, a great number of trial judges have begun to depart from all the criteria used by the Court of Cassation. They thus tend to liquidate the *danno morale* in a few words, without much of an explanation. In terms of amount, and as stated above, this heading of damage tends to equal half (or less) the amount given to the victim for the compensation of *danno biologico*.

---

[200] Scalfi, Resp. civ. prev., 1988, 223.

[201] In this regard see the accurate review by Grappiolo, Nuova giur. civ. comm., 1989, 224.

[202] Cass. 6 April 1983, no. 2396, Resp. civ. prev., 1983, 760, on a case of noise pollution.

[203] Cass. 7 October 1980, no. 537, Foro it., 1980, I, 1051.

[204] Cass. 11 October 1985, no. 4947, Arch. giur. circ., 1986, 110.

[205] Cass. 28 April 1967, no. 774, Resp. civ. prev., 1967, 572.

[206] Cass. 13 October 1980, no. 5484, Resp. civ. prev., 1981, 403; 21 Cass. 11 July 1979, no. 3996, Resp. civ. prev., 1980, 436.

[207] Cass. 13 October 1980, no. 5484, Resp. civ. prev., 1981, 403.

This kind of reasoning and this kind of behaviour, again, raises the problem of equality in the treatment of victims. If moral suffering cannot be the object of evidence, why compensate victims in different ways without any justification?

In order to solve this problem, the Court of Genoa uses tables also for the calculation of the amount of *danno morale*, while other courts appear to have followed suit. But, as is the case with the liquidation of *danno biologico*, the tables followed are not the same in all the courts.[208] The regional variations must thus remain a cause of concern.

---

[208] See Court of Genoa, 13 January 1988 (unreported), quoted by Grappiolo, n. 201 above at 242.

# 3    Special damages: past losses

## English law

### Introduction

In English law the expression 'special damages' can, as we stated in the Introduction, have several meanings. In this chapter it refers to the amounts payable by a tortfeasor to his victim for the pecuniary losses actually suffered between the date of the accident and the date of trial or, in the case of less serious injury, the date of recovery. Thus the basic principle is that the claimant must prove, on the balance of probabilities, either what he has lost in financial terms (as for example in loss of earnings), or what sums he has had to pay, or become liable to pay, in order to meet expenditure directly incurred as a consequence of his injuries.

It is not, of course, every penny expended which is recoverable as damages. The court will look to see whether those payments were reasonably necessary. The principle was explained by Megaw LJ in *Donnelly* v. *Joyce*.[1] While the claimant may say, and believe, that it would aid his recovery to travel in the style and comfort of a Rolls Royce motor car and to spend an extended holiday in a five-star hotel in the Caribbean, the court is most unlikely to accept that it was reasonably necessary for him to do so. However, judges are disinclined, where the matter is marginal, to say that it was unreasonable for the claimant to have taken a certain course if he has actually expended the money. Past losses are likely to be viewed less strictly than claims for future losses where the money has not yet been

---

[1] [1974] QB 454 at the text: 'The Plaintiff's loss is not the expenditure of money to buy the special boots or to pay for nursing attention. His loss is the existence of the need for those special boots or for those nursing services, the value of which for purposes of damages – for the purpose of the ascertainment of the amount of his loss – is the proper and reasonable cost of supplying these needs.'

expended and where the sums are likely to be greater. But the size of the expenditure is not, of itself, necessarily going to make it unreasonable. Thus, receiving treatment in New York rather than London has been held to be reasonable,[2] as has been treatment at home even if it would have been cheaper to treat the victim at an institution.[3]

## Loss of earnings

The principles are precisely the same for past as for future loss of earnings. This subject will be covered extensively in relation to future loss in the next chapter so the reader is referred to the discussion found therein. One must, however, note that in this instance the exercise is much easier in so far as (a) the multiplier is clearly known and is fixed by reference to the time that has lapsed between injury and trial, and (b) the same is (approximately) true of the multiplicand in so far as it can be ascertained what the injured person/claimant would have been earning at the time of the trial. But one must remember that what is given to the claimant is his net loss i.e., his gross lost earnings minus taxation[4] and social security contributions.[5]

## Past medical care

### Medical treatment and therapies

An injured claimant is entitled to recover the costs incurred by him in obtaining appropriate treatment and therapy for his injuries and disabilities. The question is whether the expenses were reasonably incurred. This crucial question is implied by section 2(4) of the Law Reform (Personal Injuries) Act 1968.[6] The availability of treatment on the National Health Service is to be ignored.[7] A claimant is not obliged to use the service even though he could be treated free of charge.

The one exception to that rule is that if the injury occurred in a motor accident on the highway or other public place the defendant's insurer is liable to reimburse the National Health Service, up to a maximum of

---

[2] *Winkworth v. Hubbard* [1960] 1 Lloyd's Rep. 150.     [3] *Rialas v. Mitchell* (1984) 128 SJ 704, CA.

[4] *British Transport Commission v. Gourley* [1956] AC 185.

[5] *Cooper v. Firth Brown Ltd* [1963] 1 WLR 418. This includes the employee's own contributions to whatever pension scheme to which he belongs: *Dews v. National Coal Board* [1988] AC 1.

[6] See also, *Winkworth v. Hubbard* [1960] 1 Lloyd's Rep. 150; *Cunningham v. Harrison* [1973] QB 942.

[7] Law Reform (Personal Injuries) Act 1948, s. 2(4). In relation to future treatment it is for the claimant to prove that he will undergo private treatment rather than availing himself of the National Health Service: *Woodrup v. Nicol* [1993] PIQR Q104.

£2,856 for in-patient treatment and £286 for out-patient treatment.[8] The insurer must, however, have already made some payment in respect of the injury and know of the hospital treatment.[9]

## House care etc.

Individuals who suffer personal injury may require nursing care or, at a lower level, assistance at home with the ordinary tasks of daily living such as personal hygiene, cooking, laundry, housework, shopping and the like.

English courts approach this head of loss by considering evidence of how many hours of care have been required for each day which has passed between the time when the individual concerned was discharged from hospital and the date of trial or the date of recovery. The amount of care frequently varies as the individual makes a partial or complete recovery. It is normal for expert evidence to be obtained as to precisely what level of care has been necessary from the beginning.

The expert witness will produce for the court a schedule of how much care has been required during that period. The level of expertise required of the carer will also be considered. So, for example, an individual with a broken leg may very well need assistance with simple household tasks for which a home help is sufficient. On the other hand an individual who is bedridden, but capable of living at home, may require nursing assistance at least for part of the time. The victim of a catastrophic injury may require more than one carer in order to enable him to be turned, lifted or put into the bath. In those circumstances it may be reasonably necessary to employ someone with nursing training.

In the cases of brain injury it is often reasonably necessary to employ someone with special training to cope with the particular needs and difficulties of the victim.

The recoverable damages will be the amount which the court accepts was reasonable to expend on paying for the appropriate level of assistance for the appropriate number of hours.

The support needed may take other forms. Thus, there is also much authority to support the view that an injured housewife is entitled to claim the cost of employing domestic help.[10] Indeed, a Canadian decision

---

[8] Road Traffic Act 1988, s. 157.

[9] *Barnet Group Hospital Management Committee* v. *Eagle Star Insurance Co. Ltd* [1960] 1 QB 107.

[10] *Daly* v. *General Steam Navigation Co. Ltd* [1981] 1 WLR 120; *Shaw* v. *Wirral Health Authority* [1993] 4 Med. LR 275.

recently awarded such a claimant the cost of her husband doing some of this work (even though the minority objected that the tasks performed by the husband were not, really, performed for his wife but for the household which they shared).[11] The Law Commission has proposed that in these circumstances of 'loss of . . . ability to do work in the home', the claimant should be able to recover for the costs of work done in the past by friends or relatives and the claimant should then have a personal liability to account to those helpers for that work done. Where the claimant has 'soldiered on' and done the work himself, the Law Commission prefer to treat such damages as non-pecuniary loss, in line with pain, suffering and loss of amenity.[12]

In many cases care has not actually been provided by paid third parties but by members of the claimant's family who provided it through their natural concern, love and affection for the victim. In those circumstances the court calculates the commercial cost of the care which has been provided and then applies a discount, which will normally be 25 per cent.[13] The cost of care is recoverable by a claimant irrespective of whether he or she is under any legal liability to make recompense to the person or persons who have provided the care. Most spouses or family members would provide the care without any consideration of whether they have a legal entitlement to be paid for it. Nevertheless, the claimant is entitled to recover under this head subject only to the discount. Any money received is, technically, held in trust for those who provided the care.[14] In the vast majority of cases, however, that principle is honoured more in the breach than the observance. Most family members decide that they do not want the money for themselves and that it is better used providing a fund for the future of the injured person. That is their decision. It is not open to a defendant to say, after judgment, that the money should be paid back to them because the claimant is in breach of trust. That accords with the principle that it is no business of the defendant how a claimant actually spends the general damages which he recovers.[15]

---

[11] *Kroeker* v. *Jansen* (1995) 123 DLR (4th) 652.

[12] See Law Com. No. 262 (1999), paras 3.87–3.93.

[13] *Evans* v. *Pontypridd Roofing Ltd* [2001] EWCA Civ 1657.

[14] *Hunt* v. *Severs* [1994] 2 AC 350, vindicating twenty years later the position first advanced by Lord Denning in *Cunningham* v. *Harrison* [1973] QB 942 at 952, but rejected by a differently constituted Court of Appeal in *Donnelly* v. *Joyce* [1974] QB 454.

[15] This position in 'practice' comes closer to the current state of the law in Australia which has refused to follow *Hunt* v. *Severs*. Thus see *Kars* v. *Kars* (1996) 141 ALR 37; *Fitzgerald* v. *Ford* [1996] PIQR Q72.

The above rules do not apply to compensate a spouse who gives her services to the claimant's business in consequence of the injury.[16] The reason for the distinction is that in such a case it is the business and not the individual who has suffered the loss. The word 'business' is, perhaps, insufficiently precise. If the spouse is trading as a sole trader, the loss is recoverable but not if the business is a partnership or a company.

In the case of family members there may be an alternative method of calculating the loss. If the carer has given up paid employment to care for the claimant there is an entitlement to the net loss of earnings of that individual rather than the discounted cost of care. The overriding principle is one of reasonableness. The question to which the court requires an answer is whether it was reasonably necessary for the family member concerned to give up work in order to care for the victim. Plainly, in some cases it may appear disproportionate for the individual concerned to have given up an extremely well paid job in order to provide the level of care actually required. The court may well be sympathetic to the fact that, for example, the mother of a young child has stopped work in the immediate aftermath of the accident and not returned for a period of months, or in some cases even years. That will depend upon the nature of the injury, the level of care required and the strength of the evidence generally. The court is far more likely to be sympathetic in the case of a mother-child or husband-wife relationship than in others. It is impossible to provide any hard and fast rule.

In normal circumstances the loss of earnings will be capped at the level of the cost of commercial care had it been provided. Now, for example, the court will have to assess the level of care required and what it would have cost had it been provided by an outsider. That figure will then be the ceiling of the claim for loss of earnings by the member of the family.[17] It does not follow that because a family member gives up work that would have occupied him or her for eight hours but actually provides twenty-four-hour care that she should be paid more than the amount which she would have received in employment. On the other hand, in one case the trial judge reached the conclusion that the claimant's wife, who was a nurse, had probably being doing the equivalent of the work of two full-time nurses. He awarded one and a half times the net amount which she would have earned in employment as a nurse.[18]

---

[16] *Hardwick v. Hudson* [1999] 1 WLR 1770.
[17] *Housecroft v. Burnett* [1986] 1 All ER 332; *Fish v. Wilcox and Gwent Health Authority* [1994] 5 Med. LR 230.
[18] *Hogg v. Doyle*, CA, judgment of 6 March 1991 (unreported).

### Personal expenses

This category covers claims for such items as additional heating costs where an injured individual feels the cold[19] or spends more time at home; the provision of special clothing; extra clothing and extra costs of holidays. That list is not intended to be exclusive.

The principle is precisely the same as it is in other areas, namely whether there is, on all the evidence, a reasonable requirement for the additional expenditure and whether the costs actually expended are themselves reasonable.

In cases of more serious injury special clothing may be required. It may also be necessary to wash clothes or bed clothes far more often than before as a result of incontinence or sweating.[20] In such case the household is likely to use more electricity and soap powder and have to replace the washing machine with greater frequency than normal.

Equally, a seriously injured individual may need to be accompanied on holiday by a carer who will inevitably incur extra fares and additional accommodation costs. Furthermore, the type of holiday undertaken may well be more expensive. A younger person may have been used to going camping or sharing a cheap apartment with others. That may well, as a result of his disabilities, no longer be feasible. It must be remembered that in accordance with general principles it is only the additional costs incurred which are recoverable.

In relation to clothing one of the arguments, in the case of younger individuals, which is frequently put forward by a defendant is that the young person would, but for the accident, have spent a lot of money on fashion clothes which he no longer does and that that is to be offset against the claim under this head. Whether that argument succeeds depends upon the judge's impression of the evidence.[21]

### Travel costs

In the case of past losses, this heading falls to be discussed under three sections.

First, are costs incurred by the claimant himself in travelling to and from hospital, medical appointments with his treating doctor and the like. Secondly, the claimant is entitled to recover monies expended by immediate relatives in travelling to visit him in hospital or, where reasonably necessary, accompanying him to hospital and medical appointments. In

---

[19] *Hodgson* v. *Trapp* [1989] AC 807.     [20] *Leong San Tan,* 1986 (unreported).
[21] *Donnelly* v. *Joyce,* n. 14 above.

both cases it is a matter of evidence as to how much has been expended. Although some evidence is required, a court does not necessarily expect to see a written receipt for every single journey by taxi or every single bus ticket. It applies its common sense in assessing what is reasonable.

Thirdly, the claimant can recover monies expended on his own travel if they are more than he would have expended had he not been injured. At the lower end of the scale that may be the cost of taxis used to go shopping or to get to and from work because the claimant is unable to utilise public transport as a result of his injuries. Whether they were necessarily incurred will depend very largely upon whether the medical experts accept that it was reasonably necessary for the claimant to utilise the more expensive form of travel.

Moving higher up the scale, it may be necessary for a claimant to purchase a larger motor car than that which he previously owned or even to adapt a vehicle. Those costs are calculated by looking, first, at whether, on the medical evidence, a larger or adapted vehicle was actually required. The costs of that type of vehicle or the adaptations will then be assessed but there must be offset against them what the claimant would, but for the accident, have spent on buying and/or replacing a motor vehicle.

As with other heads of damages it is for the judge to decide what is reasonable. One matter which is frequently taken into account is that it is generally necessary for an injured individual to have as reliable a car as possible. Thus, the student using an elderly motor car prior to the accident may reasonably require a newer, more comfortable and more reliable vehicle as a result of his disabilities.

If the replacement vehicle costs more to insure and run than that used by the claimant prior to the accident those additional costs will also be recoverable on the same principles.

There exists a government scheme called the Motability Scheme whereby government assistance is given for the purchase and running of a motor vehicle. Such costs can and will be taken into account in assessing what the claimant is reasonably entitled to recover. We consider this issue further in chapter 5.

### Aids and equipment

An injured individual may require all manner of aids and equipment to assist him to get about, to help with day-to-day living in the home, or even to amuse himself. The overriding principle is the same here as in what was said before: has a reasonable need been demonstrated on the evidence for purchasing, maintaining and replacing these items?

Expert evidence is almost invariably required to deal with these items. The range is enormous, proceeding from major items such as special baths and hoists to incontinence pads. The evidence will have to provide answers to these questions:

(a) Was it reasonably necessary for the claimant to purchase or hire the various aids and items of equipment claimed in his schedule?

(b) If so, was the type and model of each item reasonable or ought he to have purchased something cheaper?

(c) Even if a particular item of equipment was purchased as a result of the accident was that item something which the claimant would probably have acquired in any event? So, e.g., in modern times the court will be dubious about a claim that an individual has purchased a mobile telephone – or cordless telephone – purely as a result of the accident. The same might be said of a claim for subscriptions to one of the multichannel television companies or the purchase of a computer. However, each case must be looked at on its own particular facts and the surrounding evidence.

### Accommodation

There is, inevitably, an overlap between past and future costs of accommodation. In those cases in which all that is required are minor adaptations to a property, the expenditure may well already have been incurred. However, where it is necessary to purchase a property and/or carry out major alterations, the injured individual is unlikely to have been able to afford to meet such expenditure out of his own pocket. In general, therefore, the accommodation is likely to have been provided out of interim payments which are advances against the total sum of damages which he is likely to recover at trial.

Thus, those costs are more properly considered when looking at the damages recoverable for long-term losses. One must restate the general proposition against allowing the total cost of new accommodation.[22]

It is, however, appropriate to consider the type of case in which the claimant resides in rented accommodation and has moved to a larger or better property since the accident. As with all the other categories, the court has to consider whether the move has been justified. That will require looking at the medical evidence about the nature of his disabilities; whether a resident carer has had to be engaged (be it a member of the family or an outsider employed at commercial rates) or whether there

---

[22] Cf. *Cunningham* v. *Harrison* [1973] QB 942 and *Moriarty* v. *McCarthy* [1978] 1 WLR 155 at 163.

were deficiencies in the property in which the claimant originally lived. For example, if it was on the third floor of a block of flats without a lift and the claimant has difficulty in walking, the move will be justified.

The amount recoverable in such a case is the difference between the rent which the claimant was paying prior to the accident and the rent which he is paying at the date of trial.

### Other possible headings

In these days of greater numbers of cases of brain damage leading to mental disability, one can claim fees payable to the Court of Protection which often manages the sums awarded as damages.[23] The Court of Appeal, however, has recently been unwilling to treat as allowable expenses the sums that the victim was ordered to pay in matrimonial proceedings that followed the breakdown of her marriage as a result of her injury.[24] The decision, apparently based on considerations of public policy, is not, however, convincing; and the earlier contrary decision of *Jones* v. *Jones*[25] seems preferable.

## German law

### Loss of earnings

Lost earnings will be calculated on the basis of the theory of difference (*Differenzhypothese*) i.e., by comparing the victim's actual state with that in which he would have been but for the injury. The principle, it should be noted, is the same for future, pecuniary losses though its application to the present situation covering the period from injury to trial poses few problems since it can be done on objectively available data and requires no hypotheses and speculation.

### Past medical care

### Generally

Among the principles for medical treatment we note the following.

Treatment is compensable if it is *necessary* for the recovery of the victim, or for the improvement of his state of health, or – at least – if it mitigates

---

[23] Substantial sums can be awarded under this heading. See e.g., *Jones* v. *Jones* [1985] QB 704, CA (£28,000 including the Official Solicitor's administration costs).

[24] *Pritchard* v. *J. H. Cobden Ltd* [1987] 2 WLR 627.

[25] [1985] QB 704 (where, however, the defendant had conceded the point).

his suffering.[26] Even unconventional methods (like acupuncture) have been held to be necessary.[27] 'Necessity' is determined according to medical standards – the doctors' opinion will be followed. If a treatment, medicament or an aid has been recommended by a doctor, it has to be paid for by the wrongdoer even if it has turned out to be ineffective or even counterproductive.[28]

Only actual expenses have to be compensated; the victim has (in the realm of §§ 249, 251 BGB) no freedom in the disposition of the money (cf. below).[29] If the treatment has not yet been performed or the aid not yet been purchased, the victim has to declare his serious intent to do so.

These principles apply also to the question whether the victim may avail himself of private treatment instead of being treated under the national health scheme. The wrongdoer has to pay the additional costs if private treatment enhances the chance of recovery – again, the doctors' view will be taken into account and it will be asked whether a reasonable man in the special circumstance of the case would choose this alternative. The kind of injury and the normal standard of living of the victim may be important,[30] too. Furthermore, the courts will ask whether the victim would have chosen private treatment even if he had had to carry the financial burden himself, or if he has taken out a special insurance for these costs.[31] Private treatment or better accommodation in the hospital will not be paid for if the victim simply wants more comfort and had relied on the compensation by the wrongdoer.[32]

If the victim is a foreign citizen, treatment by medical experts from his home country may be appropriate in severe cases;[33] members of allied forces in Germany are entitled to choose the army hospital even if the costs are higher than in a German hospital.[34]

---

[26] Erman/Kuckuk (10th edn, 1999), § 249 BGB no. 40.

[27] LG Karlsruhe 11 July 1997, VersR 1998, 1256.

[28] BGH 8 June 1999, NJW 1999, 2819, 2820; BGH 8 January 1965, VersR 1965, 439; Erman/Kuckuk § 249 BGB no. 41 (the risk of success is with the wrongdoer).

[29] BGH 14 January 1986, BGHZ 97, 14.

[30] Cf. BGH 19 February 1991, NJW 1991, 2340, 2342 = Basil Markesinis and Hannes Unberath, *The German Law of Torts: A Comparative Treatise* (4th edn, Oxford, 2002), p. 546 (henceforth referred to as *GLT*). For further references see Staudinger and Schiemann § 249 BGB no. 238.

[31] Erman/Kuckuk § 249 BGB no. 41.

[32] OLG Düsseldorf 28 May 1984, VersR 1985, 644.

[33] BGH 23 September 1969, NJW 1969, 2281; OLG Hamburg 7 August 1987, VersR 1988, 858.

[34] BGH 18 October 1988, NJW-RR 1989, 670, 672 (British soldier).

## Fringe costs of hospitalisation

Apart from medical treatment, the time in hospital is generally unpleasant for patients. The tortfeasor has to pay for aids and facilities which allow the victim a decent life in hospital.[35] For example, the victim may need additional personal equipment such as pyjamas, dressing-gown, slippers or an additional set of cosmetic tools. The tortfeasor has to pay the full amount necessary for the acquisition, if the items will no longer be used after the hospitalisation; otherwise – if the victim uses them later on at home – only a proportional amount has to be paid.[36]

The victim may also need entertainment to distract him from his miserable situation and long, tedious days in bed. The courts have awarded compensation for a rented television or radio;[37] lump sums for reading materials have been denied by some courts,[38] but are paid by the insurers voluntarily, at a modest level.[39]

If entertainment equipment is bought and later on taken home (e.g., a television), the above-mentioned rules apply. The costs of lengthy phone calls to friends and relatives cannot be reimbursed.[40]

For claims concerning aids and equipment see p. 113; for claims concerning costs related to new accommodation see p. 114.

### Travel costs

## Travel expenses of the victim himself

Such expenses have to be compensated according to § 843 I BGB (special needs) if they occur permanently (e.g., increased dependency of a handicapped person on public transportation).[41] Travel expenses in connection with the accident which are not permanent (cost of visits to the doctor or to the hospital) are part of the damage which is recoverable under §§ 249, 251 BGB.

---

[35] MünchKomm-BGB/Oetker § 249 BGB no. 386.
[36] MünchKomm-BGB/Oetker *ibid*. Cf. BGH 19 May 1981, NJW 1982, 757, 758: an aid which would be useless for a healthy person has to be paid in full (e.g., a lift for handicapped people in a private home); if the aid fulfils a basic function for everybody (a motorcar, apartment), the tortfeasor has to pay only the surplus of the costs caused by the handicap.
[37] OLG Köln 13 April 1988, NJW 1988, 2957; OLG Düsseldorf 19 November 1993, NJW-RR 1994, 352.
[38] OLG Köln 4 October 1989, VersR 1989, 1309.
[39] MünchKomm-BGB/Oetker § 249 BGB no. 384 (€10–20 per week).
[40] MünchKomm-BGB/Oetker §249 BGB no. 384.
[41] BGH 10 November 1964, NJW 1965, 102.

## Travel expenses of other persons[42]

*Basic approach*

Travel costs incurred by relatives or others to visit the victim or to take him to the hospital, doctor etc., are expenses which do not fall upon the victim himself but upon the relatives. As a matter of principle, German tort law does not compensate for indirect damages to third persons; nor does it provide compensation for pure financial loss – the exceptions laid down in §§ 843–845 do not apply in this context. The courts, nevertheless, feel that such expenses should be compensated; and for a long time now have resorted to the idea that the visits of the relatives are intended to meet the special needs of the victim for personal contact, consolation and emotional support. These needs, and accordingly the appropriate costs to meet them, are thus considered to form part and parcel of the damages of the victim himself.[43]

Notwithstanding the above, the Federal Court feels uneasy with this approach. It thus tends to add that this exception to general principles has to be construed narrowly. The expenses as such and the actual amount are thus recoverable only insofar as they were 'unavoidable' in the given circumstances.[44] Since 1991, this has become the guiding criterion for German courts; it is also supported by § 254 II BGB (duty of the victim to mitigate damages). It controls all the specific issues which are discussed below.

*Necessity of travels/visits*

Since the starting point of reference is the needs of the victim, only such visits by others are held to be compensable which are 'medically necessary for the recovery of the patient'.[45] The Federal Court tries to distinguish this medical necessity not only from the wishes of the relatives to see the victim (which would constitute only a 'third party damage'), but also from other needs of the victim himself, in a psychological or physical sense. This has been criticised as disregarding the fact that medical recovery and

---

[42] For further details (and a translation of the leading decision of BGH 19 February 1991, NJW 1991, 2340) see *GLT*, pp. 42–548 and 909.

[43] While this is the unanimous position of the courts, some authors would prefer a different dogmatic approach: judge-made expansion of the statutory scheme in §§ 844, 845 BGB (Larenz and Canaris (1994) p. 586), or analogy to these provisions (Staudinger and Schiemann (1999) § 249 BGB no. 240). For attempts to establish a direct claim on the part of the relatives see p. 113.

[44] BGH 13 February 1991, NJW 1991, 2340, 2341 = *GLT*, case no. 58, p. 544.

[45] BGH *ibid.*; OLG Bremen 31 August 1999, FamRZ 2001, 1300, 1301.

psychological factors are inextricably intertwined.[46] The line which the Federal Court purports to draw causes problems, especially where the influence of visits on the recovery cannot be proved (as would be the case with visits to patients who are in coma)[47] or where there is no medical chance of recovery. Likewise, should the visits paid to a dying child by its parents be compensated?[48] If one were to apply the criteria set out by the Federal Court, the answer would have to be 'no'. But the result seems so harsh that it finds no support even in the courts. In one case before the Court of Appeal of Bremen,[49] the infant was incurably damaged by the doctor's malpractice. The personality of the child was, in fact, destroyed forever. Although the child had to be placed in an institution, the parents continued to visit the child or to take the child home over the weekend. The court reiterated and confirmed the principles set out by the above mentioned decision of the Federal Court of 1991, which would preclude compensation in this case. But then the court allegedly found a loophole and ordered compensation of the travel expenses of the mother.[50] Her duty of personal care and to remain in contact with her child (§ 1606 III S. 2 BGB) could – in this case and because of the injury – be performed only by continuous travel between the mother's home and the institution. Thus, these journeys were seen as responding to the special, permanent needs of the child, which are the basis for compensation under § 843 BGB. The result seems equitable, and the way it was reached ingenious. But since the Federal Court had not distinguished in its 1991 decision between temporary (§§ 249, 251 BGB) and permanent needs for visits (§ 843 BGB), the decision of the Court of Appeal of Bremen in reality marks a deviation from the decision of the Federal Court. The way out of the apparent impasse created by the decision of the Federal Court was thus achieved using distinguishing techniques which would be most familiar to common lawyers. And the fact that the Federal Court refused an application to review the decision of the Court of Appeal[51] would suggest that a first exception to the 'medical necessity' principle has now been accepted by the Federal Court itself.

---

[46] Wolfgang Grunsky JuS 1991, 907, 909 rejects the 'medical-necessity approach' altogether.

[47] Visits compensable: OLG Saarbrücken 23 October 1987, NZV 1989, 25; LG Saarbrücken 18 December 1987, NJW 1988, 2958 (same case).

[48] Yes: MünchKomm-BGB/Oetker § 249 BGB no. 380 (but not travels to the burial); Grunsky JuS 1991, 907, 908.

[49] FamRZ 2001, 1300.      [50] As to the father see p. 110.

[51] Publisher's note FamRZ 2001, 1301.

In addition, the Federal Court restricts the necessity of visits to cases where the victim had to stay in hospital for some time.[52] This has been criticised because it might be medically necessary for the victim to see his relatives even if he is treated outside of a hospital but away from home.[53]

### Scope of 'relatives'

While the hitherto prevailing practice used to speak of 'close relatives', the expenses of which would be compensable, in 1991 the Federal Court narrowed the concept to the 'closest relatives'.[54] The exact definition of this group remains in doubt. Generally speaking, parents, spouses or registered partners (§ 11 I Lebenspartnerschaftsgesetz 2001) are regarded as 'family members'. In one case the distinction has been made between parents with or without parental authority.[55] Although, in general, siblings would also qualify, they have been excluded in the context of travel expenses.[56] Engaged partners, on the other hand, are said to be 'close family',[57] while de facto cohabitants are an especially disputed group.[58] On the other hand, one should note that the current tendency seems to be to look not so much at the legal relationship between the victim and the 'visitor' but at the personal and emotional bonds between them. In the light of the requirement that there is a 'medical necessity' for such visits, this seems to be a preferable approach.[59] Though desirable, visits by friends, colleagues or other persons who have social contacts with the victim do not fall under this heading.

### Frequency of visits

In the light of 'medical necessity' and 'unavoidability', this question is especially difficult to answer. There is much agreement that the answer depends on the facts of each case: age of the victim, the nature of his

---

[52] BGH 19 February 1991, NJW 1991, 2340, 2341 = *GLT*, p. 544; OLG Bremen 31 August 1999, FamRZ 2001, 1300, 1301.

[53] MünchKomm-BGB/Oetker § 249 BGB no. 380; Soergel and Mertens § 249 BGB no. 42.

[54] BGH 19 February 1991, NJW 1991, 2340, 2341 = *GLT*, p. 544 (nearest family).

[55] OLG Bremen 31 August 1999, FamRZ 2001, 1300, 1301 (see p. 109: The travel expenses of the unmarried father of the child were excluded from compensation); cf. MünchKomm-BGB/Oetker § 249 BGB no. 378: if there are two parents, only the costs of the 'cheaper' parent are compensable.

[56] OLG Karlsruhe 11 July 1997, VersR 1998, 1256, 1258; Palandt/Heinrichs (62nd edn, 2003) § 249 BGB no. 11.

[57] Palandt/Heinrichs § 249 BGB no. 11, vor § 249 BGB no. 71.

[58] Included: LG Münster 12 June 1997, NJW 1998, 1801.

[59] MünchKomm-BGB/Oetker § 249 BGB no. 379.

injury, the environment in which he is placed, the closeness of the relative, the amount of costs for each visit. Daily visits are considered to be an exception, but they may be necessary where young children are severely injured.[60] In other cases, the courts have accepted as 'reasonable' two or three visits per week,[61] or visits every other day.[62]

If frequent or even daily visits are necessary, an alternative to visits which is increasingly offered by the hospitals would be allowing parents to 'live in' with their injured children. There seems to be no decision in Germany which deals with claims concerning the expenses of such an arrangement. But it is very likely that the compensation would be granted under the same principles and with the same caveats that apply to visits in general.[63]

*Compensable costs*
According to the principles outlined above (see p. 108), only the 'unavoidable costs' for visits or travels are compensable. The relatives have to choose the cheapest means of transportation, accommodation etc.[64] If there are two parents of comparable importance to the child, the visit of only one parent at a time is 'necessary'.[65]

*Travel costs*  The 'cheapest means of transport' is not an absolute standard, but open to exceptions depending on the particular circumstances of each case. Within a certain range, the relatives keep the freedom of choice. Thus, the relative may use a private car if this is not substantially more expensive than using public transportation. In this case, the compensation would be calculated on the basis of kilometres travelled.[66] In exceptional cases, even the costs of an aeroplane ticket have to be paid.[67]

---

[60] OLG Köln 9 January 1978, VersR 1979, 166 (six-year-old child); LG Saarbrücken 18 December 1987, NJW 1988, 2958 (daily visits for over one year); cf. OLG Frankfurt 2 November 1979, VersR 1981, 239, 240 (severely injured spouse).
[61] OLG München 29 October 1980, VersR 1981, 560; OLG Koblenz 23 March 1981, VersR 1981, 887; LG Münster 15 May 1985, ZfS 1988, 69 (three visits).
[62] LG Augsburg 11 March 1988, ZfS 1988, 239.
[63] The regular costs of living at home would have to be deducted, however.
[64] BGH 19 February 1991, NJW 1991, 2340, 2341 = *GLT*, p. 544.
[65] MünchKomm-BGB/Oetker § 249 BGB no. 378; but see BGH 21 December 1978, NJW 1979, 598, where the spouse, the child and the mother of an injured woman had temporarily moved to the place where she was hospitalised (the BGH remanded the case).
[66] OLG Hamm 2 June 1995, VersR 1996, 1515; OLG Bremen 31 August 1999, FamRZ 2001, 1300, 1301; LG Münster 12 June 1997, NJW 1998, 1801.
[67] OLG Düsseldorf 18 June 1973, NJW 1973, 2112 (severely injured, temporarily unconscious child).

*Overnight accommodation* This is covered when overnight stays are unavoidable, which in Germany is considered to be an exception.[68] The relatives have to make use of opportunities to stay with family or friends; otherwise, they must choose a reasonably cheap but adequate hotel.[69]

*Costs of meals* They may be covered, if necessary, but only to the extent that they exceed the costs which the relatives would have incurred at home.[70]

*Loss of earnings* A loss of earnings caused by the visit has, as a matter of principle, to be compensated, but the loss must have been avoidable. The relative must use all means to avoid the loss[71] e.g., by changing his working hours[72] or by making up for the uncompleted work after his return. However, the relative is not required to use his annual paid leave in order to visit the injured.[73]

Only the loss of salary or lost profits (in the case of self-employed persons) is compensable.[74] Other professional disadvantages suffered by the visiting relatives are not covered. These would include the greater stress in getting his work done, loss of chances or set-backs in professional promotions or the necessity to postpone the opening of a business.[75] No compensation will be granted for the sacrifice of spare time.[76]

Borderline cases include visits by a non-employed, housekeeping parent. Although he or she does not suffer a loss of earnings, the non-performance of housework may be compensated in other contexts: injury to the housekeeper himself (see p. 150), or personal care rendered gratuitously to an injured family member (see p. 155). Visits to a hospitalised family member, however, are equated by the Federal Court with the use of spare time. Normally, the housework can be done before or after the visit.[77] Probably the courts would decide otherwise if there were no opportunity to make

---

[68] BGH 19 February 1991, NJW 1991, 2340, 2341 = *GLT*, p. 545.

[69] MünchKomm-BGB/Oetker § 249 BGB no. 378.

[70] BGH 19 February 1991, NJW 1991, 2340, 2341 = *GLT*, p. 545.

[71] BGH 19 February 1991, NJW 1991, 2340, 2341 = *GLT*, p. 545.

[72] BGH 21 May 1985, NJW 1985, 2757; this is increasingly possible in Germany not only for self-employed persons, but also for employees.

[73] MünchKomm-BGB/Oetker § 249 BGB no. 377.

[74] The courts will grant compensation for the actual loss in a given case; more restrictive Staudinger/Schiemann § 249 BGB no. 241: only the average hourly salary of employees.

[75] BGH 19 February 1991, NJW 1991, 2340, 2341 = *GLT*, p. 545; for a critical view see Grunsky, JuS 1991, 907, 909.

[76] BGH 22 November 1988, NJW 1989, 766.

[77] BGH 19 February 1991, NJW 1991, 2340, 2342 = *GLT*, p. 545.

up for lost work, and substitute home help had been paid for. Thus, the courts have ordered reimbursement of the costs of a babysitter during the time of visit.[78]

This rich case law gives some indication of how detailed, indeed, sophisticated, the German law of damages has become through the development of detailed legal rules over many years of court practice.

*Freedom of the victim to dispose of the money paid*

As stated earlier, the costs of visits of relatives can be claimed by the victim himself. There is no direct claim of the relatives against the wrongdoer.[79] A recourse to §§ 683, 670 BGB[80] is rejected by the prevailing view.[81] Others would apply § 255 BGB by analogy, which would give the relatives a claim against the victim for assignment of the compensation claim.[82] The majority position, however, is that the victim is not obliged to pass on the money to his visiting relatives. Prima facie a difference with English law must be noted. However, because of the restriction of compensation to visits of 'close relatives', the problem has little practical importance.[83] If the victim is a minor child, the parents as legal representatives can assign the claim of the child to themselves[84] or can simply use the money for the family.[85]

*Aids and equipment*

Aids and equipments are an integral part of the medical treatment of the victim: compensation for such costs has to be paid according to §§ 249, 251 BGB, permanent costs according to § 843 BGB (see below) – a difference exists only with regard to the method of calculation and payments.[86] One and the same need can be satisfied in one or the other way: by paying an annuity for continuing handicaps (§ 843 I BGB), or by financing the acquisition of equipment which can assist the victim to cope with the handicaps (§§ 249, 251 BGB).[87] The acquisition of such equipment has to

---

[78] BGH 24 October 1989, NJW 1990, 1037.    [79] Seidel, VersR 1991, 1322–4.

[80] See *GLT*, p. 909; Völcker, JuS 1992, 176.

[81] Cf. BGH 21 December 1978, NJW 1979, 598/9; Staudinger/Schiemann vor § 249 BGB no. 56 with further references.

[82] Selb, Schadensbegriff/Regressmethoden (1963), p. 71; Erman/Schiemann § 843 BGB no. 20; Soergel/Zeuner § 843 BGB no. 29. Similar Hermann Lange and Gottfried Schiemann, *Schadensersatz* (3rd edn, 2003), § 11 C V, pp. 753–4 (claim for assignment based on the internal relations between victim and relatives).

[83] Cf. p. 110.    [84] Lange and Schiemann, n. 82 above at § 11 C V, pp. 753–4.

[85] § 1649 II BGB.    [86] Illustrative MünchKomm-BGB/Stein § 843 BGB no. 38.

[87] BGH 19 May 1981, NJW 1982, 757.

be compensated if they have already been bought or if the victim intends to buy them (§§ 249 II, 251 BGB); maintenance and periodical replacement will be covered by the annuity payable under § 843 I BGB (see p. 4). The standard for compensation is again 'necessity', not the 'optimum' or 'desirability'. The point of comparison for the necessity is the quality of life the victim has enjoyed before the injury.[88] For details see below.

### Accommodation

The tortfeasor has to pay the expenses if the existing apartment of the victim has to be adapted to his special needs after the injury e.g., the installation of a lift[89] or even an indoor swimming pool.[90]

Sometimes, however, the victim has to look for another apartment which is better suited to his handicapped living. In this case, the moving costs are recoverable as well as a rent increase, compared to his previous rent.[91] Problems arise if the victim buys a new apartment or home. In principle, the costs of acquisition have to be compensated too, but not to the full extent: the tortfeasor owes compensation, but does not have to contribute to the enrichment of the victim.[92] The Federal Court has found two aspects to be relevant: first, the normal costs of the use of a home have to be deducted; secondly, the tortfeasor has to make possible the *use* of the new home, but not the *ownership* of the victim. Thus, his share of the burden of costs is limited to the costs of acquisition with the exclusion of the property factor.[93] How this share has to be calculated is not entirely clear – the court refers to § 287 ZPO as last resort. One criterion mentioned by the Federal Court as an example would be the costs of the bank loan and the monthly instalments to be paid by the victim, which include the interest as well as repayment of the capital.[94] The method of payment may vary: an annuity may be ordered under § 843 I BGB or a lump sum may be preferable (§§ 249 II, 251 BGB), with which the victim could (in part) repay the loan.[95]

---

[88] BGH 8 November 1977, VersR 1978, 149, 150; OLG 17 September 1987, Köln VersR 1988, 61, 62; MünchKomm-BGB/Stein § 843 BGB no. 39.

[89] Mentioned in BGH 19 May 1981, NJW 1982, 757, 758.

[90] OLG Nürnberg 7 November 1969, VersR 1971, 260.

[91] BGH 19 May 1981, NJW 1982, 757, 758; OLG Celle 22 January 1962, VersR 1962, 292.

[92] A leading case is BGH 19 May 1981, NJW 1982, 757.

[93] BGH, *ibid.* at 758: *'bereinigter Anteil an den Baukosten'*.

[94] BGH, *ibid.* at 759; the inclusion of the repayment part of the instalments seems to be inconsistent with the basic premise of the BGH: in the end the tortfeasor has paid for the new property of the victim.

[95] BGH, *ibid.* at 758 (not very clear with regard to the relation between §§ 843 III and 249, 251 BGB).

## Italian law

As stated in the Introduction, Italian law does not *appear* to make a clear and rigid distinction between past and future losses. Though the first, covering the period from accident to trial, are easily ascertainable and can, in most cases, be supported by bills and invoices, whereas the later amounts (arising from claims from trial to the moment the victim dies) are open-ended, Italian judges tend to award one sum for both and fail to specify in their judgments how their figures have been reached. If, as a result of this approach, the reader fails to discover indemnifiable items of damage comparable to those that exist in his own system, he must not jump to the conclusion that they are left uncompensated in Italian law. For one must never forget that the amounts awarded under the umbrella notions of *danno biologico* and *danno morale* can be fairly substantial; and in some instances could well be covering losses which in the common law would receive individual attention. We offer this suggestion in a tentative manner, more on the basis of our collective and individual readings of each other's materials, than basing it on specific judgments (which, in the light of the above, is impossible). If this way of handling matters makes Italian law more opaque, it does not mean that it also makes it 'worse' than others. Each system has to operate within its own tradition; and all we wish to suggest is that understanding the solutions of a foreign system often requires evaluating its rules within their wider context.

# 4 Future pecuniary losses

## English law

### Introduction

In addition to general damages for pain, suffering and loss of amenity an injured individual will be compensated for pecuniary loss suffered by him as a direct consequence of his injuries and residual disabilities. The various heads of loss are considered later in this chapter. In essence they fall into two categories; monies which the claimant would have received but for the accident, and expenditure which he would not have incurred but for the accident. The court, inevitably, is involved in a degree of speculation. It is incumbent upon the claimant to prove, on the balance of probabilities, what would have happened in the future or what is likely to have happened in the future. The court considers the position as it is at the date of trial and makes its assessment at that date. Save in one exceptional case neither side has the opportunity to return to court to review the level of damages. Once the damages are paid it is entirely a matter for the claimant how the money is spent.[1] The defendant is not entitled to insist that the money be used for any specific purpose nor is he entitled to return to court to complain that the claimant has not, in fact, done what he said he was going to do in the course of the evidence. Thus, for example, if a claimant persuades a court that he needs a certain sum of money for a property but then, in fact, buys it for less – or remains in rented accommodation – it is not open to the defendant to complain.

---

[1] *Fitzgerald v. Ford* [1996] PIQR Q72.

*Principle of full compensation*

According to classical contract doctrine,[2] 'where a party sustains a loss by reason of a breach of contract, he is, so far as money can do it, to be placed in the same situation, with respect to damages, as if the contract had been performed'. Tort law, by contrast, seeks to put the victim in the position he was in before the tort.

In personal injuries cases, full compensation is achieved by making damages earnings-related and by insisting that these represent, so far as possible, the full amount of the loss. The difference from social security compensation is thus marked *whenever* the latter tends to work on the basis of flat rates. For the tort system, more tailored as it is to the demands of individual claimants rather than 'average models', such methods of compensation appear unfair. For flat-rate benefits, unlike earnings-related benefits, do not enable victims to maintain their pre-accident standard of living. For example, a man who has taken out a mortgage or entered into a number of hire-purchase agreements on the basis of his earnings will not be able to continue meeting his commitments if after his injury his compensation is unrelated to his pre-accident earnings but is, on the contrary, determined by pre-arranged flat rates. Moreover, flat-rate benefits, depending as they do on some single figure selected from all earners, are likely to lead to undercompensation for most and, perhaps, overcompensation for a few. The inadequacies of social security flat-rate benefits are, to some extent, avoided whenever certain additional payments are made on an earnings-related basis. But here, too, compensation is unlikely (in all cases) to be full, since ceilings tend to be imposed on earnings-related benefits.

The proclaimed aim of full compensation is not always achieved in practice, since three factors seem to have watered it down.

The first is that when awards are made for future economic loss, judges tend to 'discount' their awards to take into account a number of contingencies. The fact that our system of awards takes the form of a lump sum makes this inevitable since the court has to try to make an educated guess as to certain contingencies (possible life of the victim and his dependants, his future earnings, etc.) and the tendency, apparently, is to reduce awards too much rather than too little. Empirical studies that substantiate this argument are sadly lacking, though certainly cases can be

---

[2] *Robinson* v. *Harman* (1848) 1 Exch. 850 at 855; 154 ER 363 at 365, per Parke B.

cited where awards which appeared generous at the time of the trial have, with the passage of time, proved to be inadequate. In fairness, however, one must also note that the reverse may also be true i.e., the lump sum award may turn to be excessive, something which will occur whenever the victim dies earlier than expected at the time of calculation of his damages.

The second factor that might lead to less than full compensation is the refusal of judges to calculate damages on systematic actuarial evidence. Though such evidence is admissible in court, the more rough-and-ready method of multiplier and multiplicand, which will be explained below, has always been preferred.[3] There is, however, no conclusive evidence to support this approach. What is more likely, however, is that damages tend to be less adequate in all cases where the period of expected future loss is great. This was clearly in the minds of the members of the Pearson Committee who, by a majority, proposed a 'modified multiplier' system. But Lord Hailsham LC informed the House of Lords[4] that consultations with the members of the legal profession had revealed great hostility to this complicated proposal, so the government was not going to recommend its acceptance.

The third and final factor undermining full compensation has been inflation. Courts tend to ignore it in their calculations except in the most extreme cases, and the reasons they have given, though not entirely convincing, are also not without value.[5] Yet it is a matter of fact that inflation, especially in the late 1970s and early 1980s when it reached record levels, did eat into awards which, at the time they were made, appeared generous, if not excessive.[6] Nowadays, inflation rates are very low and have been successfully kept under control so this factor is of diminished importance.

---

[3] For criticism by a leading actuary, see Prevett (1972) 35 MLR 140 at 257. In *Mitchell v. Mulholland (No. 2)* [1972] 1 QB 65 at 77, Edmund Davies LJ put it as follows: 'actuary and accountant may to a limited degree provide the judge with a means of cross-checking his calculations, and in arriving at the appropriate multiplier'. In *Auty v. National Coal Board* [1985] 1 WLR 784, Oliver LJ used even stronger language when he said: 'As a method of providing a reliable guide to individual behaviour patterns or to future economical and political events, the predictions of an actuary can be only a little more likely to be accurate (and will almost certainly be less interesting) than those of an astrologer' (at 800–1). See, however, the criticism of the traditional method by Thorpe LJ in *Wells v. Wells* [1997] 1 WLR 652.

[4] Hansard (HL) 1982, 621.

[5] *Taylor v. O'Connor* [1971] AC 115; *Lim Poh Choo v. Camden and Islington Area Health Authority* [1980] AC 174 at 193, per Lord Scarman.

[6] For an earlier recorded instance see *Thurston v. Todd* (1966) 84 WN Pt 1 (NSW) 231.

## Method of calculation

The basic method of calculation for all but the most speculative of heads of claim is the multiplier-multiplicand approach. How does that work? It is best to discuss this topic under three subheadings.

### General observations

The assessment of damages for the loss of future (prospective) earnings is, inevitably, less precise and fraught with difficulties to which we have already alluded. These are largely due to the number of imponderables: in addition to those set out above, they may include such questions as: how long would the plaintiff live? How long would he continue working and at what rate? Would he be promoted and receive a rise? Conversely, might he lose his job? What will the rate of inflation be in the future? Would there be any significant change in his personal tax status? This tries to discover so far as possible the net annual loss suffered by the victim (the 'multiplicand')[7] and arrive at a figure for the award of lump sum damages by applying to this a 'multiplier', which must reflect not only the predicted number of years for which the loss will last but also the elements of uncertainty contained in that prediction and the fact that the plaintiff will receive immediately a lump sum, which he is expected to invest. Actuarial techniques are now built into this process since the adoption by the courts of a set of tables (the Ogden Tables) which give the multiplier applicable to the claimant depending upon the circumstances of the case. The tables cover all aspects of damages for loss for life, loss up to various retiring ages, loss of pension and loss for a number of years certain. The discount rate is fixed by the Lord Chancellor pursuant to section 1 of the Damages Act 1996. It is currently set at 2.5 per cent as explained below.

The guiding principle is that the damages must be assessed on the basis that the total sum awarded will be exhausted at the end of the period contemplated and that during that period the plaintiff will be expected to draw upon both the income derived from the investment of the sum awarded *and* upon part of the capital itself. Any other calculation which

---

[7] Note the comments of Lord Lloyd in *Wells* v. *Wells* [1999] 1 AC 345 at 377F, that careful scrutiny is needed of the elements which go to make up the multiplicand, especially since 'the effect of reducing the rate of discount is to increase the multiplier in every case'. This case was decided before the Lord Chancellor had set the discount rate. At that time it fell to the courts to set the rate and *Wells* was the case in which the House of Lords had to deal with the first substantial challenge to the long established rate of 4.5 per cent. See below.

did not require the simultaneous use of income plus capital would result in part of the capital remaining intact at the end of the contemplated period and, consequently, in overcompensation of the plaintiff. This method of calculation, however, also means that the chosen multiplier will be less than the number of years taken as the period of the loss.

## The multiplicand

The multiplicand is the annual figure representing each head of loss. So, for example, if the injured individual requires care in the medium to long term, evidence will be received of the current annual cost at the date of trial. That is the multiplicand. In certain circumstances there may be more than one multiplicand for a particular head of loss. Staying with future care as an example, the evidence may well be that the claimant will require a certain level of care for a number of years but, when he gets to say sixty-five, more will be required and the cost will be greater. In those circumstances the court will consider two multiplicands, one for the period immediately following trial and one for a much later date. The number of multiplicands is not limited. There may be any number. However, that approach is only adopted in circumstances, such as care, where there is a high degree of probability that by or at a certain date a specific state of affairs will exist.

## The multiplier

As already stated, the guiding principle is that the damages must be assessed on the basis that the total sum awarded will be exhausted at the end of the period contemplated and that during that period the plaintiff will be expected to draw upon *both* the income derived from the investment of the sum awarded *and* upon part of the capital itself. Any other calculation which did not require the *simultaneous* use of income plus capital would result in part of the capital remaining intact at the end of the contemplated period and, consequently, in overcompensation of the plaintiff. This method of calculation, however, also means that the chosen multiplier may be less than the number of years taken as the period of the loss.

For many years the courts assumed that the lump sum would be invested in equities which, on average, yield a rate of return of around 4 to 5 per cent per annum, and reduced the multiplier accordingly. In *Wells* v. *Wells*[8] the House of Lords, in a decision which one expert commentator

---

[8] [1999] 1 AC 345 (reversing the Court of Appeal [1997] 1 WLR 652).

described as 'the most important decision in personal injury litigation since the Second World War',[9] overturned this approach. The former practice had been based on the assumption that the victim should be taken to be in the same position as any other ordinary prudent investor. However, as Lord Lloyd explained:

> Granted that a substantial proportion of equities is the best long-term investment for the ordinary prudent investor, the question is whether the same is true for these plaintiffs. The ordinary investor may be assumed to have enough to live on. He can meet his day-to-day requirements. If the equity market suffers a catastrophic fall, as it did in 1972, he has no immediate need to sell. He can abide his time and wait until the equity market recovers.
>
> The plaintiffs are not in the same happy position. They are not 'ordinary' investors in the sense that they can wait for long-term recovery, remembering that it was not until 1989 that equity prices regained their old pre–1972 level in real terms. For they need the income, and a portion of the capital, every year to meet their current care.[10]

His Lordship concluded that it was more appropriate for the court to assume that the victim would invest most of the lump sum in index-linked government securities. These offer a guarantee of protection against future inflation but, in part because of this protection against inflation, also offer a lower rate of return than equities. On this basis, he said that the multiplier should be calculated on the assumption of a rate of return of 3 per cent per annum instead of the hitherto 4 or 4.5 per cent. The change has led to an inflation in the size of awards. Section 1 of the Damages Act 1996 confers a power upon the Lord Chancellor to set by order the expected rate of return which the courts should follow in such cases, in the interests of achieving greater certainty and consistency of practice; on 25 June 2001, the decision was taken by the Lord Chancellor to set the discount rate at 2.5 per cent,[11] which has inevitably further increased the level of awards. The Lord Chancellor also has the power to alter the

---

[9] David Kemp, 'Damages for Personal Injury: A Sea Change' (1998) 114 LQR 571 and which the press of the time thought would bring an unprecedented increase in the level of awards (The Times, 17 July 1998).

[10] [1999] 1 AC 345 at 366.

[11] Damages (Personal Injury) Order 2001, SI 2001/2301. It is, nevertheless, possible for the courts to take a 'different rate of return into account if any party to the proceedings shows that it is more appropriate in the case in question' (Damages Act 1996, s. 1(2)). However, early evidence suggests that the courts are extremely reluctant even to hear arguments that a different rate is more appropriate: see Warriner v. Warriner [2002] EWCA Civ 81; [2003] 3 All ER 447, where accountancy evidence as to the correct rate was refused.

discount rate in the future if he deems it appropriate to do so, but this is unlikely to occur for a number of years.

The Ogden Tables are now updated on an annual basis by the Professional Negligence Bar Association. This confirmed the trend towards a growth in the size of damages awards, heralded by the *Wells v. Wells* decision.[12] There are a number of different tables setting out the appropriate multipliers for the whole of the individual's life; for working life to aged sixty; for working life to aged sixty-five for a term certain or for future loss of pension. Different tables exist for men and women.

The court is not entitled to deviate from those tables although it may, in certain cases, apply a further discount for certain eventualities.[13] That is, however, really only applicable to loss of future earnings. The rationale for that approach is that the court will already have received and taken into account evidence about what is likely to happen in the future in setting both the multiplier and the multiplicand.

The multiplier will also be affected by the age of the victim at the time of the tort. Clearly, the older the victim the smaller the multiplier, the younger the victim the greater the multiplier. It is equally obvious that this method of calculation, despite the tendency to itemise awards, will in the end only lead to approximate compensation for future pecuniary loss. In fact, the number of imponderables in the calculation makes it likely that, the longer the period of the expected future loss, the less adequate the damages. Of the many imponderables, inflation is probably most to blame, though in these days of reduced inflation levels this is not likely to be as great a concern as it was in the late 1970s.

It is now clear that inflation beyond the date of the trial is not taken into account when determining the multiplicand. In *Cookson v. Knowles* the Court of Appeal held, and the House of Lords subsequently agreed, that for the purposes of calculating the dependency in fatal accident cases, as

---

[12] The escalation of damages awards was subjected to criticism in Harvey McGregor on *Damages* (16th edn, London, 1997, as updated by the 3rd Supplement, 2001): see paras 1601A–1601H especially at 1601E–1601G, who argued that the 2.5 per cent rate would lead to escalation 'to a degree that is far higher than proper compensation'. The main argument seemed to be that investment advice would be accepted by claimants recovering substantial damages, who would 'end up with a portfolio largely of equities, thereby leading to over-compensation as history shows that in the long term the total return on equities has always outstripped that on gilts, index-linked or otherwise'. One will have to wait to see whether the more recent volatility of the stock markets will return to the lessons of 'history' before assessing whether these consequences will be the result of the new discount rate. Current evidence suggests that they are not.

[13] *Page v. Sheerness Steel Co. Plc, sub nom. Wells v. Wells*, n. 7 above.

well as for the purposes of calculating loss of earnings in non-fatal cases, the loss should be divided into two parts, the first from the date of the death (or injury) to the date of trial, and the second from the date of trial into the future. In determining the rate of earnings of the deceased (or plaintiff) for the assessment of the first part of the loss, any increase in earnings due to inflation, which he would have received but for the death (or injury), should be taken into account. As to the second part of the loss i.e., from the trial onwards, this should be assessed on the basis of the assumed rate of earnings at the time of the trial (in our example, £5,000), with no addition for further inflationary increases in the future.

In certain circumstances the court may decline to adopt the multiplier-multiplicand approach at all. That is limited to the circumstance in which the head of loss is undoubtedly genuine but is too speculative to be susceptible to the usual method of calculation. In those circumstances the court awards a lump sum which is more to do with instinct and experience than any mathematical or scientific approach.[14]

## Future loss of earnings

This is a head of damage which probably causes more difficulty and debate than any other in the field of future pecuniary losses.

The essential basic principle is easily stated, namely that an injured claimant is entitled to recover the net sum which he would have earned but for the accident. In this context the word 'net' means after deduction of income tax and national insurance.[15] The court does not speculate as to changes in the levels for incidents of tax or national insurance after the date of trial. Earnings which have not been declared to the Inland Revenue are, nevertheless, recoverable but tax and national insurance at the appropriate rate must be deducted from the sums which the claimant would have received.[16] If, however, the earnings were derived from some unlawful act they will not be recoverable at all. The distinction is that in the former case the money came lawfully into the hands of the claimant and his unlawful act occurred subsequently when he failed to declare it to the Inland Revenue. In the latter case he never received the money lawfully at all.[17]

---

[14] Cookson v. Knowles [1979] AC 556; Blamire v. South Cumbria Health Authority [1993] PIQR Q1.

[15] British Transport Commission v. Gourley [1956] AC 185; Cooper v. Firth Brown Ltd [1963] 1 WLR 418.

[16] Duller v. South East Lincs Engineers [1981] CLY 585.

[17] Burns v. Edman [1970] 2 QB 541; Hunter v. Butler [1996] RTR 396.

At the lowest level this will involve an investigation of the length of the period for which the claimant, on the balance of probabilities, would be unable to return to his pre-accident employment. It may be that his injury is comparatively minor, in which case he will simply be absent from work, post-trial, for a matter of months. It may be necessary, however, for him to have a gradual return to work, first undertaking light duties at a lower wage than before. In those circumstances his loss is the difference between what he is actually able to earn and what he would have earned had he been fully fit. That includes the loss of opportunity to work overtime. It matters not that the claimant has no absolute contractual right to overtime payments. It is sufficient if, on the evidence, he would have been likely to earn overtime. That is, quite simply, a matter of evidence.

In the case of the more seriously injured individual the question is likely to be far more complicated, although the overriding principle remains the same.

In the case of a claimant who will never be able to return to work the loss is his annual net earnings, including overtime and pecuniary benefits, at the date of trial, times the appropriate multiplier. That figure will depend upon the age of the claimant at the date of trial and the date on which he would probably have retired.[18] That depends on the evidence. A date may be specified in the claimant's contract of employment. The court is, nevertheless, entitled to receive evidence that the particular employer generally permits employees to work beyond that date.

If the claimant is unable to return to his pre-accident employment but is, nevertheless, capable of undertaking some work it will be a question for the judge to decide what he is capable of undertaking and how much he is likely to earn in such a post. In those circumstances the loss of earnings will be the difference between what he is capable of earning and what he would have earned but for the accident. The claimant is not, of course, compelled to undertake employment. But he does have a duty to mitigate his loss. In those circumstances he is not entitled to say that the jobs which he is capable of doing are beneath him. Plainly, however, it may not be realistic for someone with a high-flying career pre-accident to undertake the most menial of tasks in the sense that no one will actually employ him. It is always worthwhile a claimant making job applications, and being turned down, in order to provide the court with evidence as to what is actually available to him. The court will also take account of such

---

[18] Ogden Tables 3–10.

matters as the level of unemployment in the area in which the claimant resides. Mitigation of loss does not involve his having to move from one end of the country to the other in order to obtain low paid employment.

Difficulties arise in this area in the case of individuals who are on a career ladder or who contend that they have lost a chance of promotion. In the case of an individual on a career ladder the court is likely to adopt different multiplicands, and reduced multipliers, for each stage of his likely career. Thus, the multiplier will be divided into a number of different periods during each of which the claimant may be earning substantially higher figures.[19]

In the case of promotion the court will have to evaluate the percentage chance of the promotion having been achieved. It will then recalculate the multiplicand for the relevant period, subject to a discount for the prospect of the lost chance.

A defendant is entitled to provide evidence, or to argue, on the basis of the claimant's own evidence, that his employment record is poor and that he would have been unlikely to have remained in employment for the whole of his working life. If such evidence is accepted by the court then the multiplier may be reduced.

Females, even nowadays, present a further problem in relation to the likelihood of career breaks to have and/or bring up children. There is not and cannot be any hard and fast rule. The matter must be looked at upon the available evidence in each case. Would she have returned to work immediately? Would she have sought to work part-time or become a full-time mother? In either of the latter events would that have impinged on the progression within her career? Those are all factors which fall to be taken into account by the court.

What is the situation in the case of a young person who has not yet embarked upon a career at all? In such a case the court will need to look at his educational attainment prior to the accident and any stated intention as to likely employment. It will also look, where appropriate, at the type of employment in which his parents and siblings have engaged in order to try and ascertain what type of work the claimant would, on the balance of probabilities, have done.

The younger the claimant the more uncertain the position. In such a case it may be necessary for the court to abandon the multiplier-multiplicand approach altogether and simply award a lump sum on the basis that

---

[19] *Brittain* v. *Garner, The Times*, 18 February 1989, but see for an alternative approach where the court used an average figure, *Housecroft* v. *Burnett* [1986] 1 All ER 332.

anything else is pure guesswork.[20] It is, however, more usual these days for the court to take an average figure for the general type of employment which the claimant's family has undertaken as the multiplicand and to use an appropriate multiplier.

In addition to loss of future earnings the court is entitled, in an appropriate case, to award an additional lump sum for the fact that the claimant is handicapped in the labour market. This head of damage only applies to an individual who is capable of returning to some form of employment but who, because of his disability, may find it more difficult than the average person to obtain further employment on his losing his job.[21]

This head of damage is not calculated in a scientific fashion. The court makes a broad assessment of how long it is likely to take the claimant to obtain further employment. It then awards net earnings for that period. Awards vary between three to six months and three years.[22]

### Medical treatment and therapies

The principle in relation to recovery of the costs of medical treatment or therapies is the same for the future as for expenditure prior to trial. The guiding principle, as always, is that of reasonable need. The claimant must also establish that he will, or probably will, require or undergo the treatment for which he claims.[23] He may be entitled to the cost of alternative therapies provided that he proves on the balance of probabilities that he will undergo them.[24]

The mere fact that a particular type of therapy (e.g., hydrotherapy) may be desirable does not make it reasonably necessary. Furthermore, the mere fact that the claimant would benefit from regular swimming does not make the cost recoverable if either he would have been likely to go swimming in any event or the cost replaces another sporting or athletic activity in which he might have taken part had it not been for the accident.[25]

On the other hand, the court is prepared to accept, e.g., a claim for IVF in the case of a claimant who is in an established relationship but is no longer able to procreate.

As with other future losses the court will utilise the multiplier-multiplicand method of calculation for future medical expenses. In the

---

[20] Blamire v. South Cumbria Health Authority [1993] PIQR Q1.

[21] Moeliker v. A. Reyrolle & Co. Ltd [1977] 1 WLR 132; Smith v. Manchester Corporation [1974] 17 KIR 1.

[22] A helpful table of awards and reasons is to be found in Butterworths Personal Injury Litigation Service, vol. I Part I.

[23] Woodrup v. Nicol [1993] PIQR Q104.    [24] George v. Stagecoach [2003] EWCH 2042.

[25] Cassell v. Riverside Health Authority [1992] PIQR Q168.

case of surgical procedures which do not require to be undertaken annually, the calculation is similar to that used for aids and equipment.

Prospective medical expenses will be estimated as accurately as possible[26] and will be awarded as part of the damages. Moreover, in accordance with section 2(4) of the Law Reform (Personal Injuries) Act 1948, failure to use the facilities of the National Health Service will not affect the 'reasonableness' of the plaintiff's expenses. As Slade J put it in *Harris* v. *Brights Asphalt Contractors Ltd*,[27] 'when an injured plaintiff in fact incurs expenses which are reasonable, that expenditure is not to be impeached on the ground that, if he had taken advantage of the facilities under the National Health Service Act 1946, these reasonable expenses might have been avoided'. But if advantage is in fact taken of the NHS, then the plaintiff will not be allowed to claim what he would have had to pay if he had contracted for such services or facilities.[28] In a society like ours the victim's right to be compensated for private hospitalisation is understandable, though some feel that this should not be allowed since even private hospitalisation is nowadays subsidised by the state.[29] What is less easy to justify, however, is the victim's right to claim such compensation, take advantage of free NHS facilities, and use the award for other purposes. This point, however, rarely arises in practice as far as the pre-trial medical expenses are concerned since at this stage plaintiffs are never sure that the defendant's insurers will pay and, therefore, rarely risk incurring the expenses themselves.

The Law Commission's Consultation Paper on *Damages for Personal Injury: Medical, Nursing and other Expenses*[30] recommended the retention of section 2(4) of the 1948 Act, and also proposed that the NHS should be able to bring a claim against tortfeasors for the costs of caring for their victims.[31] In its final Report on this issue,[32] the Law Commission stood by this provisional view,[33] although no concrete proposals on the recoupment issue were put forward. It should be noted, however, that during the consultation period prior to the final Report, the Road Traffic (NHS Charges) Act 1999

---

[26] *Lim Poh Choo* v. *Camden and Islington Area Health Authority* [1980] AC 174.

[27] [1953] 1 QB 617 at 635.    [28] *Woodrup* v. *Nicol* [1993] PIQR Q104.

[29] The Pearson Committee (Cmnd. 7054–1, 1978) paras 339–42 felt that such expenses should be recoverable only if private treatment was reasonable on medical grounds. Note, also, the Administration of Justice Act 1982, s. 5, discussed below.

[30] Law Com. No. 144, 1996.    [31] See *ibid.*, paras 4.2 and 4.3.

[32] *Damages for Personal Injury: Medical, Nursing and Other Expenses; Collateral Benefits* (Law Com. No. 262, 1999).

[33] See *ibid.*, paras 3.18 (on the retention of s. 2(4) of the 1948 Act) and 3.43 (on recoupment by the NHS).

was passed, which provides a working example of how such recoupment might operate on a broader basis (including tariffs determining costs to be recouped and an appeals procedure). It is understood that the discussions surrounding the Law Commission's work in this area contributed to the formulation of the 1999 Act.[34] Most recently, the Department of Health has issued *The Recovery of National Health Service Costs in Cases involving Personal Injury Compensation: A Consultation*.[35] This draws heavily on Law Com. No. 262, especially in using the Road Traffic (NHS Charges) Act 1999 as a basis and poses a number of questions for consultation (covering the types of costs to be recovered,[36] whether industrial illness should be included, how to take account (if at all) of any findings or compromises on contributory negligence and whether the proposed scheme should apply to all relevant compensation payments or only to cases covered by insurance). This suggests a relatively strong political will to adopt this scheme and may be seen to fit in with the current government's priorities in achieving a more stable financial base for the public provision of health services. Equally, the impact on insurance companies and, ultimately, the customers who must pay their premiums, must be recognised as the source of this finance for the NHS. The progress of these proposals is to be awaited with interest.

### Third parties taking care of the claimant's needs

Not infrequently, relatives or friends come to the assistance of a victim and thereby incur *financial* loss (e.g., of wages) or expenses. The usual reason for this is to ensure that the plaintiff/victim receives proper medical and nursing care. To do this, the third party may have to give up his or her paid job. In such cases, these third parties cannot claim these losses in their own name, for as against them the tortfeasor has committed no tort. The question thus arises whether the 'primary' or 'direct' victim[37] can recover these sums and, if so, is he under a legal or (merely) moral duty to reimburse his benefactor (the third party)? In *Roach* v. *Yates*[38] the Court of Appeal had no difficulty in awarding such compensation to the 'primary' victim since 'he would naturally feel he ought to compensate

---

[34] *Ibid.*, para. 342.    [35] September 2002, available at www.doh.gov.uk/nhscosts

[36] NHS and ambulance costs only or also those incurred by GPs, etc.

[37] In what follows, we refer to the injured person/claimant as the 'primary' or 'indirect' victim to distinguish him from the volunteer who comes to his aid (usually giving up his job in order to nurse him) since, in a sense, he too is a victim (albeit indirect) of the tort.

[38] [1938] 1 KB 256.

[in that case his wife and sister-in-law, who had given up their employment in order to nurse him] for what *they* had lost'. The italicised word 'they' could be taken to suggest that the loss in question was, in fact, the third party's (benefactor's) though, for technical reasons, it was claimed by what we have called the 'primary' or 'direct' victim of the tort. Indeed, this position was adopted by Lord Denning in *Cunningham* v. *Harrison*[39] where he also added the rider that the sum thus collected (by the 'primary' victim/claimant) would then be held on trust for the third party (benefactor). By a strange coincidence, however, one day later, in *Donnelly* v. *Joyce*,[40] a differently constituted Court of Appeal reached the same final result (i.e., that the tortfeasor should pay the loss of the third party/benefactor) but via a different route. This was, quite simply, that the loss was that of the *primary (direct) victim* and it consisted not of the expenditure itself, but of the *need* for the nursing services.

The *Donnelly* v. *Joyce* ruling, which held sway for the next twenty years, was probably prompted by the desire to put an end to uncertainties which had crept into the practice of the law and concerned how the award thus gained by the 'primary' victim should be handled (i.e., kept by him or held in trust in the name of the benefactor, and should the latter course be open only when there was a formal agreement to such effect between the 'primary' victim and the third party). These difficulties were, apparently, avoided by making it clear that the claim for the award was that of the 'primary' victim and not the third party/benefactor and it was then entirely for him to decide how, in fact, the money would be used. But as Lord Bridge put it in *Hunt* v. *Severs*,[41] the decision which terminated the reign of the *Donnelly* judgment:

By concentrating on the plaintiff's [primary victims] need and the plaintiff's loss as the basis of an award ... the reasoning in *Donnelly* diverts attention from the award's central objective of compensating the voluntary carer. Once this is recognised it becomes evident that there can be no ground in public policy or otherwise for requiring the tortfeasor to pay to the plaintiff, in respect of services which he himself has rendered, a sum of money which the plaintiff must then repay to him.

---

[39] [1973] QB 942.
[40] [1974] QB 454. In *Donnelly* v. *Joyce* the young plaintiff claimed the cost of special boots, which he needed as a result of the accident and which had been bought for him by his parents, and for his mother's lost earnings as a result of her giving up her job to look after him. The defendant conceded the first claim but contested the second on the ground that the plaintiff was under no legal obligation to reimburse his mother.
[41] [1994] 2 AC 350 at 363.

One reason why the House of Lords felt obliged to return to the Denning rationale (that what is at issue here is the benefactor's and not the 'primary' victim's loss, so that the primary victim held the damages recovered under this heading on trust for the carer)[42] were the unusual facts of the case which revealed a basic flaw in the *Donnelly* approach, and which clarify the last sentence of Lord Bridge's statement. For in the *Hunt* case the volunteer offering the services (and suffering the loss) was the plaintiff's husband who was also the defendant tortfeasor in the action! So, if the *Donnelly* reasoning had applied, the claimant (wife) would have claimed the loss suffered by her husband who gave up his job to look after her. But the husband, it will be recalled, was also the tortfeasor who had injured her in the first place so, on this kind of reasoning, he would be paying damages for his own loss. The House of Lords was able to avoid this result in the instant case while preserving intact the basic principle that in the more run-of-the-mill kind of case, claimants will still be able to recover for the gratuitous provision of services by third parties.

The logic of *Hunt* v. *Severs* is clear enough, but the House of Lords' decision gives rise to numerous problems in the case where the defendant is also the provider of care for the claimant.[43] One is that the ruling apparently does not apply if the victim and the carer enter into a contract under which the latter becomes obliged to render the services in question, in return for agreed remuneration. The courts have consistently taken the view that it would be undesirable to place the victim and carer in the position of being required to make a contract of this kind,[44] yet that is precisely the effect of *Hunt* v. *Severs*. The ruling also provides a disincentive for accident victims to accept gratuitous care from close relatives who may be in the best (and most cost-effective) position to provide it for them.[45] These were among the considerations that led the Law Commission, in its Consultation Paper on *Damages for Personal Injury: Medical, Nursing and*

---

[42] This is similar to the approach taken in Scotland: see Administration of Justice Act 1982, s. 8, although this section involves only a *personal* liability on the claimant to account to the carer. For a discussion of the 'trust' or 'personal liability' issue, see Law Com. No. 262 (1999), para. 3.55 ff. (esp. 3.62), where the Law Commission recommends legislation to make this a personal liability only (and then only for past, not future, care).

[43] See David Kemp, 'Voluntary Services Provided by Tortfeasor to his Victim' (1994) 110 LQR 524; A. Reed, 'A Commentary on *Hunt* v. *Severs*' (1995) 15 OJLS 133.

[44] See, in particular, *Donnelly* v. *Joyce* [1974] QB 454 at 463–4 (Megaw LJ); *Hunt* v. *Severs* [1993] QB 815 at 831 (Sir Thomas Bingham MR).

[45] In support of the need to promote such voluntary care, see Colman J's observation in *Hardwick* v. *Hudson* [1999] 1 WLR 1770 at 1777, that 'personal physical care can often be most effectively and economically provided by a family member or close friend'.

*other Expenses*,[46] to recommend that *Hunt* v. *Severs* should be reversed by statute, in favour of a rule to the effect that the defendant's liability for the claimant's nursing care should be unaffected by any liability which the claimant might incur to pay those damages back to the defendant, and the final Report on this issue stood by this recommendation.[47]

It could also be said that there is an air of artificiality to the reasoning in *Hunt* v. *Severs*: in practice, it is not the defendant who would have to pay the damages in question (and then have them repaid by the plaintiff), but the defendant's insurance company. The effect of the House of Lords' judgment, then, was that 'plaintiff and defendant were unable collectively to call upon the proceeds of the defendant's indemnity insurance to cover the cost of caring for the plaintiff'.[48] Both the House of Lords[49] and the Law Commission[50] rejected this line of argument, on the traditional grounds that the courts should not be influenced in setting the extent of the defendant's liability by the fact that the defendant was carrying third party insurance in respect of the loss in question. While this approach may be correct in principle, in a case like *Hunt* v. *Severs* it runs the risk of producing a result that is both unjust to the parties immediately concerned and perverse in the incentives it creates for future parties in the same position. Consideration of a number of these factors led to the Law Commission's proposal to reverse the result in *Hunt* v. *Severs*, as discussed above.

The assessment of the award for the services given to the plaintiff by these third parties has also posed a difficult dilemma. The dilemma is this: should these services (of the third party) be valued at nil (which is what happened prior to *Donnelly*) or at their full – and hence high – commercial rate? The Court of Appeal's compromise suggestion can be found in *Housecroft* v. *Burnett*.[51] There, the measure of the loss was said to be 'the proper and reasonable cost' of taking care of the plaintiff's needs. In practice this means the relative's lost earnings (where he or she is engaged in gainful employment), with the commercial rate applicable to

---

[46] Law Com. No. 144 (1996), para. 3.68.
[47] Law Com. No. 262 (1999), para. 3.76, which should be read with the earlier recommendation that the claimant should be under a personal obligation (laid down by statute) to account to the carer for past care which has been provided gratuitously (see para. 3.62). The 'carer' would have to be a 'relative or friend', which is wider than the current position in Scotland (which includes only 'relatives').
[48] Law Com. No. 144 (1996), para. 3.65.    [49] [1994] 2 AC 350 at 363 (Lord Bridge).
[50] See e.g., Law Com. No. 262 (1999), para. 3.74.
[51] [1986] 1 All ER 332 at 343 per O'Connor LJ and see discussion in relation to past losses at 345.

such services serving as an upper limit. But where this 'caring' relative does not give up paid employment, the commercial rate will be inappropriate.[52] In its recent report, the Law Commission refused to propose the setting of any limits or thresholds on such damages and did not suggest any legislative changes to the assessment of such damages. However, it did stress that the commercial rate for such caring services represented a 'good starting point' and that the courts should be wary of discounting from this too extensively (to take into account tax and other commercial expenses). Finally, the courts were encouraged to 'be more willing to award damages to compensate carers for their lost earnings even though these exceed the commercial cost of care'.[53]

Finally, in this context, section 5 of the Administration of Justice Act 1982 should be noted. This provides that any saving to the injured person which is the result of his being wholly or partly maintained at public expense in a hospital or nursing home or other institution should be set off against any income lost by him as a result of his injuries.

American, Canadian and German courts have also been called to address a complicated variation of the *Donnelly* problem, where what is at issue is not financial loss but physical injury sustained by the third party/volunteer in the interests of the 'primary' victim. Typically, in these cases a person has had a kidney negligently removed in hospital. Unfortunately (for everyone concerned), this 'primary' victim turns out to have one kidney only (apparently something that occurs in one out of 100 people) and thus is in need of an immediate transplant or else he will die. So a close relative (e.g., father/the benefactor) is asked and agrees to donate one of his kidneys in order to save the life of the 'primary' victim. Can the 'primary' victim claim for such harm suffered by the third party/volunteer? The fact that the volunteer's (relative's) loss was the result of his own, voluntary act can present legal difficulties; and the decision to donate an organ, coming after due deliberation, distinguishes these cases from the typical rescue cases (where the intervention is on the spur of the moment and unaccompanied by the certainty of hurt) which, otherwise, would appear the closest legal concept which could be used as a starting point in the reasoning process. Yet, despite these difficulties, the Canadian and German courts have allowed for the compensation of the donors – a much better solution (it is submitted) than by channelling the claim through the

---

[52] *McCamley v. Cammell Laird Shipbuilders Ltd* [1990] 1 WLR 963 at 966–7.

[53] Law Com. No. 262 (1999), paras 377–86. But this is not reflected in the case law. See nn. 50, 51 above.

primary victim.[54] It must be hoped that if, or rather when, such a case comes before our courts they will be willing to take note of the rich foreign case law on this topic.

*Future loss: home care or an institution?*

The guiding principle is, as with all heads of loss, what is reasonably required by the claimant. It is important to take full account of reasonableness. The court is entitled to, and does, consider the quality of life which the claimant would be capable of enjoying. A judge is not going to be impressed with an argument put forward by a defendant that a severely injured individual needs nothing more than a roof over his head and his physical needs taken care of. Thus, an institution may not be able to provide facilities or care that would stimulate the individual and give him what little enjoyment of life he can manage. Home care may thus, in many instances, be preferable.

Does this mean then that a claim to adapt or even change the home may in some cases be accepted? We look at this question below. Here, suffice it to say that in some circumstances this may, indeed, be allowable; but the *total* cost of acquiring new accommodation (e.g., moving from a two-storey house into a bungalow) is, it is submitted, rightly viewed with disfavour.[55] Courts are certainly unlikely to react favourably to such claims if they obtain the impression that the family of the victim really cannot cope with the injured individual at home and comes to the conclusion that they are only seeking enhanced accommodation (perhaps accompanied by a large team of commercial carers) for their own benefit.

The dilemma of whether to reside at home or go into an institution is, in most cases, more apparent than real. In most instances, there is broad agreement between the medical and other experts as to whether the claimant should reside in some form of institution or whether he is capable of being maintained in his own home or otherwise within the community. Most families are equally realistic about such matters and, in practice, are remarkably unselfish in caring for their injured relatives.

---

[54] Thus, *Urbanski* v. *Patel* [1978] 84 DLR (3d) 650 (Canada); BGH JZ 1988, 150 (Germany) (English translation in Basil Markesinis and Hannes Unberath, *The German Law of Torts: A Comparative Treatise* (4th edn, Oxford, 2002), p. 660 (henceforth referred to as *GLT*); cf. *Sirianni* v. *Anna*, 285 N.Y.S. 2d 709 (1967); *Moore* v. *Shah*, 458 N.Y.S. 2d 33 (1982); *Ornelas* v. *Fry*, 727 P.2d 819 (Ariz. App. 1986).

[55] Cf. *Cunningham* v. *Harrison* [1973] QB 942 and *Moriarty* v. *McCarthy* [1978] 1 WLR 155 at 163.

A slightly different problem relates to adaptations to the home to enable the injured individual to return there, from time to time, for short visits. There are no hard and fast rules on this and the matter can only be resolved on the evidence put forward in each particular case.

If the claimant is to reside in an institution, he will not recover the totality of the costs and the full amount of his loss of earnings claim. That is because, but for the accident, he would have expended part of his income on providing himself with accommodation and the ordinary necessaries of everyday life out of his income. The court is careful, therefore, not to permit double counting and to make a deduction from the amount awarded under one or other of those heads of damage. The matter has now become more complicated as a result of two first instance decisions, neither of which has been the subject of an appeal.[56] In both cases, the court was concerned with the obligations of local authorities under the National Assistance Act 1948 to provide care for the disabled. In both cases, the court held that the local authority was not entitled to have recourse to damages received by the claimant in a personal injury action notwithstanding that it was those injuries which imposed upon the local authority their obligations under the 1948 Act. That has led defendants to argue that the cost of an institution will be borne by the local authority and that, therefore, the claimant should not recover any damages from them. The point has, thus far, not been decided. Such claims have tended to settle on an apportionment of the risks found by the trial judge.

*Accommodation*

## Adaptations

The claimant is entitled to recover the reasonable costs of adapting a property to meet his needs by, e.g., installing a lift, widening doors to admit a wheel-chair, installing ramps and the like. The amount recoverable is simply a matter of evidence.

If, however, the nature of the adaptation is likely to enhance the value of the property by, e.g., adding an extension to the existing building, the full capital costs would not be allowed. The amount claimable would then be calculated in exactly the same way as if capital was being used for the purpose of purchasing a new property.

The converse is equally true. Many adaptations needed for an injured person will actually reduce the value of the property. Its prospective purchaser is likely to wish to restore the property to its ordinary condition.

---

[56] *Bell* v. *Todd* [2002] Lloyd's Rep. Med. 12; *Ryan* v. *Liverpool Health Authority* [2002] Lloyd's Rep. Med. 23.

If it be proved that the adaptations have actually diminished the value the claimant is entitled to the difference between the value of the property as it was and the value of the property as it is after the adaptations have been carried out.[57]

## Accommodation: purchase of a property

In cases of serious injury, it is often the case that the accommodation in which the claimant has resided up to the date of the accident proves to be too small or otherwise unsuitable for him. To give the simplest example: a tetraplegic cannot be expected to live in a flat on the third floor of a block which has no lift. It is necessary, therefore, for accommodation suitable to his post-accident needs to be purchased.

In English law, he is not simply entitled to a capital sum to purchase the new property. The reason lies in the nature of damages. They are there to compensate for a loss and not to provide a benefit or to enrich the victim or his estate. Since real property, historically, retains its value, the victim, or more probably his estate, would be enriched by the capital value of the property on his death or when he no longer needs it.

In order to overcome that problem the courts have adopted what may be regarded as a somewhat artificial approach. The court decides, first, on the capital sum required by the claimant to provide himself with suitable accommodation. From that figure it then deducts the amount which he would have spent on providing himself with housing, including any mortgage which he might have obtained, had the accident not occurred. The latter figure is then deducted from the capital sum required to provide the new house. The court allows a figure of a notional 3 per cent interest on the excess capital.[58] The 3 per cent becomes the multiplicand and the multiplier is used to calculate the global amount.

An example can help illustrate this reasoning process:

| | |
|---|---|
| Cost of accommodation post-accident | £100,000 |
| Amount which claimant would have expended before the accident | £40,000 |
| Excess required | £60,000 |
| 3% of £60,000 = | £1,800 |
| Multiplier for life = 24 | |
| General damages for accommodation £1,800 × 24 | £43,200[59] |

---

[57] *Brown v. Merton, Sutton and Wandsworth Health Authority (Teaching)* [1982] 1 All ER 650.
[58] *Thomas v. Brighton Health Authority, sub nom. Wells v. Wells*, n. 7 above.
[59] *Roberts v. Johnstone* [1989] QB 878.

How does a claimant, in fact, fund the necessary balance? That is not a matter for the courts but the practical answer is either that he does so out of his general damages for pain and suffering and loss of amenity, or by making savings in some other area, or by taking out a mortgage for the balance and paying for it out of the investment income which he receives on the totality of his award.

Costs which do not provide any sort of capital value are recoverable in full. Thus, removal expenses and legal and estate agents' fees are recoverable as a subsidiary head of damage.

Equally, the additional costs of running a larger establishment than the claimant would have required had he not been injured are recoverable. The court will look at the additional amount, at the date of trial, and apply the whole life multiplier. The price of the property and its value is, again, a matter of reasonableness. Where, e.g., the claimant purchased a house which happened to have a swimming pool, the defendant's attempt to reduce the capital cost of the house by its increased value attributable to the swimming pool failed because the overall purchase price was reasonable.[60]

## Future loss: aids and equipment

The claimant is entitled to the cost of purchasing, maintaining and ultimately replacing aids and equipment which he reasonably requires in order to assist him with the ordinary tasks of daily living. The items may vary from a motor car to a two-handled drinking cup with a lid. The same principle applies however large or small the item. The first task of the court is to decide, on the evidence, whether a particular item is reasonably required. It must also decide, in an appropriate case, which make or model is reasonably required. Plainly, there may be a considerable variation in the cost of larger or more expensive items of equipment, from motor cars to reclining chairs, electric wheel-chairs and similar items.

Having decided that the equipment is reasonably required the court then looks, first, at the cost. That sum is recoverable as an immediate capital requirement. Secondly, the court must then consider the evidence as to how frequently the item may require to be replaced. That is then converted into an annual figure to which the appropriate multiplier is applied. Thirdly, the court will consider what, if any, annual maintenance is required for that particular item of equipment. Again, the appropriate multiplier is applied to that figure.

[60] *Willett v. North Bedfordshire Health Authority* (1992) 143 NLJ 745.

The following example may be of some use:

| | |
|---|---|
| Cost of electric wheel-chair | £6,000 |
| Replacement every six years – annual cost | £1,000 |
| Annual maintenance | £300 |
| Whole life multiplier = 24 | |
| Recoverable damages: | |
| Initial capital payment | £6,000 |
| Replacement cost £1,000 × 24 | £24,000 |
| Annual maintenance £300 × 24 | £6,000 |
| Total recoverable | £36,000 |

The replacement figure may be reduced in cases in which the claimant is unlikely to require the particular item of equipment for the entirety of his life. The court will then look at how many times the item will in fact be replaced and apply a different multiplier, namely one for a period of years certain. So, e.g., if a thirty-year-old claimant would be unlikely to use an electric wheel-chair after the age of sixty, it will utilise the multiplier for the term certain for thirty years.

### Loss of pension

There is no difference in principle between loss of pension and loss of future earnings.

The question, of course, is whether the claimant was, or would have been, in pensionable employment. That may not be such a straightforward question as it first appears. As one example, a secretary for a large organisation may, at the date of the accident, be in pensionable employment. If, on the evidence, her employers would have shut that office so that she would have been made redundant some two years after the accident in any event, could she have obtained other pensionable employment? That is a very open question and would need to be the subject of both factual and expert evidence.[61] In the actual case, the opinion of the employment expert was that she would have been likely to obtain pensionable employment within nine to twelve months of the notional date of redundancy. If, of course, there is no loss of pension rights there is no claim.[62]

One approach is to establish, first, what pension and lump sum the claimant would have received had he retained his pre-accident employment to pensionable age. Consider, on the evidence, what pension provision the claimant is in fact likely to obtain, if any. The court can then adopt

---

[61] The above is a real example from a case which settled shortly before trial.
[62] *Dews* v. *National Coal Board* [1988] AC 1.

one of two approaches. One is to make enquiries in the insurance market as to the cost of a deferred annuity to meet the net loss of pension to claim that sum.[63] Alternatively, the court can receive evidence as to the likely pension loss and then apply a multiplier from the Ogden Tables. That was the approach adopted, at first instance, by Dyson J in *Page* v. *Sheerness Steel Co. Plc.*[64] The discount to be adopted for imponderables will vary according to the age of the claimant at the date of trial. The younger the claimant the greater the discount rate. For example, in *Page* v. *Sheerness Steel* (above) Dyson J assessed the discount at 10 per cent.

### The lost years

In the case of a claimant who has a substantially reduced life expectancy, which means that his working life will be foreshortened, the court awards a reduced sum by way of future loss of earnings for the period after the expected death of the claimant. Why is the award reduced? In the ordinary case an individual would expend his earnings partly for his own benefit, partly for the joint benefit of himself and his family and partly for the sole benefit of his family. In consequence of his death, the expenditure of the household will be reduced. Thus, in the case of a married person, the earnings for the lost years will be reduced by 50 per cent. Where there are children it will be reduced by 31.6 per cent.[65] In the case of a young child who has not yet embarked upon employment, no award will be made.

## German law

### Future pecuniary losses

### Basic approach

The method of calculation depends on the form of payment: annuity or lump sum (see p. 42). In both instances, however, the starting point is the 'differential method'(*Differenzhypothese*) which is the basic principle underlying §§ 249–252 BGB.[66] This principle applies equally to compensation for loss of earnings or increased needs. The question asked is 'what would the economic situation of the victim be but for the injury?'. In assessing the difference (= disadvantage to the victim), all known or foreseeable factors

---

[63] *London Ambulance Service NHS Trust* v. *Swan*, CA, judgment of 12 March 1999 (unreported); *Auty* v. *National Coal Board* [1985] 1 WLR 784.

[64] [1996] PIQR Q26. Upheld by the House of Lords, *sub nom. Wells* v. *Wells*, n. 7 above.

[65] *Harris* v. *Empress Motors Ltd* [1984] 1 WLR 212.

[66] See Hermann Lange and Gottfried Schiemann, *Schadensersatz* (3rd edn, 2003), § 61, p. 248.

or likely future developments have to be taken into account. This includes such things as pay rises, professional promotions, risks of labour market, changes in inflation rate, end of gainful employment, etc.[67]

## Periodic payments

The annuity payable according to § 843 I BGB for all continuing and future losses is *in practice* calculated on a monthly basis.[68] Although § 843 I BGB provides for a uniform annuity, which covers both lost earnings and increased needs (even though the basis of calculation of the two is different), the courts nowadays have to distinguish explicitly in the judgment between these two parts of the compensation package. This is because the annuity for lost *income* is subject to income tax, whereas the annuity for increased *needs* is not.[69]

With regard to the loss of earnings, the judge has to prognosticate future developments as accurately as possible.[70] If a child is injured, the likely beginning of gainful employment has to be determined, as well as the date when the victim would have given up such employment. If not otherwise indicated, this will be the age of 65, after which the victim will be entitled to an old age pension (the contributions to the pension scheme have to be paid by the tortfeasor, because without the injury they would have been paid by the victim out of his salary and (partly) by his employer).[71]

As to the *value of the lost income*, two alternative points of reference may be used: the income the victim would have earned but for the injury, or the market value of his work.[72] The latter approach is important where the victim was not, actually, working for a salary at the time of the injury – for instance a spouse engaged in housework – but must still be compensated for the loss of his or her working ability.[73] With regard to the former approach, two methods of calculation are adopted by the German courts, the result of which are essentially the same: according to the '*Bruttolohnmethode*', the calculation proceeds from the (hypothetical)

---

[67] BGH 17 January 1995, NJW 1995, 1023, 1024.
[68] Despite §§ 843 II, 760 II BGB, which would call for a three-month period.
[69] MünchKomm-BGB/Stein § 843 BGB no. 43; cf. pp. 42–3.
[70] BGH 20 December 1960, BGHZ 34, 110, 118.
[71] BGH 26 September 1995, NJW 1995, 3313; BGH 27 June 1995, NJW-RR 1995, 1272; cf. pp. 142–3.
[72] '*Konkrete/abstrakte arbeitswertorientierte Betrachtungsweise*', see MünchKomm-BGB/Stein § 843 BGB no. 25, 27.
[73] See p. 143.

gross income, but costs and expenditures which the victim (as compared to an actually working employee) does not have to incur will be deducted.[74] The 'Nettolohnmethode' proceeds from the net income, but the court will add all payments which the victim as an employee would have paid out of his gross salary to the state (taxes) or social security and which he now has to continue to pay.[75] The Federal Court has declared both approaches to be equivalent methods of calculation which – if applied properly – do not produce different results.[76]

Periodical payments based on *increased needs* are especially difficult to calculate. If the necessary costs vary from month to month, the court has to assess an average amount of monthly costs.[77] If the needs can be expected to end after some time, the court has to set a time limit for the periodical payments.[78] In case of foreseeable changes, the court may define different periods of time with different amounts of monthly payments, respectively.

The plaintiff must, to the extent that this is possible, itemise and prove his increased needs.[79] Therefore, he may not claim an overall excess payment as compensation for future inflation – he has to show the specific costs which will be necessary to meet his needs.[80] If the future needs are not foreseeable at the time of trial, he may, instead of suing for damages, bring an action for a declaratory judgment (*Feststellungsklage*, § 256 ZPO), which declares the defendant liable for all future damages caused by the injury to be proved by the plaintiff at a later stage (see p. 43).

The plaintiff may also confine his claim to certain items of his damages, and later bring another claim with regard to other parts of his damages (*Teilklage*, § 258 ZPO).[81] In pursuing this tactic, however, plaintiffs must keep a watchful eye on the danger of claims becoming statute barred (see pp. 191–2).

If, after a court decree ordering periodical payments, the health or economic situation of the victim changes, either party may return to court and ask for a modification of the judgment (§ 323 ZPO).[82] Since the original judgment was – by necessity – based on a prognosis of future developments, a 'change of facts' (§ 323 I ZPO) requires that the actual

---

[74] Cf. BGH 22 January 1980, NJW 1980, 1787.    [75] BGH 12 July 1957, VersR 1957, 574.
[76] BGH 15 November 1994, NJW 1995, 389, 390.
[77] Gerhard Küppersbusch, *Ersatzansprüche bei Personenschäden*, no. 183.
[78] MünchKomm-BGB/Stein § 843 BGB no. 44.
[79] BGH 13 January 1970, MDR 1970, 315; BayObLG 11 July 1968, BayObLGZ 1968, 184, 187.
[80] OLG Köln 19 May 1988, VersR 1988, 185, 186.
[81] Thomas/Putzo/Reichhold, ZPO (24th edn, 2002) § 323 nos 39, 40.
[82] BGH 20 December 1960, BGHZ 34, 110, 118; Palandt/Thomas § 843 BGB no. 17.

development was substantially different from that prognosticated in the original judgment.[83]

## Compensation by means of a lump sum

As long as the parties agree on some kind of capitalised compensation, the courts will not interfere – the issue is left to contractual freedom. Legal rules exist only insofar as a lump sum has to be assessed by court decree according to § 843 III BGB. As a basic principle, the capital payment is to put the victim in the same position as if he were receiving periodical payments owed by the tortfeasor under § 843 I BGB. This means that he should not receive less nor, on the other hand, should he end up getting more money than he would have received under the annuity system. As in English law, therefore, the capital has to be calculated in such a way as to equal the amount that he would receive at the end of the estimated period of monthly payments. The general idea is thus to avoid any 'enrichment' which could follow from an unused part of the capital remaining at the end of the relevant period and after the annual losses of the victim had been taken care of.[84]

Payments made in this way entail risks (and opportunities) for both parties which are associated with the well-known difficulties associated with any system of lump sum payments. Thus, unlike the annuity system, which allows a return to the court for an upward or downward adjustment of the award, the BGH has held that the parties do not have this right if they have opted for a lump sum payment.[85]

The calculation in detail follows very much the 'multiplicand and multiplier method' found in English law, though it is not explicitly called this.[86] Thus, at first instance the compensable damage and its value per year expressed in periodical payments have to be assessed. The relevant factors taken into account are lost income or alimony and increased needs. In addition, the hypothetical time of periodical payments has to be determined. The result may be called the 'multiplicand', which then – in a second step – has to be multiplied by a *Kapitalisierungsfaktor* (multiplier), which also takes account of the income the victim can expect

---

[83] BGH 20 December 1960, BGHZ 34, 110, 118; see also chapter 1.

[84] Cf. BGH 8 January 1981, NJW 1981, 818, 820: 'A lump sum is largely nothing else than the cash value of the owed periodical payments.'

[85] BGH 8 January 1981, NJW 1981, 818, 820; for a different view see MünchKomm-BGB/ Stein § 843 BGB nos 49, 62.

[86] Cf. Gerhard Küppersbusch no. 650 ff.; Schlund, 'Juristische Aspekte der Kapitalisierung von Renten- und Unterhaltsansprüchen', BB 1993, 2025; Eckelmann-Boos, Versicherungsrecht 1978, 210.

from the capital sum, and other aspects of risk allocation. Last but not least, one must recall the imperative that the capital itself must be exhausted at the end of the (hypothetical) periodical payments. The private practice of the insurance companies has established detailed and comprehensive *Kapitalisierungstabellen*[87] which though they have no legally binding force have much persuasive authority. Since the future income from the capital is not exactly predictable, an average income of between 5 to 5.5 per cent is usually taken as the basis of calculation (*Abzinsungsfaktor*).[88] These principles may be illustrated by a practical example. A five-year-old child is severely injured and entitled to a monthly income for the rest of his life. The income would be €2,500 per month (= €30,000 per year). The statistical life expectation is seventy-eight years (for 2000), the duration of periodical payments would therefore be seventy-three years. The overall value of such payments would be 73 × €30,000 = €2,190,000. The multiplier (*Kapitalisierungsfaktor*) according to the established tables would be 19,755. The annual damages (€30,000) have to be multiplied by this factor; consequently, a lump sum of €592, 650 would have to be paid.[89]

If, as sometimes happens, the *Kapitalisierungsfaktor* expresses only the period of (hypothetical) annuities, the income from the capital has to be deducted in addition (*Abzinsungsfaktor*).

The Federal Court has stressed that all dates in actuarial tables are no more than a starting point for the judge and may be modified according to the circumstances of the case and the overall economic situation. His discretion to do so and to fix a certain amount of capital as a lump sum is based on § 287 ZPO.[90]

## Loss of earnings

### In general

The basic rule is that the defendant who is bound to make compensation must restore the situation which would have existed if the circumstances making him liable to compensation had not occurred (§ 249 sentence 1 BGB). The claimant is to be put in the same position as if he had not been injured, which also includes his hypothetical economic position, in particular the loss of future earnings.[91] This principle is specified in the

---

[87] See, e.g., Schneider, Schlund and Haas, *Kapitalisierungs- und Verrentungstabellen* (2nd edn, 1992); Gerhard Küppersbusch p. 283.

[88] Cf. Schlund BB 1993, 2025, 2027; BGH 8 January 1981, NJW 1981, 818, 821.

[89] Example taken from Gerhard Küppersbusch no. 650 (adapted to the euro currency).

[90] BGH 8 January 1981, NJW 1981, 818, 821.     [91] See *GLT*, p. 909.

context of tort law in §§ 842, 843 BGB (cf. p. 138). The 'damage' which is to be compensated as loss of earnings is the difference between the economic position after the accident and the hypothetical economic position if the injury had not occurred. Thus, the award and the calculation of future loss of earnings are based on the court's conclusion: what the claimant would have earned but for the injury.

## Principles

*Concrete loss/damage*

Compensation for future loss of earnings requires that the claimant would have worked in the future or had other income but for the injury. Therefore, the claimant cannot recover a loss of earnings merely due to the fact that the injury to body or health causes the destruction or diminution of his earning capacity. His loss does not result from the destruction of the earning capacity as such, but from the non-utilisation of it in return for payment.[92] Likewise, damages are not awarded if the claimant would have lost his income in any event e.g., through an imminent dismissal or because of the insolvency of the employer.[93] The 'loss of a chance' to make a profit is not yet considered to be a compensable damage under German law (but see pp. 144–5).[94]

The injury may, additionally, cause pecuniary benefits for the claimant; alternatively, the loss of earnings may be compensated by other persons. If so, the claimant actually does not suffer a loss or, at the very least, his loss is correspondingly decreased if we compare his current economic position with his hypothetical economic position if not for the injury. The rule in this respect is that even though the victim is to be indemnified for his loss he must not make a profit from his injury. Thus, pecuniary benefits due to the injury may exclude or decrease his claim if the rule of '*Vorteilsausgleichung*' is applicable. This is the case if the victim receives benefits due to the injury, these benefits do not contradict the purpose of the damages and a deduction of these benefits from the award is reasonable.[95] From there, the court must deduct tax advantages, tax or social security contributions which the claimant may no longer have to incur[96]

---

[92] BGH 20 April 1999, VersR 2000, 233, 234.
[93] See *GLT*, p. 909; BGH 17 January 1995, NJW 1995, 1023, 1024 (insolvency); BGH 13 May 1953, BGHZ 10, 6, 9 ff. (dismissal).
[94] For a different view see Gerald Mäsch, *Chance und Schaden – Zur Dienstleisterhaftung bei unaufklärbaren Kausalverläufen* (Mohr Siebeck, Tübingen, 2004).
[95] MünchKomm-BGB/Oetker § 249 BGB no. 227.
[96] Palandt/Heinrichs, vor § 249 BGB no. 144 ff. with a summary concerning deductible tax advantages.

or saved expenses such as the community expenses[97] from the award, unless these deductions are unreasonable. Furthermore, if the claimant's loss is compensated by an innocent absentee, the court must take into account that this may cause a transfer of the victim's rights to the innocent absentee.[98]

### Contributory fault

According to § 254 II BGB, the claimant is obliged to mitigate his loss as much as reasonably possible.[99] So if, as a result of the injury, the claimant works in another, but less well paid job, he can merely ask for the difference between his former and his current earnings. Likewise, the claimant cannot recover the full amount of earnings he had earned before the accident if he is unemployed but does not look for or take up any available and reasonable employment. The court must consider the circumstances of the claimant, e.g., the family situation, the kind of injury, age, professional training or the employment situation in general, in order to assess if and to what extent the claimant is obliged to work. According to this rule, the claimant can be obliged to change his profession and thus submit himself to retraining, unless this would substantially worsen his professional and social status.[100] The decision on this point, however, is objectively reached and it is not sufficient for the claimant alone to say that the alternative occupation falls below his professional standards and status. Furthermore, the Federal Court has said that even a move to another town or city could be reasonable in exceptional cases.[101] If the claimant does not look for or take up reasonable employment, the court will take into account what the claimant hypothetically could have earned from such alternative employment. On the other hand, if the injured person has earnings from an alternative employment, which he would not have been obliged to take up, the court will not take them into account.[102]

### Evidence

The claimant has to prove that he would have continued to work in the future and also show what he would have earned but for the injury. In cases in which damages are to be awarded, the burden of proof is alleviated by § 287 ZPO and § 252 sentence 2 BGB to the effect that the court has a

---

[97] BGH 22 January 1980, NJW 1980, 1787.    [98] For further information cf. pp. 189–92.
[99] See *GLT*, pp. 905–7.    [100] MünchKomm-BGB/Stein § 843 BGB no. 34.
[101] BGH 3 July 1962, VersR 1962, 1100.    [102] BGH 25 September 1973, VersR 1974, 142.

discretion to estimate the amount of damages. However, this 'damage' must be based on an ordinary (or probable) course of events. Thus, the claimant has to prove that a loss of earnings is likely to have happened.[103] In doing so, the claimant must show facts, indications or circumstances as to what he would have earned but for the injury. Furthermore, he must produce the facts of what happened after the injury but no later than the end of the trial, since the court considers the position as it is at the time of the trial and makes its assessment at that time.[104]

Under German law as it stands today, the compensation of 'lost chances' is a question of likelihood of lost income. If the court decides in favour of the plaintiff, it is not the chance which is compensated but the income the plaintiff would probably have had.[105]

How does one determine what is 'likely' to have happened in the future but for the injury? The Federal Court stated that there is no fixed standard of likelihood. The claimant's burden of proof, therefore, differs from case to case.[106] However, a loss of earnings is not proven if it is not based on a course which is at least more probable than any course from which a loss of earnings can be excluded. On the other hand, the Federal Court has insisted that the assessment whether or not the claimant would have suffered a loss of earnings should not be subjected to overrigorous proof at the expense of the claimant.[107] If the injury prevents a reliable prediction, the court must consider the fact that a rigorous standard of proof would benefit the defendant who is actually responsible for the claimant's injury and the difficulty he faces in proving the resulting loss.

By contrast, the burden of proof falls upon the defendant with respect to the reasons which may exclude (or reduce) the loss of earnings. Therefore, the defendant must show facts which may suggest why the claimant would not have worked, or that the claimant would have earned less than actually claimed by the latter. If the victim cannot continue to work in his former profession, the defendant must also prove that an alternative employment

---

[103] BGH 22 September 1992, VersR 1993, 55, 56; BGH 17 January 1995, NJW 1995, 1023, 1024.

[104] BGH 20 April 1999, VersR 2000, 233, 234; BGH 24 January 1995, VersR 1995, 469, 470.

[105] For a detailed account of German law in comparison to French law see Helge Großerichter, *Hypothetischer Geschehensverlauf und Schadensfeststellung* (Beck, München, 2001); cf. p. 143.

[106] BGH 22 September 1992, VersR 1993, 55, 56; BGH 17 January 1995, NJW 1995, 1023, 1024.

[107] BGH 20 April 1999, VersR 2000, 233, 234; BGH 17 January 1995, NJW 1995, 1023, 1024; see *GLT*, p. 909.

would be available and reasonable.[108] In this context, the claimant must first show what he has done in order to take up an alternative employment.

## Calculation

As already stated, §§ 287 ZPO and 252 BGB are applicable and the court has a discretion to evaluate the damage. Therefore, the problem is rarely the calculation of earnings, but the conclusion as to what the victim would have earned but for the injury. Generally, the court can assume that the claimant would have earned as much as before if he was employed at the time of injury. If the claimant was unemployed before the accident, he must prove that he would have taken up a certain employment. If so, the court would award the usual income that would result from such employment. In addition, the court must also consider the possible rise of wages (or other income) in the future.[109] In doing so, the court will normally resort to collective labour agreements or the German civil service pay scale, if applicable to the claimant's hypothetical employment.[110] Nevertheless, if substantial and non-foreseeable facts should occur later on, and these facts would reduce or increase the loss of earnings, the claimant and/or the defendant can, under § 323 ZPO, ask for a judgment to modify the original award for the future. As to the method of calculation in particular, see pp. 138–9.

## Particular problems

*Promotion and substantially increased earnings in the future*
In the case of a claimant who asserts that he would have been promoted or had substantial earnings in the future, the court has to consider his professional skills and his employment record in order to determine if this is likely to have happened. In accordance with § 287 ZPO and § 252 sentence 2 BGB, promotion and increased earnings can be expected according to the ordinary course of events and, therefore, are likely to happen for a diligent person with a good professional record up to the moment of the accident. On the other hand, the hypothetical prognosis may be negative and this may well be inferred for a person with a poor employment record. Nonetheless, even a less qualified claimant can also prove that he probably could have had higher earnings by showing plausible facts for the alleged course of events, e.g., his efforts to gain further job training[111] which

---

[108]  BGH 23 January 1979, NJW 1979, 2142.
[109]  BGH 20 December 1960, BGHZ 34, 110, 118 ff.
[110]  MünchKomm-BGB/Stein § 843 BGB no. 15.
[111]  BGH 20 April 1999, VersR 2000, 233, 234; BGH 24 January 1995, VersR 1995, 469, 470.

he can pursue even after the accident. Even if the victim failed in his efforts for further job training, the award for loss of earnings can include increased earnings if it can be shown that he would have been successful but for the injury.[112]

If a reliable prediction is not possible, the court will assume that the claimant would have had average success in his profession but for the injury.[113] Thus, pay rises or promotions which can regularly be expected in the occupation which the victim had chosen before the injury have to be taken into account.[114] Relevant provisions in collective agreements or statutes (for public employees), which link the rise or promotion to age or seniority, are thus used as guidelines by the courts.[115] However, in the absence of such guidelines, difficulties may arise. The court thus cannot say that a claimant who was a professional football player would not have earned money as a football team manager for an indefinite time after his playing career had come to an end because such a change is unlikely to have happened. To put it differently, the court cannot assume that the claimant would not be successful at finding a permanent job as team manager. Since the claimant is prevented from proving himself as team manager due to the injury, and because the injury is caused by the defendant, the court must assume that the claimant would have had at least average success. However, the Federal Court stresses that the remaining risks concerning the claimant's professional course could, eventually, justify proportional deductions if a reliable prediction cannot be made.[116]

*Children and apprentices*
The claimant has to supply convincing facts for a hypothetical career in the course of which he would have earned money. In the case of children or apprentices, these facts could be their performance at school (or during the employment training period) prior to the injury or their skills, interests or career aspirations. In one case the Federal Court[117] accepted the lower court's decision that the claimant would have found employment as a teacher in a primary school despite an excess supply of teaching staff, even though she had not yet finished her first year in university to become

---

[112] BGH 20 April 1999, VersR 2000, 233, 234; BGH 24 January 1995, VersR 1995, 469, 470.
[113] BGH 17 February 1998, VersR 1998, 770, 772.
[114] BGH 2 April 1963, VersR 1963, 682.
[115] BGH 20 March 1962, NJW 1962, 1054, 1055; BGH 28 April 1992, NJW-RR 1992, 1050.
[116] BGH 20 April 1999, VersR 2000, 233, 234; BGH 17 February 1998, VersR 1998, 770, 772; BGH 24 January 1995, VersR 1995, 469, 470.
[117] BGH 5 July 1983, VI ZR 269/82 (unreported).

a teacher and her grades had not been outstanding. In another decision
the Court of Appeal of Saarbrücken[118] awarded compensation for a loss
of earnings on the basis that the claimant would have been a motor mechanic, although the claimant did not finish his job training. The court was
convinced that the claimant, who was injured at the age of sixteen, would
successfully have completed his apprenticeship as a motor mechanic. The
reason for this conclusion was evidence concerning the claimant's career
aspirations, technical interests and skills and his performance in school.
However, if there is no indication at all for the hypothetical professional
development of the victim, it is then acceptable to take into account the
profession of the parents, brothers or sisters of the victim.[119]

But the younger the injured claimant the more uncertain is the hypothetical course of events. For this reason German courts reject claims
(Leistungsklage) for the loss of earnings, if the plaintiff is not yet old enough
to embark upon a career.[120] The victim, however, can ask for a declaratory judgment (Feststellungsklage) that at a later stage of his life he will be
entitled to damages for lost earnings, if such losses can be established.[121]

*Self-employed persons*
The Federal Court pointed out that the loss of earnings of a self-employed
person is to be based on the loss of profits from his business. His loss of
earnings cannot be simply calculated by means of the costs for an equivalent substitute.[122] The claimant must show his loss of profits by means
of the operating results in the past years from which the court can calculate the loss as best it can.[123] In doing so, it is recommended that the
claimant bring forward as much evidence as possible. This should include

---

[118] OLG Saarbrücken 27 November 1997, OLGR 1998, 381.
[119] OLG Karlsruhe 25 November 1988, VersR 1989, 1101, 1102; cf. also BGH 23 March 1982,
VI ZR 85/81 (unreported): the court accepted the award of the OLG Köln 29 January
1981, 7 U 85/80 where the claimant was injured right from his birth and became deaf.
In this case, the victim, who had become a public servant on an inferior level, was
entitled to additional payments as compensation for lost higher earnings. The court
held that the claimant would have entered a more successful career as a public servant
but for the injury. One of the reasons for this award was that his brother was a lecturer
(Studienrat), his sister was a doctor and his father was a judge.
[120] RG 5 April 1906, JW 1906, 359, 360; RG 27 September 1906, JW 1906, 718, 719; cf.
Steffen, DAR 1984, 1.
[121] BGH 3 December 1951, BGHZ 4, 133, 137; OLG Köln 19 May 1988, VersR 1988, 1185,
1186.
[122] BGH 5 May 1970, BGHZ 54, 45, 53; for a different view see MünchKomm-BGB/Stein § 843
BGB no. 29.
[123] BGH 6 February 2000, NJW 2001, 1640 ff.; BGH 10 December 1996, NJW 1997, 941 ff.

the balances, profits and loss accounts (*Gewinn- und Verlustmeldungen*), income tax assessment notices and tax returns *(Einkommensteuerbescheide und -erklärungen)*, advanced notification of purchase tax and purchase tax notice within the crucial period of time (*Umsatzsteuervoranmeldungen und - bescheide für den maßgeblichen Zeitraum*).[124] It is not sufficient, if the claimant only supplies the sales figures *(Umsatzzahlen)* of his business.[125] In this regard it is important to note that there is no fixed rule as to which period of time is crucial to determine the future loss of earnings – this depends on the circumstances of each case.

On the other hand, a self-employed person can recover the costs of a substitute (*Ersatzkräfte*), if he actually employs one. The employment of such substitutes causes additional costs which reduce the profits. However, the employment must be reasonable from an economic point of view.[126] Given that the employment is reasonable, it is irrelevant whether or not the claimant's business operates less well with the substitute. But even if the operating results achieved by the substitute are better, the court can assume that the claimant would have done as well but for the injury.[127] Therefore, the court does not apply the rule of *Vorteilsausgleichung* in such cases.

If family members or friends take over the claimant's job without asking for compensation, the claimant is entitled to demand the market price for necessary substitutes (with regard to personal care, see pp. 156–7). However, he can only recover the net sum, since his family or friends do not have to pay taxes or social security contributions.[128]

Even if the self-employed person had not made any profits up until the date of his injury, he could claim loss of earnings provided he can prove that profits were likely to have occurred from business connections and that these connections were broken up by the injury.[129] To that end he must deliver plausible facts, e.g., the establishment of business connections and expected orders likely to result from such connections. However, it will not be convincing if the claimant merely proves that he was in touch with two companies, but received orders only for a few months or days over a period of two years.[130]

---

[124] Küppersbusch, *Ersatzansprüche bei Personenschäden* (7th edn, 2000), no. 97.
[125] OLG Brandenburg 24 October 1995, OLGR 1996, 76, 77.
[126] BGH 10 December 1996, NJW 1997, 941, 942.
[127] BGH 10 December 1996, NJW 1997, 941, 942; BGH 31 March 1992, NJW-RR 1992, 852.
[128] OLG Oldenburg 10 November 1992, NJW-RR 1993, 798.
[129] BGH 3 March 1998, NJW 1998, 1634, 1636; BGH 6 July 1993, NJW 1993, 2673.
[130] BGH 3 March 1998, NJW 1998, 1634, 1636.

*Female claimants*

In the case of female claimants, two questions have to be distinguished.

The first is to decide whether a housewife suffers a loss of earnings and if so, how is that to be calculated. Secondly, how should a court approach a claim by a woman who may either give up work altogether, work part-time, or have breaks in her career, in order to bear and/or rear her children? It should be noted that this traditional approach nowadays strikes many as being sex-oriented discrimination. Even more commentators, however, would regard it as being substantially incorrect, for housework is not necessarily done by women (Germans prefer to speak of the 'home-spouse' = *Hausgatte*) and the statutory leave for the upbringing of small children (*Elternzeit*) is, nowadays, available to both parents, even cumulatively. This should not, however, obscure the fact that the likelihood of such events occurring is still much greater where females are concerned.

*Housewife* According to the original concept of the BGB, the wife had the statutory duty to keep the house and to care for the children. If she was injured, the husband lost her 'service' and could claim under § 845 BGB. Under modern family law, the spouses are partners with equal rights; housekeeping is not a service owed by one spouse to the other, but an alternative and equivalent way of contributing to the family support: § 1360 sentence 2 BGB. Taking this as a starting point, the Federal Court has found that housewives suffer a loss of earnings as well, which has to be compensated according to § 842 BGB.[131] A loss of earnings can be claimed if the injured party cannot perform his or her domestic work which is considered to be an economic value by which he or she is able to fulfil his or her maintenance obligation towards the family. Household chores are in this context an economic activity which is comparable to any other gainful employment.[132] Nevertheless, it has to be pointed out that an injured homemaker cannot ask for damages, if the domestic work is performed without a legal maintenance obligation, e.g., within a

---

[131] BGH 25 September 1962, BGHZ 38, 55, 57; BGH 25 September 1973, NJW 1974, 41, 42.

[132] BGH 25 September 1962, BGHZ 38, 55, 57; BGH 25 September 1973, NJW 1974, 41, 42: 'Nicht schon die Betätigung der Arbeitskraft als solche, sondern nur die für andere in Erfüllung einer gesetzlich geschuldeten Unterhaltsverpflichtung geleistete Haushaltstätigkeit ist eine der Erwerbstätigkeit vergleichbare, wirtschaftlich ins Gewicht fallende Arbeitsleistung und stellt somit einen Erwerbsschaden dar'.

non-marital partnership[133] or in cases of voluntary care of the grandson by the grandmother.[134]

Though the dogmatic approach to these problems nowadays seems to be settled, the problem of calculation of the actual loss still remains to be solved.

The victim is entitled to claim the costs of a substitute, but the calculation of the costs of an adequate substitute causes further difficulties. In this context the tables of Schulz-Borck and Hoffmann are very helpful.[135] These tables provide information about the labour time of a homemaker in relation to the number of family members and standard of living of the family (*Anspruchsstufe des Haushalts*), the time a substitute is needed (considering the claimant's injury) and lastly the market price of qualified substitutes. The Federal Court[136] has accepted the application of these tables, if the court knows and uses them as an aid in order to assert the real or concrete loss and not in order to evaluate an abstract loss. Moreover, the claimant can demand the gross costs including social security contributions, which he has to pay as employer for his employee, if he actually employs a substitute. If the claimant does not hire a substitute, she or he is only entitled to ask for the net costs.[137] (Compare the slightly different situation where family care is concerned, pp. 156–7).

*Pregnancy and child care*
*Pregnancy and birth*: the defendant cannot argue that the female victim would have had no earnings during the time of her pregnancy if maternity protection rules are applicable. The German *Mutterschutzgesetz* (now backed by EC law[138]) provides for maternity pay whenever an employee is unable

---

[133] OLG Köln 11 March 1982, ZfS 1984, 132; against it OLG Karlsruhe 6 March 1992, DAR 1993, 391; the BGH has not ruled on this question yet but it stated that the loss of earnings of a claimant who was injured before her marriage is realised at the time she celebrates the marriage, since the partial destruction of her earning capacity subsequently lowers her contribution to the maintenance of her family, BGH 25 September 1962, BGHZ 38, 55, 57; in another case the BGH held that the household chores of a widow in a subsequent non-marital partnership was not to be seen as a gainful employment or something comparable, BGH 19 June 1984, NJW 1984, 2520. Domestic work is therefore not comparable with a gainful employment as long as the claimant is not married or living in a registered partnership.
[134] OLG Celle 12 November 1981, VersR 1983, 40.
[135] Cf. Schulz-Borck and Hofmann, *Schadensersatz bei Ausfall von Hausfrauen im Haushalt* (5th edn, 1997).
[136] BGH 10 October 1989, NJW-RR 1990, 34.    [137] BGH 10 October 1989, NJW-RR 1990, 34.
[138] Directive 92/85/EC of 19 October 1992 [1992] OJ L348/1, 28 November 1992.

to work because of her pregnancy, especially six weeks before and eight weeks after the birth. Therefore, she would have had earnings during this time. Pregnancy and birth are not facts which exclude earnings in this regard.[139]

*Child care*: the Federal Court has not yet ruled on this matter for the time after birth, but the Court of Appeal of Zweibrücken[140] has held that the mother is entitled to claim compensation for loss of earnings, unless it appears that she would not have been able to perform her paid work and the child care cumulatively. Thus, it has to be asked if the claimant would have had a break in her career in order to care for the child. According to the court, the claimant must show that she would have handled employment and child care together, for instance by support of her family or by sending the child to the *Kindergarten*. Today, the burden of proof might have changed because more and more women manage to reconcile child care and professional work, and the state provides more assistance in this respect. But there is no recent court decision on this point.

Even if a female claimant has had a career break to raise a family, she can still recover loss of earnings as a homemaker under the preconditions stated above. The Federal Court[141] has also decided that the victim could recover the costs of a housekeeper as loss of earnings while she was studying, as she was unable to combine child care and her studies, but she would have managed both but for the injury.

*Key man in an incorporated business*
It is disputed how the court should compensate the 'key' man or woman in a small, incorporated business where the real loss is that of the company and not the individual. The company is not entitled to recover its economic losses under § 823 BGB. According to § 823 paragraph 1 BGB, only the injured can claim compensation for an economic loss which results from a violation of his interests and rights protected by the above-mentioned statute. Even though the established and operating business[142] is protected by § 823 paragraph 1 BGB as 'another right', it is not a direct interference with the business if an employee of the company is injured by the tortfeasor.[143] On the other hand, § 823 paragraph 2 BGB requires the violation of a 'protective law', i.e., that the defendant must violate a

---

[139] LG Hamburg 19 January 1979, MDR 1970, 670.
[140] OLG Zweibrücken 24 February 1978, VersR 1978, 1029 ff.
[141] BGH 4 December 1985, VersR 1985, 356 ff.      [142] See *GLT*, pp. 71–3.
[143] BGH 19 June 1952, BGHZ 7, 30, 35 ff.

statutory provision designed for the protection of the claimant. However, there is no statutory provision which protects the economic interests of the employer in the working ability of his employees. Only § 826 BGB may, in exceptional cases, serve as a basis for a claim of the company (intentional injury to an employee in order to cause damage to the company).

The 'key' person himself may claim compensation for lost earnings according to the rules stated above. If he is not an employee in terms of labour law but had worked for the company as shareholder or company organ (executive director), the calculation of his lost income may cause problems.[144] But, as a matter of principle, the key person can only claim his own damage, not the damage of the company (no *Drittschadensliqui-dation*[145]). The Federal Court, however, insists that there is one exception to this general rule,[146] although its case law has been strongly criticised in academic literature. Under certain circumstances the Federal Court considers the damage of the company to be part of the damage of the 'key' person.[147] For this to happen certain conditions must be satisfied.

First, the injured party must hold all (or the crucial majority) of the shares of the company. To put it differently, in practical terms the company must be owned by the injured party. Secondly, the injured party, prior to the accident, must have been working for his company. Lastly, he must show that he would have earned money for his company but for the accident. Under these circumstances, the defendant has to compensate the hypothetical profits of the company. The Federal Court has thus held that in this case the incorporated company is nothing but a part of the claimant's assets (*Sondervermögen*) which the claimant has set apart for reason of tax, liability, and so on. If the injury causes a damage in this special asset, because the claimant is prevented from working for his company, he also suffers a personal loss which is a set-back for his personal assets. In the first decision of the Federal Court it remained doubtful whether the claimant was entitled to claim damages for himself or in the name of his company.[148] Later, the Federal Court pointed out that only the injured partner is entitled to recover the company's loss in respect of his shares

---

[144] For details see Staudinger/Schiemann (1998) § 252 BGB nos 50–52; Vorbemerkung zu § 249 BGB no. 61.

[145] For a discussion of this notion see *GLT*, pp. 64 ff.

[146] BGH 13 November 1973, NJW 1974, 143 ff.; BGH 8 February 1977, NJW 1977, 1283 ff.; BGH 6 October 1988, VersR 1989, 94 ff.; BGH 15 November 1990, VersR 1991, 678 ff.

[147] Cf. Karsten Schmidt, *Gesellschaftsrecht* (4th edn, 2002), § 40 III 4: '*gesellschaftsfreundlicher Durchgriff*'.

[148] BGH 13 November 1973, NJW 1974, 134.

and thus neither the company nor other partners can claim compensation.[149] Therefore, the defendant has to make payments to the claimant and not to the claimant's company.

### Future medical care

### In general

If the injured person needs care by others, he or she can claim the resulting costs from the tortfeasor. According to § 843 I BGB the costs have to be paid in the form of an annuity. If, however, the injured person can show convincing reasons, he may ask for (and receive) a lump sum, § 843 III BGB (see chapter 4 as to the method of calculation).

The 'damage' which is to be compensated under § 843 I BGB is not the costs of the care, but the *special needs* of the injured party caused by the wrongful act.[150] The plaintiff has to show and prove these needs;[151] then the court will award damages on the basis of actual or future expenses which are deemed necessary and reasonable to meet such needs.

### What care is adequate?

Adequate care in this sense does not mean the cheapest alternative. Although the injured person/claimant is generally expected to mitigate his loss as much as is reasonably possible (§ 254 II BGB), the question of proper care is to a large extent a personal decision; and it is accepted that the law of damages may not impinge on the freedom of choice of the injured party as to how he wants to live (or how his representatives think it best for him to live). According to a fundamental principle of the law of damages, adequate compensation has to take the dignity of the victim and his right to adequate compensation into account.[152] On the other hand, adequate care does not mean 'optimal care' either. If the decision of the victim is reasonable (within a broad range of discretion), it will be accepted and form the factual basis of his compensation claim.[153] If the costs of the chosen lifestyle are disproportionately high, the injured party will not be

---

[149] BGH 8 February 1977, NJW 1977, 1283 ff.; BGH 6 October 1988, VersR 1989, 94 ff.; 15 November 1990, VersR 1991, 678 ff. For a detailed discussion and critique see Staudinger/Schiemann (1998), Vorb. vor § 249 BGB nos 59, 60 with further references.

[150] RG 23 May 1935, RGZ 148, 68, 70/71; BGH 29 October 1957, NJW 1958, 627; BGH 15 December 1970, VersR 1971, 442, 444; MünchKomm-BGB/Stein (3rd edn, 1997), § 843 BGB no. 40.

[151] BGH 13 January 1970, MDR 1970, 315.    [152] BGH 19 May 1981, NJW 1982, 757, 758.

[153] BGH 8 November 1977, VersR 1978, 149; OLG Stuttgart 30 January 1997, VersR 1998, 366; OLG Bremen 21 April 1998, NJW-RR 1999, 1115, 1116.

able to recover the full amount.[154] Hence, the costs of care within the family have to be compensated even if they are higher than institutional care, because they are outweighed by personal and emotional benefits for the injured.[155] On the other hand, the tremendous costs of permanent total care in an institution are no argument against full compensation, if such an arrangement is chosen by the representative of the injured party and is medically indicated.[156]

## How are the costs of care calculated?

### Professional care

If the victim intends to rely on professional care, the recoverable costs include not only the net salary of the carers, but also their tax and social security contributions.[157]

### Family care

*Principle* If the care is performed by family members (spouse, parents, children), it is normally free of charge vis-à-vis the victim, notwithstanding the possibility that the care is based on a regular employment contract – in this case the same rules apply as with regard to professional care. If the family help is gratuitous, this does not preclude a compensation claim by the victim. It is his special needs which justify the claim, not actual expenses (see p. 154). The explanation for this rule is simple: the Federal Court sees no reason why the altruistic help of family members should relieve the wrongdoer of his liability. In addition, the court refers to the principle underlying § 843 IV BGB: support by family members is not to be deducted from the amount of damages which the wrongdoer has to pay to the victim.[158] It does not matter whether the family members would have a profitable income but for the care-taking – the value of the care as such has to be compensated, even if it is performed by a housewife or by a retired or otherwise not gainfully employed person.[159]

*How are the damages assessed in these cases?* If there is a loss of earnings on the part of the carer, this may be indicative of the value of the care, the market

---

[154] OLG Bremen, *ibid.* [155] OLG Bremen 21 April 1998, NJW-RR 1999, 1115, 1116.
[156] BGH 25 June 1996, NJW 1996, 2508; cf. OLG Bremen *ibid.*: monthly DM42,000
(= €22,000)!
[157] BGH 10 November 1998, NJW 1999, 421, 422/3.
[158] BGH 22 November 1988, NJW 1989, 766; see also BGH 8 November 1977, VersR 1978,
149, 150; BGH 24 November 1995, NJW 1996, 921; BGH 4 March 1997, NJW 1997, 1853;
BGH 8 June 1999, NJW 1999, 2819.
[159] BGH 8 November 1977, VersR 1978, 149.

value of the care being the upper limit. The market value is the decisive standard for the assessment of damages in all cases: how much would the victim have to pay for comparable care by professional persons?[160]

*Restrictions and modifications* The courts apply this standard, albeit with some restrictions. The first concerns that part of the salary which is deducted for tax and social security contributions: since a non-employed family member does not have to pay these contributions, they are not awarded by the courts.[161] This has been criticised in the literature, because, as a general principle, the amount of damages is not determined by the actual expenses but by the special needs of the victim (see p. 154). The compensation is to enable him to buy the necessary care 'in the market' – this would include the gross payments to an employed carer.[162] The Federal Court has confirmed its position recently, but – at the same time – indicated some doubts and allowed an exception to the net salary rule.[163] In that case, a severely injured daughter was cared for by her mother, a housewife who was never in gainful employment. The statutory regulation of care insurance, introduced in Germany as a new branch of the social security system, tries to instigate home care instead of institutional care, and therefore pays benefits for family members who provide the necessary care which otherwise would have to be performed by professional (and paid) staff.[164] The payments made by the insurer to family care-takers mirror the salary for gainful employment, including contributions to the old age pension insurance (so the carer may acquire pension rights in his own right). When it comes to the scope of tortious liability, the Federal Court then argues in the usual way. The fact that the social security has a statutory duty to pay the family carer should not relieve the tortfeasor of his duty to compensate all the damages caused by him. The damage of the daughter is her need of intensive care, and this need persists even if it is (professionally) met by others. As a result, the defendant has to reimburse all payments which the care insurer has made (and will have to make) to the mother, including contributions to social security.[165] It is unclear whether this judgment could be regarded as a first step away from the established net salary rule of the court.

---

[160] BGH 15 October 1985, VersR 1986, 264; BGH 10 November 1998, VersR 1999, 252.
[161] BGH 29 March 1988, NJW 1988, 1783, 1784; BGH 10 October 1989, NJW-RR 1990, 34; BGH 24 April 1990, NJW-RR 1990, 962.
[162] MünchKomm-BGB/Stein § 843 BGB no. 30.
[163] BGH 10 November 1998, NJW 1999, 421.
[164] § 3 S. 1 Nr. 1 a Sozialgesetzbuch VI (Rentenversicherung; Retirement Insurance Act); § 44 Sozialgesetzbuch XI (Pflegeversicherung; Geriatric Care Insurance Act).
[165] For subrogation rights see chapter 4.

The second restriction concerns the level of compensation for a family carer. Some courts tend to allow further deductions from the 'market price' for adequate care. More precisely, they argue that: (a) care within the family unit is less burdensome to the provider (no distance to the workplace, less time-consuming); (b) some care is owed by the relatives anyway (basic personal contact and help); and (c) the 'market salary' is calculated for professional staff while family members usually are untrained and cannot provide the same quality of care.[166] It seems doubtful whether these decisions are compatible with the leading principle of § 843 I BGB (see p. 154).

The third restriction draws a delicate line between compensatory care by family members and emotional or psychological attachment and help which only close relatives are able to provide and which, accordingly, cannot be bought for money on the commercial market. Interpersonal emotions and love cannot be measured in economic terms.[167] The Federal Court speaks of 'non-fungible functions' of parents, which include time spent for conciliation, appeasement, distraction or some training for rehabilitation.[168] The court admits that even such functions can be performed by professionals, but they are compensable only if (a) professional care would be of comparable quality, and (b) professional care would have been reasonably considered in the given circumstances. If parents spend an additional hour per day with the injured child, professional care would rarely be considered as a substitute – the time spent is therefore not recoverable care.[169]

*Care performed by the wrongdoer* If the injury has been caused by a family member (e.g., negligent supervision of a child), this relative may provide the necessary care later on.[170] Although the wrongdoer may feel himself under a moral duty to take over the care, there is no such duty in German law. According to §§ 251 I, 843 BGB the victim has to be compensated in money, the tortfeasor does not owe personal care. But such an obligation may arise from family law.[171] In any event, if the tortfeasor

---

[166] OLG Hamm 17 August 1993, NJW-RR 1994, 415 (allowing, however, a special bonus for the mother who had undergone special training to care for an injured child); OLG Bremen 21 April 1998, NJW-RR 1999, 1115; see also BGH 22 November 1988, NJW 1989, 766, 767.

[167] BGH 22 November 1988, NJW 1989, 766, 767 (cf. *GLT*, p. 909).

[168] BGH 8 June 1999, NJW 1999, 2819, concerning destruction of the teeth by sugared baby tea.

[169] BGH 8 June 1999, NJW 1999, 2819, 2820.    [170] Cf. *Hunt* v. *Severs* [1994] 2 AC 350.

[171] OLG München 30 May 1995, NJW-RR 1995, 1239, quoting §§ 1601, 1610 II BGB in a case where a mother has negligently caused the injury of her child.

actually takes over the care, he or she fulfils the claim of the child for proper care '*in natura*' – there is no right of the child to obtain additional financial compensation.[172] On the other hand, the carer cannot charge a salary because, in one or the other way, he or she is liable to provide adequate care and has chosen this alternative to meet his or her responsibility.

A problem arises if others are liable as well. In the only case reported in Germany, the negligent mother had taken out liability insurance and, according to § 3 no. 2 Pflichtversicherungsgesetz, the injured child had a claim against his mother and the insurance company as joint and several debtors. In the internal relationship between the debtors, it is the insurance company which has to carry the burden of compensation in the end (§ 3 no. 9 Pflichtversicherungsgesetz). Since the mother has already satisfied the needs of her child for personal care *in natura*, the financial claim of the child against both debtors switches by *cessio legis* to the mother (§ 426 II BGB), who can then claim from the insurer an appropriate sum for her care (see p. 152).

*Is the victim bound to use the money he has received for adequate care, or can he do with it as he likes?*

### In general

German law in this respect seems to be somewhat inconsistent. If a person is injured, the tortfeasor owes in principle '*restitutio in integro*': § 249 S. 1 BGB. Alternatively, the victim may ask for a sum of money in order to organise the reparation himself: § 249 II 1 BGB. This applies to damage to property as well as to personal injuries.[173] But whether the victim is then free to dispose of the money he receives is, according to the case law, answered differently: in the case of *damage to property*, the owner may take the money and leave his property, e.g., his car, unrepaired.[174] This rule has been implicitly confirmed by the latest statutory reform, which now denies the claim of the owner with regard to the VAT (which is to be paid only in case of actual repair), but thereby acknowledges the claim in all other respects (§ 249 II 2 BGB).

In case of *personal injury*, a comparable freedom of disposition is denied by the courts, because money paid for an operation or medical treatment which is not performed would amount to non-pecuniary damage, which

---

[172] OLG München *ibid.*    [173] See *GLT*, p. 907.
[174] BGH 23 March 1976, BGHZ 66, 239, 241; BGH 4 May 1982, NJW 1982, 1864, 1865.

is recoverable only under special circumstances (see p. 60).[175] If the victim receives the money, but does not have the operation, he has to pay the money back.[176]

These rules do not apply, however, if damage can be claimed under § 843 BGB (Financial compensation for persisting special needs, see p. 160). The legitimating basis for compensation under this provision is not the actual expenses of the victim, but his existing, additional needs caused by the injury (see p. 154). Thus, if the victim needs someone to help him or care for him, and collects money which is to enable him to pay for future care, he is entitled to keep the money if later on he decides to manage without help[177] – but only if and as long as the need for care continues to exist. Should the care become unnecessary from an objective point of view, the tortfeasor can ask for a judgment to modify the original award with effect for the future (§ 323 ZPO).

## Money received as compensation for family care[178]

The victim recovers the money as compensation for his *own* damage (i.e., his special needs, see p. 154), but in reality the economic loss is on the side of family members. Does the victim have to reimburse them?[179] There seems to be no published court decision on this issue, and the views expressed by academic writers are split. Some would base a claim by the relative on §§ 683, 670 BGB (agency without mandate). Yet this is not without its difficulties since the relative did not act with the (necessary) intent to do the 'business' of the tortfeasor; and this would make it difficult to reply on these provisions of the Code.[180] Other authors try to rely on provisions of family law analogously, which would give the carer a claim against the victim: § 1648 or § 1607 III BGB.[181] But these theories seem to have little practical relevance where personal care is provided by family members. For in these cases there exists a functioning family unit with

[175] BGH 14 January 1986, NJW 1986, 1538 = *GLT*, case no. 142; OLG Köln 19 May 1999, VersR 2000, 1021; Hermann Lange and Gottfried Schiemann, *Schadensersatz* (3rd edn, 2003) § 5 IV 6, pp. 228–30; cf. *GLT*, p. 908.
[176] *Condictio ob rem*, § 812 I 2 Alt. 2 BGB, MünchKomm-BGB/Oetker (4th edn, 2000), § 249 BGB no. 355; Lange/Schiemann, n. 175 above, § 5 IV 6, pp. 228–30.
[177] RG 23 May 1935, RGZ 148, 68, 70/71; RG 11 June 1936, RGZ 151, 298; BGH 15 December 1970, VersR 1971, 442, 444; KG 15 February 1982, VersR 1982, 978, 979; Erman/Schiemann, *BGB* (10th edn, 2000), § 843 nos 11, 12.
[178] For the dogmatic problems under German law, see *GLT*, pp. 546–7.
[179] See *GLT*, p. 909.
[180] Cf. Esser and Weyers, *Schuldrecht* (8th edn, 2000), II/2, p. 15; Karl Larenz, *Schuldrecht* (14th edn, 1987), I, p. 536 no. 40.
[181] Thiele AcP 167 (1967) 193, 221.

close mutual bonds. The sums recovered are considered part of the family budget which is not split up into individual claims. The distribution of the money seems to be left to family autonomy.

### Other potential heads of damage

Functions of § 843 BGB, beyond loss of earnings and the need of special care, are essentially as follows.

### Preservation of physical health; improvements through operations/medical treatment after the injury

To this end, the victim may need a special diet or better food in general,[182] or he has continuously to take medicaments, tonics and the like[183] or he has to have a medical check-up from time to time.

### Mitigation of persisting physical or emotional impairments

Under this heading, the victim may claim the costs of a sanatorium or therapy,[184] and the maintenance or replacement of various aids and equipment (wheel-chair, lift in his home, glasses, hearing aids etc., the original acquisition being financed under § 249 II BGB).

### Compensation for continuing losses or disadvantages in a professional career

The most important example in this context is the loss of earnings (see p. 70); the costs of a special school education or special vocational training may also fall under this head of damages.[185]

### Compensation for increased needs in daily life

The need for personal care is the most prominent example (see p. 154). But German courts have granted compensation in many other respects. Thus, a rent increase has been granted if the victim, because of his injury, had to move to another, more expensive apartment (see p. 114). Likewise, the increased costs of public transportation (or the use of a car) have

---

[182] RG 11 June 1936, RGZ 151, 298.

[183] BGH 29 October 1957, NJW 1958, 627; BGH 11 February 1992, NJW-RR 1992, 791.

[184] LG Bonn 12 April 1995, VersR 1996, 381, 382.

[185] BGH 11 February 1992, NJW-RR 1992, 791. If, however, it takes more time for the victim to finish his education and to enter gainful employment, this particular damage has to be compensated under § 842 BGB (loss of earnings); see also BGH 23 October 1984, NJW 1985, 791, 792; OLG Düsseldorf 30 December 1968, VersR 1969, 671.

been allowed where the circumstances so demanded.[186] An award has, likewise, been made to cover the cost of shuttling a child between the institution where they have to live and the family home.[187] The cost of professional help in the household has also been awarded.[188] Finally, to give one last illustration, maintenance work in the house or garden, if such work had previously been done by the injured himself, has also been compensated.[189]

## Lost years

Under this heading, we refer to the problem addressed in *Pickett* v. *British Rail Engineering Ltd.*[190] There is no comparable discussion in Germany: the interests of surviving relatives are taken care of with regard to lost maintenance claims against the deceased (§ 844 II BGB); the expectation of inheriting savings which the deceased would have accumulated but for his death has – as far as we can see – never been considered a potential head of damages: Germans would probably view this loss as a 'risk of life'.

Premature death, though, can influence compensation for the victim in two respects. First, the *non-pecuniary damages* awarded to a severely injured person (*Schmerzensgeld*) have been reduced by the BGH in proportion to the reduced life expectancy: the damages are to compensate for suffering, and the period of suffering is shortened by the imminent death.[191] This has been criticised by other courts and in the literature. According to these views, the loss of years should be a criterion for awarding a higher amount of non-pecuniary damages than usual.[192] Other decisions seem to steer a middle course: in cases of HIV infection, they grant annuity payments because the remaining life expectancy is too uncertain to allow the calculation of a lump sum payment. In this context the loss of years works in the way mentioned above: shorter life means less compensation.

---

[186] BGH 10 November 1964, NJW 1965, 102; BGH 18 February 1992, NJW-RR 1992, 792 ff.

[187] OLG Hamm 17 March 1994, DAR 1994, 496, 498.

[188] BGH 25 September 1973, NJW 1974, 41, 42; BGH 4 December 1984, NJW 1985, 735; BGH 18 February 1992, NJW-RR 1992, 792; OLG Karlsruhe 6 March 1992, DAR 1993, 391; OLG Oldenburg 28 July 1992, VersR 1993, 1491; KG 15 February 1982, VersR 1982, 978, 979; OLG Bremen 21 April 1998, NJW-RR 1999, 1115.

[189] OLG Koblenz 7 October 1993, NJW-RR 1994, 1049, 1050.    [190] [1980] AC 136.

[191] BGH 16 December 1975, NJW 1976, 1147, 1149 (the victim had survived the accident only for a short time); KG 26 February 1973, NJW 1974, 607, 608; OLG München 16 December 1969, VersR 1970, 643.

[192] OLG Oldenburg 19 April 1994, VersR 1994, 1071, 1072; MünchKomm-BGB/Stein § 847 BGB no. 8, 31, 32; Staudinger/Schäfer § 847 BGB no. 82.

But in calculating the monthly instalment, the courts tend to take into account the reduced quality of life of the victim, who knows that his life chances are severely impaired. Thus, the monthly payments have to be calculated generously.[193]

Secondly, premature death influences the *loss of earnings* which is compensated, as a matter of rule rather than of facts, by periodical payments (§ 843 I BGB) which end at the time when the victim is likely to die. But even in the case of compensation by a capital award (§ 843 III BGB), life expectancy is an important factor of calculation. Consequently, loss of earnings is a head of damages only as long as the victim lives; lost earnings because of lost years are disregarded in German law.

## Italian law

### Introduction

In addition to damage qualified as *danno biologico* (injury to health *per se* including loss of amenity of life, aesthetic loss, social life, etc., discussed in chapters 1 and 3) and *danno morale* (pain and suffering, in the sense explained above), which are the headings of damage of Italian law which correspond to non-pecuniary losses of the common law, the victim is also entitled to be compensated for pecuniary loss suffered by him as a direct consequence of his injuries. In Italian legal terminology this damage is referred to as *danno patrimoniale*.

The term is a product of academic writing since the text of the Civil Code, in the general rules governing damages from non-performance of obligations (article 1223 ff.), refers simply to *danno* without any adjective. Only in tort law does the Code deal with 'non-patrimonial' damages, which courts and academics refer to as *danno morale*. Two inferences follow from the above. First, all losses not qualified as 'non-patrimonial' are to be considered as 'patrimonial' (i.e., affecting the estate of the victim). Secondly, *danno morale* is awarded only in tort cases, and it is considered exceptional;[194] non-performance of a contractual obligation cannot entail *danno morale*.

Following the terminology of Roman law, the Italian law of *danno patrimoniale* is divided into two general headings: *damnum emergens* (*danno*

---

[193] OLG Hamburg 20 April 1990, NJW 1990, 2322, 2324; similar, but less clear BGH 30 April 1991, NJW 1991, 1948, 1951 (*GLT*, p. 45).

[194] Subject to the very recent liberalising decisions of the Italian Supreme Court regarding *danno morale* discussed in chapters 1 and 2.

*emergente*), which means all expenses paid by the victim and *lucrum cessans* (*lucro cessante*), which means lost profits. Roughly speaking, we can say that the first head of loss comes close to the English concept of special damages/ past losses while the second head of loss is nearer the English concept of general/future pecuniary losses. But the analogy is not complete. For *danno emergente* can refer to real, though future, losses and not to failed gains which would be part of what the English would then call general damages.

Italian (like English) judges may well be tempted to start their calculations with the first item of damages but, for the reasons given in the previous chapter, this separation does not figure in their judgments. Referring, as they do, to the future, these kind of losses involve a degree of speculation. The court must thus begin with the position of the victim at the date of the trial, and then be guided in its evaluation of the future by the evidence offered by the victim and by the reports usually prepared by different types of experts (doctors, actuaries etc.).

The court often sets out to liquidate a life annuity. This will happen if it has been requested by the claimant to do so or if it is considered as more appropriate by the court itself. As already stated, however, lump sums seem to be the rule. No control is exercised over the use which the claimant will make of any sums awarded. In practice this means that awards made to the claimant for, say, equipment or specialised care may subsequently be diverted by him to other purposes with complete impunity.

The calculation of future losses makes reference to the pre-accident earnings, and to the future possible earnings which the victim could expect, taking into account his training, education, abilities, choices and the opportunities available to him. According to the circumstances, past earnings can serve as the basis of the calculation, but the victim is allowed to give evidence that in the future his earnings could be greater.

### Method of calculation

Such calculations, inevitably, include a certain amount of speculation. In order to work out what level of earnings the victim could have reached in the future, courts use the same techniques connected with the multiplier-multiplicand approach. No statute requests the courts to use this method; but it has been in practice for many decades now.

In Italian case law, courts refer to this kind of calculation in terms of an abstract concept, which looks at the victim as a worker as an employee or self-employed person. This concept is called 'specific working capacity' (*capacità lavorativa specifica*). Before the invention of the head of loss named *danno biologico* the courts, in order to give the victim greater compensation, also used another head of loss called 'general working capacity' (*capacità lavorativa generica*) which has now been abandoned, being included in the notion of *danno biologico*.

The term 'work' includes employment, self-employment, the activity of entrepreneurs, as well as the activity of persons who do not receive regular remuneration, such as housewives, pensioners, the unemployed, minors and the like.

## Future loss of earnings (capacità lavorativa specifica, *specific working incapacity*)

### General observations

This item concerns the reduction or cessation of earnings. It may refer to the present or to the future, and it may concern merely a temporary reduction or a permanent reduction or cessation. The injured party must overcome difficult problems concerning evidence of the loss sustained by him. Case law is not based on uniform criteria related to the appreciation of evidence. Thus, we find decisions having recourse to presumption of evidence (presumed damage, *danno presunto*) and others which require, as is deemed more appropriate, evidence of *actual* damage (*danno attuale*). This, of course, must be adduced by the victim of the tort.

An example of the former trend can be found in a decision which contains the following dicta:

> The economic damage to an individual can be liquidated only if it is ascertained, even through rebuttable presumptions, that the injured party, due to the impairment of his psycho-physical integrity, will incur a loss of his specific future earning capacity.

In that case the Italian Court of Cassation confirmed the decision of the Court of Appeal which, notwithstanding the existence of ascertained disability equal to 25 per cent, had excluded future losses because the victim, instead of providing evidence of the reduction in earnings, had merely claimed an automatic economic relevance of damage to health, in particular aesthetic damage.[195]

An example of the second approach can be found in a decision of the Supreme Court of 2001.[196] According to this decision the ascertainment of after-effects, which influence the specific working capacity, does not imply the automatic obligation of the wrongdoer to compensate the economic

---

[195] Cass. 28 April 1999, no. 4231, Resp. civ. e prev., 2000, 110.
[196] Cass. 29 October 2001, no. 13409, Giust. civ. Mass., 2001, 1814.

damage consequent on the reduction of the earning capacity, as a result of the reduced specific working capacity. Therefore, such economic damage due to disability must be ascertained 'through evidence that the injured party performed or, if such person was not working yet, would presumably perform an income-producing activity. However, the damage cannot automatically be liquidated on the presumption that the reduction of specific working capacity is certain'.

This conclusion seems to be more appropriate, because it conforms to the function of compensation of civil liability rules on injury to the psycho-physical integrity of the individual. The Court of Cassation has long since maintained this opinion. Thus, in its decision of 18 November 1982, no. 6234, it stated that:

the assessment of the economic damage suffered because of personal disability by a working person, once the injury and its correlation with the damaging event have been proved, must still be based upon an actual reference-situation, because compensation for the damage deriving from torts – having the function of restoring the assets of the injured party to the same situation as they would have been without the damaging event – is based upon and limited by the actual loss incurred, to be determined on the basis of an element of certainty. Consequently, the trial judge must consider the actual amount of the injured party's earnings, and he is not allowed to replace such an element with the salary due in theory to the workers of the category to which the injured party belongs.[197]

Case law makes a distinction between methods of calculation, according to the kind of employment, if any, in which the victim was involved. So the results in the amount of damages depend upon the category in which the victim is included.

## Categories of victims

### Employees
As regards employees, proof must be given concerning the salary received. This must include the tax returns and any other evidence suitable for such a purpose. The reduction or loss of earnings is connected with the *prospective* or *actual* working capability.

Income from employment includes all earnings relevant to the worker's remuneration, namely wages (or salary), production bonuses, additional monthly payments as well as all reimbursements connected with the performance of the working activity. If the victim has two occupations (as

---

[197] Cass. 18 November 1982, no. 6234.

is notoriously frequent in Italy) the income from the second occupation must also be taken into account, provided that it does not come from an unlawful activity and, always, on condition that it can be proved (which may not always be easy to do if it was paid in 'cash' in order to evade tax). Income is calculated before tax.

The income taken into account is only earned income, not unearned income. The loss of profit must be direct and immediate. Net business income is included among the items, thereby excluding expenditure incurred for the production of such income. Social security contributions are also included (provided that they are not charged to third parties). It is disputed whether taxes are to be included or not: the Court of Cassation deems that they are not included in the event of temporary incapacity, while they are included in the event of permanent incapacity.

Social security contributions are reimbursed to the employee only if the accident has resulted in a permanent inability to work; in all other cases such costs are charged to the employer and do not affect the worker's income.

### Self-employment and entrepreneurial activities

For earnings from self-employment, the highest net income produced in the last three years is considered. However, the earnings of an entrepreneur carrying out his activity for a medium or large firm are differentiated from the income of a small entrepreneur. In the first case, it is difficult to separate earned income from capital gains. As the two kinds of income are to be differentiated – the former alone being compensated[198] – an ideal percentage of income reduction is determined. In the second case, on the other hand, where capital gains are mixed with earned income, all the net profit of the firm is to be taken into account.[199] Production costs are excluded from income and therefore from compensation.[200] For the self-employed, social security contributions are also calculated.

### Housewives

There is a dispute in case law with regard to compensation for future loss to housewives. Some judges deem that housewives are entitled only to compensation of *danno biologico*;[201] others have awarded for damages arising from the loss of future employment.[202] Yet a third group, have

---

[198] Cass. 24 May 1993, no. 5832.     [199] Cass. 13 October 1997, no. 9959.
[200] Cass. 15 November 1993, no. 11271.     [201] e.g., App. Milan, 19 October 1993.
[202] Trib. Pisa, 16 January 1985.

liquidated damages arising from the economic value of the employment of a domestic helper.[203]

The Court of Cassation has accepted this argument. It has further maintained that the housewife's work is not limited to doing the housework, but also consists of the management of family life and it has also awarded damages for the loss deriving from the impossibility of carrying out work outside the household.[204] In any event, courts state that the activity of housewives has its own dignity and is therefore considered in its economic effects, which are reduced if the housewife is impaired because of the injury. As the Supreme Court has put it:

A housewife incurs an injury, to be recognised as an economic damage in the strict sense, therefore compensatable separately from and in addition to *danno biologico*, every time the tort results in an impairment of the productive capacity, expressed in this case by fulfilment of the so-called household tasks. This conclusion is supported by the acknowledgement of the housewife's activity as a working activity in the strict sense, which is, therefore, protected by art. 4 of the Constitution, and by the principle of full compensation for personal injuries. This means that not only health, a value protected by art. 32 of the Constitution, is to be compensated, but also any injury to any constitutionally relevant interests. Such damage is to be compensated equitably by the method of capitalisation of the housewife's notional income. The income can be determined by referring to the daily income of a full-time domestic helper, or to the income of a domestic helper who works by the hour, or to the income compared with the triple of the non-contributory pension, and in any case in accordance with art. 2056 of the It. Civil Code.[205]

Compensation for damages for gains arising from unlawful activities is excluded (e.g., prostitution) even though the possibility of subjecting even this income to tax levy is now being discussed.

*Pensioners*
Pensioners are not entitled to compensation. But they can prove that they have a residual specific working capacity or that they have an occupation concurrent with their pension. In such case, compensation will be calculated in accordance with the above-mentioned rules.

*Minors*
In order to calculate the income from permanent incapacity of minors the courts used to resort to forecasts that took into consideration, in a mechanical and class-oriented way, the father's profession or employment,

---

[203] Trib. Venice, 8 June 1994.    [204] Cass. 6 November 1997.
[205] Cass. 11 December 2000, no. 15580, Resp. civ. e prev., 2001, 609.

while now other elements are taken into account such as age, social environment, social life, as well as the aptitudes and talents of the child.

The circumstances of the case are decisive in order to establish the quantum of compensation. For example, in a case concerning a young girl who had completely lost her hair, it was specified that:

this serious impairment (affecting social life) implies, besides a psycho-physical element in a strict sense, included in the scope of damage to health, an economic element as well, connected with the negative influence that such impairment has in the performance of activities ancillary to or integrating the normal working activity, causing a reduction of the so-called competition capacity of the individual.[206]

## Loss of opportunities

The prospects of income acquisition are referred to as 'loss of opportunities'. Courts are in disagreement on their qualification, i.e., whether they are actual damages or loss of profit, but it seems more appropriate to think of this as a case of loss of profit, such as future prospects for career improvement.

## Method for the calculation of compensation: lump sum, life annuity

For temporary inability to work, earnings lost for non-worked days are added up and revalued, including holidays. For future earnings, reference is made to temporary capitalisation. For total loss of income reference is made to a capitalisation ratio taking into account the future years of life of the injured party.[207] The age taken into account is the age of the individual at the time of liquidation of damages, considering the difference between physical life and working life.[208] If, however, the victim obtains a disability pension, this is to be deducted from the result of the calculation.[209] For partial loss of income the same calculations are reduced in proportion.

In the event that re-employment is possible, it is necessary to consider the kind of occupation and the relevant income that the victim will be able to obtain.[210]

As stated above, in the domain of tort law alone the Civil Code provides[211] that a settlement in liquidation can be ordered by the judge in the form of a life annuity. The judge takes into account the conditions of the

---

[206] Cass. 23 January 1995, no. 755.    [207] Cass. 18 November 1999, no. 174.
[208] These calculations are usually done by medical experts.
[209] Cass. 12 July 2000, no. 9228.    [210] Cass. 30 December 1993, no. 13013.
[211] Article 2057.

parties and the nature of the injury. In such a case, the judge shall order suitable precautionary measures. There are two conditions to be satisfied: the damage must arise from a personal injury and the injury must be permanent. Temporary inabilities are not included in the application of this rule even if they entail long periods of treatment and rehabilitation.

The annuity is considered as established for life. Temporary annuities are not allowed. Unlike French and German law, the choice between lump sum and annuity is left to the judge, who decides according to the conditions of the parties. The matter is not seen as a question of which is the best way of sanctioning the wrongdoer. The prime consideration is what best helps the recovery of the injured party. In deciding this, the judge takes into account the following factors: on the side of the victim, his age, his position in society, his culture and his hobbies. On the side of the debtor/defendant he scrutinises carefully his ability to pay the amount awarded to the claimant by the court.

The future length of the victim's life is calculated according to the average foreseeable life *in abstracto,* not *in concreto,* i.e., in connection with the seriousness of the injury that has been suffered. The average life's length is nowadays estimated as being seventy-five years.

Life annuity ordered by the judge is governed by the same provisions concerning the special contract of life annuity included in the Civil Code (article 1872). It is an aleatory contract, and the annuity can be established by the transfer of movable or immovable property or the assignment of capital.

### Medical treatment and therapies

All kinds of expenses due to medical treatment paid by the victim before the trial or in the future are considered a loss to be compensated (*danno emergente*). Evidence is usually easy to adduce. This head of damages results in a variety of items: fees paid to doctors and other professionals, nursing care, rehabilitation therapies, physical and health improvement, equipment, means of transportation to reach the hospitals where the therapies are offered, medical check-ups (whenever needed), etc. In these instances, case law seems to be mainly concerned with the causal link of these costs with the consequences of the injury. Expenses are considered recoverable if they were necessary or even only useful – terms which, in substance, come close to the common law requirement of reasonableness. The principle in relation to recovery is always the same as referred to above: the victim must be put in the same situation in which he found himself before the accident, in order to avoid any unjust reduction of the award.

The necessity or utility of this kind of expenses are evaluated *in concreto*, taking account of all the circumstances of the case. So, if serious injury can be treated abroad, courts allow the victim to be compensated for the medical treatment and for the necessary travel. If injuries are light, and the victim can be cured in national hospitals, no recovery is allowed, due to the lack of causal link, but also because the victim is under a duty to mitigate his losses (article 1227 cod. civ.).

Medical treatment can be afforded by the national health service or by private hospitals. Though some decisions have refused the award of damages for expenses incurred in private hospitals,[212] most courts allow the victim to receive private treatment, provided what he seeks satisfies the requirements of 'necessary or useful'. The debtor has to give evidence of the lack of causality between the expenses and the injury. Unnecessary expenses are those connected, e.g., with the provision of a television in a hospital room, or visits to doctors following the accident but for reasons unconnected to it. Evidence of this kind of (permissible) expenses must be submitted in written form. Evidence is not implied, but has to be adduced by the victim.[213]

Future medical expenses are recoverable if they are foreseeable according to special calculations. A claim for future private treatment will succeed, provided it satisfies the requirement of necessity; and repayment of this amount will not be possible if, in the event, the claimant decides not to use these funds for the requested purpose but diverts them to other uses.

Sums paid by private insurances relieve the debtor from paying this kind of expenses according to the principle that the victim cannot profit from a double compensation.[214]

---

[212] e.g., Trib. Trieste, 14 January 1988.
[213] Corte di Cassazione, 2 February 2000, no. 2037.
[214] Appeal Court of Rome, 12 December 1998.

# 5 Collateral sources of revenue: subrogation rights and miscellaneous matters

## English law

*Social security payments*

### General observations

In England, the recovery and deduction of benefits is governed by the Social Security (Recovery of Benefits) Act 1997. That came into force on 6 October 1997 and applies to all cases concluded after that date irrespective of when the litigation began, the accident occurred or the condition complained of was contracted.

Major changes were instituted by the 1997 Act. First, general damages for pain, suffering and loss of amenities are not subject to any deduction. Secondly, loss of earnings, cost of care and damages for loss of mobility are subject to recoupment of certain specified benefits particularly applicable to each of those heads of damage.[1] Thirdly, it is the defendant who is liable to make the repayment to the Compensation Recovery Unit, not the claimant. The full amount of all recoverable benefits must be paid irrespective of whether they have been claimed by the claimant or not. It is the responsibility of the defendants to obtain the relevant certificate from the Unit and to pay what is due. The payment which is made to a claimant must be, or is taken to be, net of repayable benefits. No interest is payable on the benefits so recouped.

That is equally applicable to any interim payments of damages agreed (or ordered to) be paid during the course of the proceedings. The defendant must obtain the relevant certificate and make the payment to the Unit of the sum recoverable by them up to the date on which the interim payment

---

[1] See s. 8 of and Sch. 2 to the 1997 Act.

is made. There is, however, a cut-off date which is five years from the date of the accident or the first claim for the relevant benefit.

The defendant is bound to repay the full amount of the recoverable benefit notwithstanding that, in consequence of a finding of contributory negligence, he is not liable for 100 per cent of the recoverable damages.

Benefits which are deductible are set out in Schedule 2 to the Act. As explained above, certain types of benefit fall to be set against specific heads of claim. In consequence, any judgment at trial must identify specifically the amounts recovered in respect of care, loss of earnings and loss of mobility. It matters not, however, whether the sums recovered are in respect of past or future loss. If a settlement is being negotiated it may be worthwhile reducing the amount recovered under specified heads of damage and loading others, if that can properly be done, in order to reduce the recoupment. That is particularly the case where a degree of contributory negligence has been accepted because, as set out above, recoupment is still 100 per cent even though the claimant does not recover 100 per cent of his damages.

## Do social security payments fall to be deducted from the award?

The position is as set out in the preceding paragraph but with a time limit of five years from the date of the accident or the date of the claim in the case of an industrial or other illness. Once the five-year period has expired no account is to be taken of state benefits. The court is not permitted to make a deduction from an award of damages for the fact that a claimant has obtained or will, in the future, obtain or continue to obtain monies from the state which will, in part, reduce his loss.

We have already considered the position of treatment available on the National Health Service in chapter 4.

### Pension losses

We have already considered, in chapter 4, what is recoverable by way of loss of pension. Retirement pensions, disability pensions or *ex gratia* pensions paid by an employer are not normally deductible.[2] That rule is, however, subject to two exceptions. The first relates to a lump sum payable to an injured person of which part is attributable to the period after retirement.[3] The second exception relates to that part of the disability pension

---

[2] *Hewson v. Downs* [1970] 1 QB 73; *Cunningham v. Harrison* [1973] QB 942.
[3] *Longden v. British Coal Corporation* [1998] AC 653.

which the claimant will receive during the period when his retirement pension would normally have been payable.[4]

## Monies provided by the employer

If an employer continues to make payments to an employee after the accident do such payments fall to be repaid or is the claim for past loss of earnings reduced? The answer depends upon the nature of the payments and the legal liability of the claimant to repay his employer.

If there is a legal liability to repay, then those monies must form part of the special damages claim.[5] The position is the same if the claimant has given an undertaking to repay his employer.

If the employer makes a voluntary payment that sum does not fall to be deducted from the special damages claim. However, if he expects to be reimbursed, and has entered into a legally binding contract with the claimant that he should be reimbursed out of the damages recovered, then the amount should be added to the special damages claim and is then usually subject to a direction that the money should be paid to the employer.

There is one exception to the exception. If, by the terms of his contract of employment, the claimant is entitled to part or all of his wages or salary during a period of incapacity, such sum then falls to be deducted from his special damages claim for past loss of earnings because he has, of course, suffered no loss. That rule applies even where the money is paid by an insurance company under a permanent disability scheme. Whether or not the payments are deductible depends upon who has paid the premiums and how the money is actually paid. So, e.g., if the employer takes out the policy and pays the premiums and the money is paid to him to be passed on to the claimant as wages or salary, the money will be deducted from any past or future loss of earnings.[6] There is no difference in principle between that situation and the one in which the less seriously injured individual is capable of doing, and in fact does, some work.

## Benevolence of third parties

Payments made to claimants by third parties as an act of benevolence are not to be taken into account when assessing damages.[7] That does

---

[4] *Smoker* v. *London Fire and Civil Defence Authority; Wood* v. *British Coal Corporation* [1991] 2 AC 502.

[5] *Browning* v. *War Office* [1963] 1 QB 750.

[6] *Hussain* v. *New Taplow Paper Mills Ltd* [1988] AC 514.     [7] *Hodgson* v. *Trapp* [1989] AC 807.

not apply when the benevolence comes from the tortfeasor himself. So, monies paid by an employer, who was the tortfeasor, out of benevolence were to be taken into account.[8]

## Insurance policies taken out by the injured person

Any monies received from such insurance policies are to be wholly disregarded by the court. That is so even if, e.g., a claimant has taken out and paid for a policy which, in the event of his incapacity, pays him a sum equivalent to his net earnings. There is no logical reason for the distinction. The courts have attempted to justify it by saying that justice demands that a tortfeasor should not be relieved of his obligations because his victim has been sufficiently prudent to pay for such a policy and that the payments are made not by reason of the accident but because of the contract between the victim and his insurer.

## Duties of local authorities

Pursuant to the provisions of section 26 of the National Assistance Act 1948 a local authority has a duty to provide, and pay for, the care of a disabled person. It is also required to recover those costs from the individual concerned unless he satisfies them that he is unable to make a full refund. However, damages paid into the Court of Protection on behalf of a patient, and the income derived from that capital, are to be ignored for the purposes of recoupment by a local authority.[9] These two decisions have led some defendants to argue that they should not have to pay for costs of care since the same will be met by the local authority. In the majority of cases the level of care which the local authority are able or willing to provide falls below that which is reasonably required by a claimant and the point does not arise. There are cases, as for instance that of an injured child who has been placed in the care of a local authority, where it is very important. There has not, as yet, been any reported authority on whether a local authority can be compelled to provide that level of care which the trial judge considers to be reasonably required by the claimant or whether the tortfeasor is liable for a 'top up' over the sums provided or to be provided by the local authority. Equally, the courts have not considered in any reported case what is to happen in the event of a change in the law absolving local authorities from this duty.

[8] *Williams* v. *BOC Gases Ltd* [2000] ICR 1181.
[9] *Bell* v. *Todd* [2002] Lloyd's Rep. Med. 12 and *Ryan* v. *Liverpool Health Authority* [2002] Lloyd's Rep. Med. 23. Neither decision has been appealed.

## Interest

The claimant is entitled to interest on general damages for pain, suffering and loss of amenity at 2 per cent per annum from the date of service of the proceedings until judgment.[10]

In the case of special damages, the rule is that the claimant is entitled to interest at one-half of the appropriate rate from the date of the accident until trial. The appropriate rate is the rate of interest allowed on money in court placed on special account. Interest is payable on the full amount of special damages without making any deduction for recoupable benefits.[11]

In exceptional cases, such as where one party or the other has been guilty of gross and culpable delay in bringing the matter to trial, the court may increase or diminish the award of interest or alter the period for which it is allowed.[12]

## Limitation periods

It is beyond the scope of this book to deal with periods of limitation other than in the barest outline.

The primary limitation period for cases involving personal injuries is three years from the date on which the cause of action accrued or the date of knowledge (if later) of the person injured.[13] Thus, in the simplest case, the claimant will have three years from the date of his accident or injury in which to institute proceedings.

The date of knowledge is defined by section 14 of the Limitation Act 1980. It is the date on which the claimant first had knowledge:

   (i)   that the injury in question was significant; and

   (ii)   that the injury was attributable in whole or in part to the act or omission which is alleged to constitute negligence, nuisance or breach of duty; and

   (iii)   of the identity of the defendant; and

   (iv)   if it is alleged that the act or omission was that of a person other than the defendant, the identity of that person and the additional facts supporting the bringing of an action against the defendant. Knowledge that any act or omission did or did not, as a matter of law, involve negligence, nuisance or breach of duty is irrelevant.

Injury is significant if the person whose date of knowledge is in question would reasonably have considered it sufficiently serious to justify

---

[10] *Wright* v. *British Railways Board* [1983] 2 AC 773.

[11] *Wadey* v. *Surrey County Council* [2000] 1 WLR 820.

[12] *Spittle* v. *Bunney* [1988] 1 WLR 847.    [13] Limitation Act 1980, s. 11.

his instituting proceedings for damages against a defendant who did not dispute liability and was able to satisfy a judgment.[14]

An individual is not required to know what the specific act of negligence was. So, e.g., a woman who knew that she had undergone a mastectomy unnecessarily, because the lump was benign, had the knowledge required to satisfy section 14.[15]

A person's knowledge is deemed to include knowledge which he might reasonably have been expected to acquire from facts observable or ascertainable by him or from facts ascertainable by him with the help of medical or other appropriate expert advice which it is reasonable for him to request. If, however, he has taken all reasonable steps to obtain (and act upon) that advice, such knowledge will not be imputed to him.[16]

If a defendant wishes to take a limitation defence he must specifically plead it. The court is not entitled to take the point of its own motion.

Once a limitation defence has been raised, the burden of proving that the claim was brought within the primary limitation period is upon the claimant. However, the burden of proof in constructive knowledge under section 14(3) as opposed to actual knowledge is upon the defendant.[17]

In the case of a person under a disability, the primary limitation period does not begin to run until the claimant is free of that disability. Thus, in the case of a child the primary limitation period is three years from the date on which he attains his majority. In England that is his eighteenth birthday. In the case of a person with a disability the limitation period may never expire. However, once time has begun to run, it does not cease to do so. If, therefore, a person becomes a patient after the date of an accident, the primary limitation period remains three years. However, in those particular circumstances the claimant may have a good case for inviting the court to disapply the primary limitation period pursuant to section 33 of the Limitation Act 1980, of which more below.

There are two exceptions to that rule. First, in the case of an intentional tort, such as trespass to the person, the primary limitation period is six years and there is no power to extend the period under section 33 of the Limitation Act 1980.[18] The second relates to claims brought under the Consumer Protection Act 1987. In that Act, a claim may not be brought

---

[14] Limitation Act 1980, s. 14(2).    [15] *Dobbie* v. *Medway Health Authority* [1994] 1 WLR 1234.

[16] Limitation Act 1980, s. 14(3). For a detailed exposition of this area of the law, see *Nash* v. *Eli Lilly & Co.* [1993] 1 WLR 782.

[17] *Nash* v. *Eli Lilly & Co.,* n. 16 above.

[18] *Stubbings* v. *Webb* [1993] AC 498. An attempt by the claimant to challenge this decision in the ECHR failed. See *Stubbings* v. *United Kingdom* [1997] 1 FLR 105.

more than ten years after the product is first supplied irrespective of the date on which the claimant acquired knowledge or whether he is or was under a disability.

As set out above, in cases not covered by the two exceptions dealt with in the preceding paragraph the court may override the primary limitation period.[19] The court is only entitled to do this if it appears that it would be equitable to allow an action to proceed having regard to the degree to which the primary limitation period prejudices the claimant balanced against the degree to which any decision which the court may make extending the limitation period would prejudice the defendant. Section 33(3) sets out the specific circumstances as to which the court is required to have regard in coming to that decision.[20]

The limitation period may also be extended in a case where any fact relevant to the claimant's right of action has been deliberately concealed from him by the defendant.[21]

If the claimant dies prior to the expiration of the primary limitation period the surviving cause of action for the benefit of his estate has to be brought within either three years of the date of the death or three years of the date of knowledge of the personal representative of the deceased.[22]

## Persons under a disability

### Generally

There are two classes of persons who are regarded, in English law, as being under a disability. They are infants and patients. An infant is a person under the age of eighteen.

A patient is an individual who is medically certified as being incapable of managing his own affairs.[23] That expression admits of no easy definition. What is clear, however, is that the fact that a claimant may not be capable of managing a very large sum of money does not make him a patient for these purposes. The test is whether he is capable of giving proper instructions to his legal team and of taking all decisions germane to the litigation, including whether or not to accept an offer of settlement.

In each case the proceedings must be brought by a litigation friend. That individual may be a parent or relation of the person under a disability or a stranger, such as a solicitor. The court must be satisfied, however, that

---

[19] Limitation Act 1980, s. 33.
[20] For a full exposition of this area of the law see *Nash v Eli Lilly & Co.*, n. 16 above.
[21] Limitation Act 1980, s. 32.    [22] Limitation Act 1980, s. 11(5).
[23] *Mastermann-Lister* v. *Jewell* [2003] 1 WLR 1511.

the litigation friend is a responsible individual. He is obliged to act in the best interests of the claimant and may be removed by the court if he does not do so.

A claim brought by a person under a disability may not be settled unless the settlement is approved by the court. Such approval will involve the judge considering all the circumstances of the case, including an opinion from counsel, or leading counsel, instructed on behalf of the claimant. That opinion is not, normally, shown to the defendant. It will normally contain a statement that counsel is of the opinion that the settlement is a proper one. It will also explain to the court, in a case where the claim is settled for less than the full amount of damages which might ordinarily be recoverable, why counsel is of the view that such a settlement is proper.

## To whom are the damages recovered paid in such a case?

In the case of a child, the monies are usually invested in court. That is so where the injury is minor, the child has made, or will make, a full recovery before attaining the age of eighteen and the damages are not enormous. The parents are entitled to apply, at the time of settlement or at a later stage, for money to be paid out of court for a specific purpose which benefits the child. It is frequently the case, for example, that the court will sanction a sum of money being paid out of the damages to purchase a particular item such as a new bicycle for a child or to enable him and his parents to go on holiday.

If the child is so seriously injured that he is likely to become a patient as soon as he attains the age of eighteen then his damages will be dealt with in the same way as that of a patient.

In the last century the Supreme Court of Judicature had jurisdiction over what were then called lunatics under a special department headed by the Master of Lunacy. Nowadays, that part of the Supreme Court is a special department entitled the Court of Protection. It has a substantial staff, headed by the Master, or when it is a woman, the Mistress of the Court of Protection. Their duty is to administer the affairs of persons under a disability. The sanction of the Court of Protection is required for any settlement of a case involving a patient. The approval of the court is also required as in the case of a child.

In the case of a patient, a receiver is appointed in addition to a litigation friend, although it may be the same person. The receiver will manage the day-to-day financial affairs of the patient and must prepare annual accounts for the Court of Protection.

While the case is continuing the Court of Protection will monitor, and must approve, any major expenditure on behalf of the patient. For example, if an interim payment of sufficient size is obtained to enable a property to be purchased for the patient and his family, the approval of the purchase by the Master of the Court of Protection, or one of his officers, is required.

Until very recently damages paid into the Court of Protection, at the time of final settlement, were invested and overseen by the Public Trust Office. As a result of its poor investment performance that role of the Public Trust Office is now being abolished. The Court of Protection will utilise outside assistance in relation to the investment strategy.

With the sanction and approval of the Court of Protection, private trusts may be set up in order to invest and administer the damages. In such a case the approval of the Court of Protection is sought for the terms of the trust, the identity of the trustees and the proposed investment strategy. That route is being used with increasing frequency because those advising patients believe that they will be able to achieve better capital growth and higher levels of income, if the damages are invested by a specialist outside agency. Lower levels of Court of Protection fees are also payable where the court is not itself administering the money.

## Miscellaneous matters

In the Introduction we mentioned the possibility of damages reaching the claimant in the form of structured settlements. Here is the place to refer to this (relatively) new institution and explain it briefly.

In the ordinary or conventional case, the court assesses or calculates the sum payable by the defendant to the claimant in respect of each head of damage. The total award is then expressed as a single lump sum payable within fourteen days of the judgment.

It is then a matter for the claimant, or the Court of Protection, to invest his damages and spend both income and capital as he thinks fit. Of course, with the vagaries of the investment market, capital can be lost. Equally, less income may be received than is either necessary or desirable. The damages can run out before, and sometimes long before, the injured individual dies.

In an attempt to overcome that difficulty, structured settlements have come into existence and, until the recent drop in annuity rates, were extremely popular.

What is a structured settlement? It is the purchase, by the parties at the time of settlement, of an annuity for the injured individual. The annuity so purchased can either be at a level rate or index-linked. The annual sum payable will then continue for as long as the claimant lives. If he survives for only a short period then the annuity dies with him subject only to one proviso. If, on the other hand, he lives for far longer than was expected at the date of trial, he will continue to receive the income from the annuity throughout his life. The one proviso is that structured settlements will generally have a guaranteed period, which may be five or more years. The annual income will then continue for the remainder of the guarantee period even if the claimant dies.

A structured settlement can only be entered into by agreement between the parties. The court is unable to impose one. In practice, it is the claimant who decides whether to structure part or all of his damages. It is of little moment or interest to a defendant since he either pays the lump sum to the claimant or his representatives or pays part or all of it to a financial institution for the purchase of the annuity.

The income from the annuity is tax free in the hands of the claimant or his representative. The money is treated by the Inland Revenue as if it was the return of capital and not as income. That has substantial advantages. Take a working example: if £100,000 purchases an annuity at 4 per cent per annum, the claimant's net income will be £4,000. In order to achieve the same figure from the investment of a conventional award an annual return of £6,000 gross would be required.

Of course, the disadvantage of the structured settlement is that the claimant has no access to the capital which has been used for the purchase of the annuity. He does not, therefore, have lump sums available to deal with major emergencies. In times when annuity rates are low, as now, an investment adviser may well be able to achieve a better overall return if he is free to invest partly for capital growth and partly for income.

Specialist advice is invariably needed before a party decides whether to structure part or all of his damages. The current practice generally entails structuring part of the award whilst leaving another part to be paid and invested in the conventional manner.

An important and radical change in the law is proposed by the amendment to section 2 of the Damages Act 1996 by section 100(1) of the Courts Act 2003. It will give the court power to order that the defendant pay for future losses by means of periodical payments. The court will be bound to consider whether it should make such an order but can only do so if it is satisfied that continuity of the payments is reasonably secure. That will be secured by section 6 of the Act. The new section 2(B) would also give the court power to vary the periodical payments in certain circumstances. From the point of view of a claimant, periodical payments would have distinct advantages since he will be assured that future costs will be met for the duration of his life and that he will not be dependent upon the success of his investment. There does not appear to be any good reason why such a regime should not work well. Both sides can take a degree of comfort from them. A claimant and his family will know that there will always be enough money to meet his needs. Insurers will know that they will not overpay as they might if the claimant lived only for a short time after the award of a lump sum. The legislation is not, however, yet in force.

The court has also used its case management powers to adjourn part of a damages claim and direct that the claimant could return for a further award of both special and general damages if they underwent additional treatment in the future.[24] The power to take that step has not been challenged in the Court of Appeal. It is likely to be used sparingly.

## German law

### Introductory observations

The guiding principle is that the injured is to be indemnified for his loss; however, he must not make a profit from his injury. The victim must not reap the benefits of double compensation.[25] Consequently, if the victim's loss is compensated by persons other than the tortfeasor, he may not be allowed to claim compensation from him as well. In order to prevent a double compensation, the court must take the following points into account.

First, the court must consider, if benefits which the victim may receive due to his injury are deductible from the award under the rule of 'Vorteilsausgleichung'. This is the case if the victim receives benefits because of the injury: these benefits do not contradict the purpose of the obligation to pay damages and a deduction of the benefits from the award is reasonable.[26]

Secondly, if the victim is compensated by a third party e.g., an insurance company, German law often provides for statutory subrogation rights.[27] Accordingly, the victim's rights are transferred to the third party *ex lege*

---

[24] A v. *National Blood Authority* [2002] Lloyd's Rep. Med. 487.

[25] See Basil Markesinis and Hannes Unberath, *The German Law of Torts: A Comparative Treatise* (4th edn, 2002), p. 904 (henceforth referred to as *GLT*); BGH 10 November 1998, BGHZ 140, 39, 42; Pickel, SGB X, § 116 no. 19.

[26] MünchKomm-BGB/Oetker § 249 BGB no. 227.

[27] e.g., §§ 116 Sozialgesetzbuch X (Verwaltungsverfahren; Administrative Procedure Act), 87a Bundesbeamtengesetz, 30 para. 2 Soldatengesetz, 6 Entgeltfortzahlungsgesetz, 67 para. 1 Versicherungsvertragsgesetz.

to the extent that he has indemnified the victim.[28] A tort action of the victim himself will then be dismissed by the court.[29] Moreover, the subrogation occurs at the moment of the accident and results in the victim automatically and immediately losing all control over the claim (or part of the claim) which he may have,[30] i.e., the victim can no longer dispose of his claim. Therefore, claims settlement between the victim and the tortfeasor or his insurer would be ineffective in respect of the 'innocent absentee'.[31] Where statutory subrogation is not provided for, the victim may be obliged to confer his claim against the tortfeasor on the insurer or another institution which has already compensated him for his loss.[32]

## Social security payments

### Vorteilsausgleichung

Payments/services which are rendered by the social security carrier may benefit the claimant, but not relieve the tortfeasor of his duty to compensate the victim.[33] Thus, it would not be reasonable, if these social security payments/services were to be deducted from the damages by way of 'Vorteilsausgleichung'.

## Subrogation according to § 116 SGB X

### Preconditions of a subrogation under § 116 SGB X
According to § 116 para. 1 SGB X the social security carrier can seek reimbursement from the wrongdoer or his insurance company, if the victim is entitled to claim compensation from the wrongdoer and if the social security carrier has compensated the victim fully or in part.

### Social security carrier
§ 116 para. 1 SGB X applies to services/payments of the social security carrier under the health insurance scheme, the retirement insurance scheme, the care insurance scheme and the accidents at work insurance scheme. The relevance of this rule can be illustrated by the following figures. In 2001, roughly 90 per cent of the population or 71 million people were

---

[28] See *GLT*, pp. 903, 904.    [29] BGH 28 September 1999, NJW 1999, 3711, 3712.
[30] See *GLT*, p. 903.
[31] BGH 30 November 1955, BGHZ 19, 177, 181; BGH 12 December 1995, NJW 1996, 726, 727 ff.
[32] 'Conventional subrogation', see *GLT*, p. 905; cf. p. 188.    [33] Pickel, SGB X, § 116 no. 19.

insured under the health insurance scheme.[34] In 1999, about 50.7 million were covered by the retirement insurance scheme which is generally applied to employees.[35] Furthermore, 36 million employees and 17 million students and pupils were insured under the accidents at work insurance scheme.[36] In addition, services/payments of the public welfare institutions (*Sozialhilfeträger*) or of the public employment agencies may also cause a subrogation according to § 116 para. 1 and 10 SGB X.

*Services/payments from the social security carrier*
The above-mentioned social security insurance schemes provide for many services in the case of their members being injured.[37] The social security carriers are obliged to compensate their insured members in many respects, for example in respect of medical treatment, loss of earnings, special needs etc. The compensation may be made *in natura* (medical treatment by doctors) or payment of money.

*Compensation must cover the victim's loss*
As to congruity of social security benefits and damages, see next paragraph.

*Kind of damage*
Subrogation occurs only when and insofar as the social security carrier has actually indemnified the victim for losses for which the tortfeasor was obliged to compensate. Two points are crucial in this context.

First, the purpose of the services and payments by the social security have to be determined. This is important to know, since the subrogation is limited to the type of loss for which the social security carrier has rendered services or compensated the victim.[38] Personal injuries often cause different types of losses, as for instance the loss of earnings or maintenance, the

---

[34] Sozialbericht [Social Report] 2001 of the German government, Teil B, no. 78 (www.bundeskanzler.de/Anlage18039/sozialbericht2001); Schulin and Igl, *Sozialrecht* (7th edn, 2002), nos 82, 155.

[35] Sozialbericht 2001, Teil B, no. 70 with reference to a statistic of the Verband Deutscher Rentenversicherungsträger. However, according to Schulin and Igl, *Sozialrecht* (7th edn, 2002), no. 82, only 44.3 million people are insured under this scheme with reference to the Sozialbericht 1997, Teil B, no. 68. These figures are taken from the Rentenversicherungsbericht [Retirement Insurance Report] 1997 of the German government.

[36] Schulin and Igl, *Sozialrecht* (7th edn, 2002), no. 82, with reference to the Sozialbericht 1997, Teil B, no. 84.

[37] *GLT*, p. 910.    [38] BGH 10 November 1998, BGHZ 140, 39, 42.

costs of medical treatment or funeral and special needs. Hence, if a victim is reimbursed for the costs of medical treatment under the statutory health insurance scheme, the carrier cannot take over the claim for loss of earnings as well but only the claim for the costs of medical treatment. As long as the social security carrier does not compensate a certain type of loss, the victim still has control over this part of the claim.[39] Accordingly, e.g., the victim's right to demand damages for pain and suffering cannot be transferred to any social security carrier, since compensation for pain and suffering is not provided for by any social security insurance scheme.[40]

Secondly, temporal congruity must also be ascertained. If the victim is prevented from working merely for two weeks, but the payments of the social security carrier were made for a longer period of time, the social security carrier can only seek reimbursement from the wrongdoer for those two weeks.[41] However, the court must take into account whether the earnings from a short period of employment would have been used for the time of unemployment and, if so, for how long. For example: if the victim who is permanently entitled to public welfare (*Sozialhilfe*) works only for a few months in a year, but these earnings are sufficient to live on for a whole year, the welfare agency can subrogate against the wrongdoer for the whole amount.[42]

### Amount of compensation

Even if a loss has been compensated by the social security carrier, the victim keeps control over his claim insofar as these payments/services did not fully cover this kind of loss.[43]

### Restrictions

*Family* A subrogation does not occur if the wrongdoer is a family member who lives with the victim and has not caused the injury deliberately (§ 116 VI SGB X). This exception has been enacted to safeguard family peace and takes account of the fact that the family lives on a common budget.[44]

---

[39] BGH 10 April 1979, VersR 1979, 640, 641; MünchKomm-BGB/Oetker § 249 BGB no. 449 (with many other examples in nos. 451–60).

[40] BGH 22 September 1970, VersR 1970, 1053, 1054; MünchKomm/Oetker § 249 BGB no. 454.

[41] MünchKomm-BGB/Oetker § 249 BGB no. 461 with reference to BGH 23 March 1973, LM RVO § 1542 no. 78.

[42] BGH 4 March 1997, NJW 1997, 2175, 2176.    [43] GLT, p. 910.

[44] For details see MünchKomm-BGB/Oetker § 249 BGB nos. 469–471.

*Contributory negligence* The social security carrier cannot recover the full amount which has been paid if there has been contributory negligence by the injured party (§ 116 para. 3 SGB X). The social security carrier can claim from the wrongdoer only a proportional amount in these cases.[45] For example: the victim had a loss of earnings amounting to €3,000 and receives €1,400 from the social security carrier. The victim's contributory fault amounts to 50 per cent. As a result, the tortfeasor's obligation to pay damages is 50 per cent out of €3,000, which is €1,500. Hence, the social security carrier can recover only the amount which it has paid to the victim in relation to the tortfeasor's fault. This is 50 per cent of €1,400 = €700. Therefore, the victim can still claim €800 in his tort action against the tortfeasor. As a result, the victim recovers €2,200 from the social security carrier and the tortfeasor.[46]

*Maximum rate of damage* § 116 para. 5 SGB X limits the subrogation or the transfer of the victim's right in respect of maximum rates of damages, as e.g., provided for in § 12 Strassenverkehrsgesetz. These rates normally include all types of loss (pain and suffering, loss of earnings etc.). If the victim's loss is higher than the maximum rate, the victim has to be fully indemnified first for 'his' part of the damages before the social security carrier can claim the part of damages the right to which has been transferred to him (preferential quota in favour of the victim, '*Quotenvorrecht*'). For example: the victim's loss amounts to €750,000 (€500,000 for loss of earnings and €250,000 for pain and suffering) and the maximum rate of damages is €600,000 (§ 12 Strassenverkehrsgesetz). So, if he receives €400,000 from the social security carrier for his loss of earnings, he still has a loss which amounts to €350,000. Therefore, he will be able to claim €350,000 in his tort action against the tortfeasor. Only thereafter can the social security carrier enforce its subrogated rights against the tortfeasor – but only up to the maximum limit of liability (€600,000), hence €250,000.

*Public welfare* (Sozialhilfe) If the victim is principally entitled to demand services from the public welfare institution and his rights are transferred to the respective carrier, even so he will be entitled to sue the wrongdoer for damages. The reason is that, according to § 2 Bundessozialhilfegesetz, social services are granted only if the victim is not capable of

---

[45] See MünchKomm-BGB/Oetker § 249 BGB no. 466.
[46] Example taken from MünchKomm-BGB/Oetker § 249 BGB no. 466.

paying for himself. Thus, the victim must first enforce his claims against the tortfeasor before he is entitled to public funds or continues to receive them.[47]

*Pension losses*

## In general

The BGH held that a loss is not to be compensated until the loss actually occurs.[48] Hence, the wrongdoer need not compensate a loss of pension until the victim has reached the age of retirement.

## Pension losses and the retirement insurance scheme

However, the tortfeasor may be obliged to prevent a future loss of pension. If the victim is employed at the time of the accident, the contributions of the employee to the social security insurance scheme, in particular the contributions to the retirement insurance scheme and the claims therefrom, are considered as part of the earnings that the victim would have made.[49] Therefore, the wrongdoer must also pay these contributions to ensure that the victim's future pension will not be decreased because of lost premiums. According to § 119 SGB X the claims to contributions to the retirement insurance scheme are transferred to the carrier of the retirement insurance scheme. As a result, it is not the victim who eventually recovers the contributions from the tortfeasor and passes them on to the retirement insurance scheme but it is the carrier of the retirement insurance scheme himself who takes over the claim. Furthermore, in accordance with § 62 SGB VI the wrongdoer must pay the contributions, even if a loss in premium would not cause a reduction of the victim's pension. This rule assumes a loss of pension which would not have occurred and is therefore criticised by some authors. Before § 62 SGB VI was enacted in 1992, the BGH, too, had denied a loss of pension in these cases, but this case law has now become obsolete.[50]

Although the legislator intended to have the amount of the contributions calculated on the basis of earnings at the time of the accident, the

---

[47] BGH 12 December 1995, NJW 1996, 726, 728.

[48] BGH 19 October 1993, VersR 1994, 186, 187; BGH 12 April 1983, VersR 1983, 663, 665.

[49] BGH 25 January 2000, NZV 2000, 252, 254; BGH 19 October 1993, VersR 1994, 186; BGH 12 April 1983, VersR 1983, 663.

[50] See now BGH 25 January 2000, NZV 2000, 252, 254; BGH 10 December 1991, BGHZ 116, 260, 267; BGH 9 May 1995, BGHZ 129, 366, 369; in the past BGH 18 October 1977, BGHZ 69, 347, 350; BGH 30 June 1987, BGHZ 101, 207, 211 denied a loss of pension.

BGH decided that the contributions have to be calculated on the basis of the earnings which the victim would have earned but for the accident.[51] However, the amount of contributions is to be diminished, if another social security carrier pays benefits to compensate for lost income (*Lohnersatzleistungen*), which also include contributions to the retirement insurance scheme (e.g., sick pay, workmen's compensation, unemployment benefits, etc.) for the victim. In these cases § 116 SGB X takes priority over § 119 SGB X and therefore the latter social security carrier will first be subrogated to the tort claim against the wrongdoer under § 116 SGB X. Afterwards, the carrier of the retirement insurance scheme can recover the balance from the defendant.[52]

The defendant must pay the contributions as long as the victim would have been in gainful employment. Therefore, he may be obliged to pay the contributions until the victim reaches retirement age.

## Pension losses and the occupational pension plan

The expenditures which the employer incurs in order to fulfil his pension promise are part of the employee's earnings which he would have had but for the injury.[53] If the employer is now obliged to continue to pay wages or premiums to the occupational pension plan, although his employee is prevented from working due to the injury,[54] he can recover these expenditures from the wrongdoer according to § 6 Entgeltfortzahlungsgesetz. Likewise, the employer can recover the expenditures, if he makes *ex gratia* payments and § 255 BGB can be applied analogously.[55]

However, if the employer is no longer bound to pay into the occupational pension plan, the victim cannot demand from the wrongdoer the expenditures which his employer would have made in order to contribute to the occupational pension scheme or to use them otherwise for himself. A resulting pension loss will not be compensated until the loss has materialised i.e., the victim has reached retirement age.

---

[51] BGH 25 January 2000, NZV 2000, 252, 253; cf. also Hauck-Haines/Nehls, SGB X/3 § 119 no. 25; Gerhard Küppersbusch, Ersatzansprüche bei Personenschäden, no. 574; but see Bundestag, Bundestags-Drucksache 9/95, 29.

[52] Cf. further § 170 I no. 2a SGB VI.

[53] BGH 7 July 1998, NJW 1998, 3276, 3278; BGH 11 November 1975, NJW 1976, 326, 327.

[54] Normally the employer must continue paying wages in accordance with the Entgeltfortzahlungsgesetz, but he can be obliged to do so also by employment contract or collective agreement.

[55] Cf. p. 188.

*Services/payments from the employer, insurer, family
and friends*

### Vorteilsausgleichung

Normally, payments/services from the employer, insurer or family and friends are granted to benefit the victim and not the tortfeasor. Therefore, a deduction of these benefits from the award by way of 'Vorteilsausgleichung' would be unreasonable, unless the payments/services are rendered for reasons other than compensation of the victim because of the injury[56] or even if the purpose of the payments/services is the relief of the wrongdoer.[57]

## Subrogation

*Services/payments from the employer*
Generally, the employer has to continue to pay the wages and salaries of his injured employees for a period of six weeks (§ 3 Entgeltfortzahlungs-gesetz). For this reason, § 6 Entgeltfortzahlungsgesetz provides for a subrogation in favour of the employer to the extent that he has paid wages according to § 3 Entgeltfortzahlungsgesetz. This includes the employee's gross earnings and the employer's part of the contributions to the social security insurance scheme. Likewise, § 87a Bundesbeamtengesetz or § 52 Beamtenrechtsrahmengesetz ensure a subrogation for the benefit of the public authorities who have similar obligations towards their injured public servants.

If the employer makes *ex gratia* payments although he is not under a legal duty to pay wages to his injured employee, he can demand that the employee cedes his claim to him. The BGH applied § 255 BGB analogously and held that the employee was obliged to cede his claim to the employer, if the employer had compensated his loss of earnings.[58] However, the employer cannot seek reimbursement for more than the gross earnings including the employer's contribution to the social security insurance scheme, even if he voluntarily pays more to the injured employee.

We have already said that under § 116 SGB X the rights of the victim are transferred to the social security carrier by operation of law at the

---

[56] *GLT*, p. 911. If the early retirement pension did not aim at compensating the victim for the consequences of the accident, but the purpose of the pension was to relieve pressure from the labour market, a 'Vorteilsausgleichung' would not unreasonably relieve the defendant, BGH 7 November 2000, NJW 2001, 1274, 1275.

[57] BGH 7 May 1975, BGHZ 64, 260, 266 in a case in which the defendant's insurer made the payments.

[58] BGH 22 June 1956, BGHZ 21, 112, 119; BGH 9 April 1964, BGHZ 41, 292, 294; BGH 23 May 1989, BGHZ 107, 325, 329.

moment of the accident. As a result, the victim cannot (fully) cede his claim to the employer who makes *ex gratia* payments. The recovery claim of the social security carrier has priority in this respect.

*Services/payments from the insurer*
See below.

*Services/payments by family and friends*
A statutory subrogation rule does not exist in this respect. Payments/ services rendered by family members or friends normally do not reduce the amount of damages which the tortfeasor has to pay. The victim is free to cede his claim, but he is not bound to do so.

## Insurance policies

There are various collateral sources of revenue in Germany, including private life insurances or insurances against the consequences of accidents.[59] The question whether benefits from such insurances have to be taken into account in assessing the damages of the victim is not regulated by statute in Germany.[60] The principles developed by the courts are summarised under the key-word '*Vorteilsausgleichung*'.[61] The courts look at the legislative intent of the rule which orders compensation and at the purpose of the contribution of third parties – are they paid for the benefit of the victim or to discharge the tortfeasor?[62]

With regard to private insurances, the following has to be distinguished: if accident insurance is taken out by the victim, the claim of the victim against the tortfeasor is transferred to the insurer when and insofar as he pays the damages (§ 67 I Versicherungsvertragsgesetz: '*cessio legis*'). From this it follows that the payments do not *reduce* the amount of damages the tortfeasor has to pay.[63] This rule does not apply, however, if the tortfeasor is a family member (§ 67 II VVG), or if the insurance has been taken out by the tortfeasor – in both cases it is the purpose of the insurance to give relief to him.

Where § 67 VVG does not apply (e.g., life insurances), the deductibility depends essentially upon the person who has taken out the

---

[59] See Hein Kötz and Gerhard Wagner, *Deliktsrecht* (9th edn, 2001), nos. 211–26.
[60] Note, however, § 843 IV BGB: maintenance payments by relatives have to be disregarded.
[61] See Christian von Bar, *Gemeineuropäisches Deliktsrecht* (1999), vol. II, p. 451 ff.
[62] The arguments in particular are very much like those put forward by British courts, see Basil Markesinis and Simon Deakin, *Tort Law* (5th edn, OUP, 2003), ch. 8.
[63] Staudinger/Schiemann § 249 BGB no. 159.

insurance: insurance taken out by the victim or by third parties to the benefit of the victim will not be taken into account.[64] This includes sickness insurance which entitles the victim to a certain amount of money per day in hospital (hospital per diem allowance insurance), or legal expenses insurance (with regard to the lawyer's fees of the victim).[65] However, if the insurance has been taken out by the wrongdoer (possibly in favour of the victim), the payments by the insurer have to be deducted.[66]

Finally, it should be noted that a liability insurance taken out by the tortfeasor may influence the amount of non-pecuniary damages awarded to the victim. Such damages have to be assessed as the court deems equitable and just in the case before it, and all factors of a case will be taken into account, including the financial situation of both parties. The liability insurance puts the tortfeasor on the same footing as 'rich' tortfeasors, and the damages will be assessed accordingly.[67]

*Interest*

Interest is payable on all damages as long as their object is the payment of money. As there are no special provisions in the law of torts, the general provisions of §§ 280 ff. BGB apply. Interest can thus be claimed for faulty delay of payment.

The payment of damages is due at the time the damage occurs. Delay of payment in principle requires the claimant to give a reminder, which is, however, dispensable in certain legally defined cases (§ 286 BGB).

If the plaintiff claims the payment of money, he is at any rate entitled to interest as from the time the suit is pending (§ 290 BGB). This also applies if the claimant makes use of the possibility to leave the amount of damages for non-pecuniary headings up to the discretion of the judge.[68]

The interest rate amounts to five points above the basis rate established by the Central European Bank (§ 288 I BGB).

A higher rate may be claimed if the plaintiff proves that he had the possibility and intention to invest the money more profitably or else that he had to borrow money at a higher interest rate for the period of the delay.[69] The basis for the claim then is § 280 I BGB as the loss of

---

[64] BGH 19 November 1955, BGHZ 19, 94, 99; BGH 17 November 1957, BGHZ 25, 322, 328; BGH 7 January 1969, VersR 1969, 350, 351; BGH 13 July 1971, NJW 1971, 2069, 2070; BGH 19 December 1978, NJW 1979, 760.

[65] OLG München 14 May 1959, VersR 1959, 957, 959; MünchKomm-BGB/Oetker § 249 BGB no. 248.

[66] MünchKomm-BGB/Oetker § 249 BGB no. 248.    [67] BGH 6 July 1955, BGHZ 18, 149, 165 ff.

[68] BGH 5 January 1965, NJW 1965, 1376.

[69] Palandt/Heinrichs (62nd edn, 2003), § 288 BGB nos. 4, 12 ff.

interest or the interest paid to the bank are a damage resulting from the delay.

The claim is, however, not to be reduced if the creditor's actual damage falls short of the standard rate as in § 288 I BGB.[70] For this claim, it is in fact not even necessary for there to have been an actual loss or payment of interest at all.[71]

## Limitation periods

### Basic rules

After the reform of the law of obligations, there is in general no special period of limitation for tort claims. The general limitation period of three years (§ 195 BGB) also applies to such claims.

According to § 199 I BGB, this general period begins at the end of the year in which the claim came into existence and the creditor has or negligently has not, any knowledge of it and of the person of the debtor.

For the existence of the claim, it is mandatory that the damage was suffered by the claimant. At that moment, the limitation period begins for all damages resulting from the tortious act, even if further damage occurs only later.[72] Knowledge of the claim in the sense of § 199 I BGB means knowledge of all facts that are the basis of its existence. These facts are essentially the violating act, the tortfeasor's negligence, the damage as such, as well as the fact that the claimant is himself affected by the damage.[73] It is, however, not required that the claimant is informed of every detail or all circumstances. It is sufficient that there are reasonable prospects for a civil action.[74]

An error in law does not prevent knowledge.[75]

## Maximum periods

Additionally, maximum limitation periods are stated in § 199 II–IV BGB. As for claims for damages, the maximum limitation period depends on the kind of injury. § 199 II BGB states that claims for damages resulting from a violation of either life, body, health or freedom, as do most claims under tort law, are limited to thirty years from the date of the tortious

---

[70] Palandt/Heinrichs (62nd edn, 2003), § 288 BGB no. 4.
[71] BGH 26 April 1979, BGHZ 74, 231.     [72] BGH 15 October 1992, NJW 1993, 648, 650.
[73] BGH 15 October 1992, NJW 1993, 648 ff.
[74] BGH 17 February 2000, NJW 2000, 1498; BGH 6 March 2001, NJW 2001, 1721.
[75] BGH 25 February 1999, NJW 1999, 2041.

act. It is of no relevance when the claim actually arose or whether the claimant had knowledge of it.

For other claims for damages, § 199 III BGB provides a double-tracked model which is independent of the creditor's knowledge or negligent lack of knowledge. According to § 199 III no. 1 BGB, the limitation period for other claims for damages than those named in § 199 II BGB is ten years from the date of their coming into existence. Additionally, there is a maximum limitation period in § 199 III no. 2 of thirty years from the date of the tortious act, regardless of the date when the victim's claim came into existence.

## Interruption and suspension of limitation periods

German civil law distinguishes between the interruption and the suspension of limitation periods (§§ 203 ff. BGB).

Subsequent to an interruption, the limitation period begins to run anew for its full length. According to § 212 I BGB, the limitation period is interrupted when the creditor acknowledges the claim or an act of judicial execution is performed concerning the claim.

The suspension only hinders the running or ending of the limitation period for the time being (§ 209 BGB). The most important cases of suspension are the filing of a lawsuit or comparable motions that aim at enforcing the claim (§ 204 I BGB). The limitation period is also suspended during negotiations concerning the claim (§ 203 BGB); in this case, the limitation period ends no sooner than three months after the end of the negotiations.

There are other reasons for the suspension of the limitation period: a persisting familial relationship between creditor and debtor, force majeure or the infringement of sexual self-determination (§§ 205–211 BGB).

### Persons under a disability

The estates and the income of a child are administered by his parents, if they have parental responsibility (*Vermögenssorge*) (§§ 1626 I, 1638–1649 BGB), otherwise by guardians who have been appointed by the court (*Pfleger*) (§§ 1909 BGB or '*Vormund*', 1773 ff. BGB). If the injured party is not a child but is unable to care for his own interests, his assets or income will be administered by persons who had been given power of agency by the injured party himself (at a time when he was still capable of acting for himself), or by a court-appointed guardian (*Betreuer*) (§ 1896 BGB).

If the *parents* act for their child, they have great discretion over how to invest a lump sum or other capital paid to the victim. According to § 1652 BGB, their investment decisions have to be economically reasonable e.g., the investment has to be safe, on the one hand, but also profitable on the other hand.[76] Within these broadly defined limits the parents are free to act on behalf of the child. The family court has the power to intervene if they disregard these limits (§§ 1666 I, II, 1667 BGB), but this power is used only in cases of severe parental mismanagement.[77] If the injured child is paid an annuity instead of a lump sum, this will be treated like income or maintenance of the child. It has to be used to meet the living expenses and other needs of the child (§ 1649 BGB).

If the administrator is a *guardian* (for a child or a disabled adult), he is less free than parents: He is bound by a statutory catalogue of the admissible forms of investment (§§ 1806, 1807, 1908 i BGB), and even then he should ask for court permission (§ 1810 BGB). He may, however, propose other forms of investment, which have to be approved by the court (§ 1811 BGB). Under no circumstances is the guardian entitled to use money received by his ward for himself (§§ 1805, 1908 i; parents are in a slightly better position: § 1649 II BGB).

The costs of property administration by third parties are part of the 'damages' which have to be paid by the wrongdoer, if the inability of the victim to act for himself is the consequence of his injury (e.g., an adult has become mentally disabled because of medical malpractice). If an already incapable person has been injured, however, the need for administration of his assets is not caused by the injury, and the costs are not compensable.

If parents are the administrators, they may not claim money for their own expenditures (§ 1648 BGB). The costs and fees of guardians are regulated in detail by a statute (§§ 1835–1836, 1908 i BGB).

These principles apply also when an injured child will never become able to manage his own affairs: until the age of eighteen, he is cared for by his parents according to the above-mentioned rules; afterwards, the court has to appoint guardians for him (these might well be the parents who, from now on, are subject to the law on guardians, but also entitled like guardians).

---

[76] Staudinger/Engler (2000) § 1642 BGB no. 7.
[77] For examples see Staudinger/Coester (2000) § 1666 BGB no. 171.

## Italian law

### Introductory observations

Under the Italian legal system as well, the guiding principle is that the victim will recover damages for his loss (qualified in legal terms and quantity). But since a balance has to be struck between the competing interests of the two sides – injurer and injured – he cannot receive more than that. As the Roman maxim put it '*nemo locupletari potest aliena iactura*'. So the victim is a creditor who cannot ask from the debtor more than is due according to law and must not end up by making a profit. This means that double compensation is prohibited; and if another person, besides the tortfeasor, performs this obligation, the victim cannot claim compensation from the tortfeasor as well.

In the case of joint liability e.g., when the injury is caused by a minor, and his parents are also liable,[78] or by an employee, and the employer is liable as well,[79] the victim can sue the tortfeasor and the person jointly liable with him. Of course, in such cases he will receive compensation only once. In special cases (e.g., car accident insurance) the victim can use the '*azione diretta*' – the direct action – against the insurer of the tortfeasor, thus saving time and effort. The solution is, of course, well known to most legal systems.

When the victim receives some profit from the accident, another principle is usually applied, '*compensatio lucri cum damno*,' so that the profit is deducted from the recovery. But this rule is not always applied in cases concerning damages for personal injury.

### Social security payments

Social security payments are provided by two national institutions, according to the state or condition of the beneficiary. The Istituto nazionale della providenza sociale (INPS) provides assistance and pensions to persons suffering from a disability. These include blind people, physically impaired persons and the elderly who are resident in Italy, have no revenue, or revenue below €4,666.41 per year. The monthly allowance amounts to €295.85.

According to article 14 of the statute governing this subject matter (Law no. 22 of 12 June 1984), the social security carrier (INPS) can be subrogated in the victim's rights and recover all the losses caused by the tortfeasor if it provides the social pension to the victim.

---

[78] On the basis of art. 2048 cod. civ.   [79] On the basis of art. 2049 cod. civ.

The national health system ('*sistema sanitario nazionale*, SSN) is governed by a special statute;[80] local hospitals are obliged to give assistance to all in need. The above-mentioned social security insurance schemes also provide for services to their members in cases where they have been injured while already members, or where they become members due to the accident.

Case law draws a sharp distinction between the sums or services offered to the victim by the social security systems and the sums due from a private insurer. The first must be given in any case, and they cannot be calculated in the recovery, except for INAIL. This means that the principle '*compensatio lucri cum damno*' does not usually apply in connection with social security services. The rules concerning INAIL form an exception to the rule introduced by case law. The reason is that the obligation arising from the health system or social pension system is based on the law, while the obligation of recovery is based on the tort.[81]

## Insurance policies

Private insurance may be connected with the consequences of the accidents. According to EC Directives, insurance for car accidents is mandatory in Italy.[82] As stated, the injured person is given a direct claim against the insurer.[83] He can receive only the maximum amount provided by the insurance contract. If the injured party cannot obtain full compensation from the insurance, he must ask for the difference from the tortfeasor. If the tortfeasor is unknown, or if he is known but did not comply with the mandatory rules concerning car insurance or, finally, if the insurance company has gone bankrupt, the injured party can claim damages from the Guarantee Fund for Car Accident Victims[84] which does not provide complete compensation for the victim, but just an indemnity which is the subject of negotiation between the victim and the Fund.

The victim who could recover damages from the insurer of the tortfeasor cannot claim damages also from the tortfeasor. All compensation received by the insurer is deducted from the amount of damages the tortfeasor has to pay.[85]

As to the insurer of the victim himself, there is not a uniform interpretation of the principles of the law applied to the cases. This uncertainty

---

[80] See Legislative Decree no. 229 of 19 June 1999.
[81] Cass. 1 July 1994, no. 6228, Riv. giur. Enel, 1996, 467.
[82] See Law no. 990 of 24 December 1969 and susbsequent modifications.
[83] *Ibid.*, art. 18.    [84] *Ibid.*, art. 20.    [85] Cass. 7 October 1997, no. 9742.

also applies to the judges of the Supreme Court, some of whom favour the application of the principle 'compensatio lucri cum damno' (as in the decision mentioned above). Others, however, believe that this principle should not be applied so they allow the victim to ask his own insurer for the compensation due for the accident.[86]

### Interest

In Italian law the violation of personality rights (e.g., injury to personal health) is considered a loss which results in a debt of 'value' (debito di valore), which is converted into a debt of money only at the moment of the liquidation of damages ('debito di valuta').[87] Since it has been converted into an obligation of money (pecuniary obligation, 'obbligazione pecuniaria'), article 1224 cod. civ. applies. Usually 'legal interest' is due, i.e., the rate determined every year by the Treasury Department.

### Limitation period

According to the Civil Code, the right to compensation for damages aris-ing from unlawful acts lapses five years from the date on which the act occurred.[88] With respect to damages arising from the circulation of vehi-cles of any kind, the right to compensation lapses in two years (article 2). In products liability cases, according to the statute concerning this sub-ject,[89] the limitation period is three years. Different limitation periods are connected with crimes, and for personal injury cases.

As to the date from which the period begins, case law draws a distinc-tion between injuries with permanent effects and injuries with temporary effects. In the first case the period begins when the temporary effects have disappeared.[90]

The Civil Code distinguishes between suspension and interruption of limitation periods.[91] In tort law, for example, the limitation period is suspended if the injury has been brought against a minor or a handicapped person, and they lacked legal representatives. It is interrupted when the creditor acknowledges the claim, or when the creditor begins any judicial execution concerning the claim.

---

[86] Cass. 10 February 1999, no. 1135.
[87] Cass. 11 June 1992, no. 7194, Foro it., 1992, I, 2079.
[88] See art. 2947 § 1.    [89] Presidential Decree no. 224 of 24 May 1988.
[90] Cass. 4 February 1992, no. 1210.    [91] See art. 2941 ff.

# 6    Conclusions

## General observations

This monograph has been concerned with the law of damages in three major European legal systems. In accordance with the proclaimed belief of one of us,[1] and in this instance also shared by all of its co-authors, this study has targeted mainly (but not exclusively) judges and international practitioners not only in order to inform them about an area of tort law of growing international significance, but also in the belief that they are the most important propagators of the comparative study of the law. Wider reflections of a more speculative nature have, on the whole, thus been restricted to the Introduction and the Conclusions; and they are concerned with mainly two issues.

The first is how to present the law of one country to lawyers of another in a way that makes sense to them. We have referred to this problem as being one of 'suitable packaging'. Readers must not be put off by a term which could be seen in a pejorative light. The packaging does not alter the product; it just makes it more saleable. National laws have their own intrinsic value. The systems under comparison also have their own long and very respectable history to support and explain their national solutions. Last but by no means least, their lawyers have their own ways of expressing their thoughts; and we are not here referring simply to

---

[1] See, e.g., Basil Markesinis, *Comparative Law in the Courtroom and the Classroom* (Hart Publishing 2003). In a similar vein, *Foreign Law, and Comparative Methodology* (1997) and *Always on the Same Path* (Hart Publishing, 2001), both containing essays in comparative private and public law, and explaining why judges rather than academics are, potentially, the most important *human* resource for promoting the study of foreign law. We italicise *human* for, naturally, impersonal phenomena, such as the current globalisation of markets and business, are providing an even greater impetus for the study of foreign law.

special features of the grammar of each national language. But all these 'individual' or 'peculiar' characteristics also make them indigestible to 'outsiders' unless 'served' in an attractive way. That is where the issue of packaging enters the scene; and it is one which raises interesting and controversial methodological issues.

Our second concern has been to warn readers that if a concept or an idea is, or appears to be, missing in one system it does not mean that the practical concern behind it is not addressed in a different way. This theme is interlinked with the previous one; and if successfully tackled, the two themes together are meant to suggest to readers – judges, practitioners, academics, students – ways of looking at foreign law in order to understand it better.

Yet even here, the transnational litigation phenomenon – in our view likely to increase and not decrease in the years to come – has not been far from our minds. And that is why in this last chapter we have broadened the brush-strokes to cover, *where necessary*, the picture in the USA. Inevitably, and to the extent that these statements refer to the situation 'in America' (as an abbreviation for the law of fifty-one jurisdictions), they are of a generalised nature. They also appear to go beyond the self-imposed parameters of this book. Notwithstanding the above, we have added them here for two reasons.

First is the fact that the gradual expansion of the American class action so as to have 'international effects' is leading American courts and American lawyers to enquire about foreign law. This is an important audience for this book. The question, which our book tries to answer, is not focused on what one could call the 'substantive' part of the (foreign) law of tort – is there a 'notion of a duty of care?', 'which theory of causation do the German courts adopt?' or 'what alternatives do we have to the tort system?' – on which there is a fair amount of academic discussion, but on the 'remedial' part of tort law which has not been well served by academic literature. Here the questions, in their simplest form, are: 'can the claimant obtain damages for this or that heading of damage?' (in this book formulated in accordance with the Anglo-American taxonomy without even pausing to ask the question if this is the same in other systems) and, if so, 'how much'?

In our view, and on the basis of the practical experience of two of the authors of this study, an American court (or practitioner) is unlikely to 'understand' the foreign solution – English, German, Italian or any other – simply by being told that, say, in Germany or Italy they do not recognise punitive damages but in England they do; or that German law (like

American law) also recognises strict liability for harm caused by defective products. Such answers, correct at one level, are inadequate or even misleading at another. For they fail to take into account a variety of other factors which affect the final result and thus give rise to wrong impressions for the 'foreign' lawyer who encounters them. Some of these factors have been mentioned in the preceding narrative; others will be touched upon in this conclusion; but they must be taken into account since they help put the foreign law in its proper context.

The American-propelled internationalisation of tort law and practice is thus one reason why we venture here into some of the features of that system's law even though otherwise it is not the main subject of our enquiry. Once again, this represents an acknowledgement of the fact that this book might prove 'of use' to American transnational litigation. 'Use' here is italicised for we think it would be of little use to provide practitioners with detailed lists of amounts of damages awarded for the loss of an eye, an imploding breast – the *Dow Corning* terminology – or total blindness. Such figures, even if they could be assembled accurately, would change over time. The law of damages is a fast moving subject, so a snapshot of it is only of a limited value. Instead, we thus chose to give our readers some idea of levels of damages but set them in the national contexts and tried to show how they are worked out, why they can be elusive, how they came to be recognised and questions of that kind. For anyone who pauses to think about these matters, this is a tall order. But that is the difference between a monograph and a loose-leaf practitioner's manual.

The second reason why we cannot allow American law to escape our mind completely is of an even more academic nature. Simply put, it is because we wish to lay the foundations for a future argument namely, that English law – in some areas of the law but not in all – is moving closer to the European systems and in many respects is refusing to espouse American ideas and trends. This is a bold thesis to stomach.[2] For Continental European lawyers often believe English and American law to be very similar; and English lawyers are romantically attached to the belief that the famous 'special relationship' between the two countries is still alive in the legal world as many believe it is in the political sphere. To achieve this aim, we have to jump out of the main area of investigation

---

[2] Perhaps less bold or surprising when one considers that European law has become so much part of the domestic law of each EU member state. So, e.g., *A v. National Blood Authority* [2001] 3 All ER 289, where Burton J looked at the Product Liability Directive 1985/374 directly rather than the provisions of the Consumer Protection Act 1987. See [2001] Lloyd's Rep. Med. 187 at 190 col. 2.

and invite the reader to reflect upon the American material against its well-known, wider background. It is precisely because this background is so well known that we feel we can refer to it without doing too much injustice to American law in its full (nuanced, complex and sophisticated) beauty. So what is this background which affects their tort law in practice and also colours their view about our laws?

## The wider background

The law of damages cannot be separated, nor properly understood, apart from the substantive law which determines whether there is a cause of action and what is its proper ambit. European lawyers, who in the 1970s were reforming their law of product liability, often fell under the fascination of American law by ignoring this simple but essential truth. The reverse is also true, namely, that the substantive law of a particular system may be explicable by the fact that its law of damages is less generous than others.[3]

This warning is even more important in international tort practice. For it is almost meaningless to try to work out the measure of damages a claimant might potentially try to claim without taking into account whether the rules of substantive law establish fault or strict liability, what role is played by social security (and other auxiliary sources of compensation), whether a particular legal system recognises subrogation rights against the defendant (or can seek recoupment from the *victim*/claimant), how litigation is financed, and the like. Ignoring these background factors can make a system look similar to another when, in fact, it is very different. Conversely, it might make a legal system seem mean or ungenerous, especially if compared to American law. This, for instance, is likely to happen when one 'forgets' that in most European countries medical expenses can (and often are) covered by the state or other social security carriers. This is not the case in American law with the result that American tort law has to be more generous than German or Italian if it is not to leave a deserving victim totally (or almost totally) without redress. Here, then, is one important difference between, on the one hand English and

---

[3] An illustration of this can be found in the domain of tortious liability for breach of statutory duties imposed on the state or other state organs. At one level, the differences between English and French law are thus substantial. At another level, however, these differences may be attenuated. The greater willingness of French law to impose liability may, in part, be explicable by the (apparently) lower levels of awards. On this, see Duncan Fairgrieve, *State Liability in Tort* (OUP, 2003), passim.

Continental European law and, on the other, American law.[4] The American reader of this work must thus make allowances for the fact that European awards are lower.

In our experience, differences (and similarities) of this kind do not (and often cannot) emerge from the mere study of books. On the contrary, they manifest themselves gradually as one gets a deeper appreciation of how the foreign system works in practice. In short, what one needs to do is to try to understand the law in action; and that does not come easily except to those who have either lived abroad, studied abroad, done business abroad or, better still, all three. This law-in-action approach thus involves looking at other branches of the law besides tort law proper. The way trials are conducted (i.e., with or without juries) is thus an issue of paramount importance, as is the question 'how is litigation financed?': through legal aid, insurance coverage, contingent fees or a combination of some or all. These are factors which may not only affect the size of awards but also ancillary rules relevant to the law of damages such as the collateral source rule (as we explain briefly later on). More importantly (and as already stated), they may make awards appear larger or smaller than they really are; and in the law of transnational tort litigation one must always try to avoid the danger of comparing 'apples with oranges'.

To these 'procedural' factors one must add the decisive, persuasive or partially significant role that other semi-official reports may play in the commencing of a legal action and, therefore, in the likely award of damages at the end of the entire process. Because of lack of space, we offer here one example drawn from our own experience; but others could easily be given.

In the *Dow Corning* international litigation, the impact of preliminary reports prepared by medical officials of the government had a significant outcome both at the level of national litigation and at the level of the final, international settlement. In England, for instance,[5] reports coming from the Chief Medical Officer of the government, to the effect that silicone had

---

[4] Conversely, the European Convention on Human Rights may have, unwittingly or otherwise, widened the ambit of those situations in which a person can be compensated for injury. The attempt by the English courts to narrow the scope of the duty of care in *X (Minors)* v. *Bedfordshire County Council* [1995] 2 AC 633 has been limited by two decisions of the ECHR, namely *Osman* v. *United Kingdom* [1999] 1 FLR 193 and *Z* v. *United Kingdom* [2000] 2 LGLR 212.

[5] In Germany, as well, similar 'official' reports were produced. Though they were vindicated by the sparse litigation that ensued from this tragedy, they did not, however, appear to have stopped it altogether as they seem to have done in England. The German and English position thus seem to be closer to one another than either is to the

not been shown conclusively to have the deleterious effects attributed to it by the claimants, seemed to have worked decisively against their attempts to obtain legal aid and commence litigation.[6] Similar reports in the USA were, on the other hand, deemed to have had much less value and thus were of less influence in commencing litigation. To put it differently, in the USA there was no preliminary hurdle to overcome in order to show that there was an arguable case in order to obtain the necessary funds to commence litigation, whereas in England there was. These are not factors which immediately spring to mind when one is considering suing in another country[7] or are taken into account when attempting to compare the generosity of the tort awards made by the respective systems. Yet they are important, as two of the authors of this work found out when they were professionally involved in two such international settlements.[8]

The law of damages, and some of its related issues such as the capping of awards, must also be examined closely with respect to the prevailing systems of social security available for accident and disease. This is important for at least three reasons.

First, an award made to the plaintiff for various types of medical expenses will invariably make American awards larger (or seem larger) than they are since many of these items are, in the European (and other) systems, covered directly by the state (or other social security carriers) and may not always and immediately be visible. One could even go further and argue that the non-existence of these (different) sources of compensation in the USA may, in part at least, justify the larger awards one often finds in that continent.

---

American. These nuances must not escape the attention of either the comparatist or the practitioner.

[6] This is not always the case. The persistent efforts of the government to promote the MMR vaccine did not prevent the Legal Services Commission from granting public funding to autistic children who claimed that their condition was due to the vaccine: *Sayers* v. *SmithKline Beecham plc* [2002] EWHC 1280.

[7] Forum shopping is limited, at least amongst European states, by the terms of the Brussels Regulation or Convention. However, courts in almost every jurisdiction can assess damages on the basis of the law of the country in which the claimant resides. Thus, American courts have accepted jurisdiction to try a tort action but applied English law to questions of quantum in a number of cases. That was, e.g., the decision of the court in Florida trying claims arising from the explosion of a motor boat at a resort in St Lucia. English claimants stayed actions in England and joined an action in Florida only to find that their award was restricted to damages recoverable in England and at the rates normally awarded in England.

[8] *Bowling* v. *Pfizer (Shiley Heart Valve Litigation)* sub nom. *Bowling* v. *Pfizer Inc.* 143 F.R.D. 141 (S. D. Ohio 1992) and 159 F.R.D. 492 (S. D.Ohio 1994) *and Dow Corning (Silicone Breast Implant Litigation)* sub nom. *In Re Dow Corning* 255 B.R. (Bankr E.D. Mich 2000).

Secondly, the existence of these parallel systems of compensation must at least trigger off thoughts (concerns?) about subrogation or return of money received by claimants. To put it differently, is it not possible that part of an award made by an American court to a French or German claimant might well end up going into the account of some other 'payer' (insurance, social security carrier)? Knowing which head of damages is covered by these rules can thus make a difference at the end of the day.[9] But on this score, the European legal systems do not speak with one voice with the result that in many cases part of these awards never actually reaches the claimant's hands.

Thirdly, and on a purely intellectual level, one must, occasionally at least, raise the question whether one could not eliminate some types of litigation by replacing the adversarial tort process with a different way of handling the vicissitudes of daily life.[10] Generosity may in some cases be best sacrificed to speed. Likewise, legal entrepreneurship may have to be made to yield to a more bureaucratic way of remedying the consequences of accidents if it means more money reaching more claimants rather than being absorbed by the actors of a legal dispute. Uniformity, finally, may win over diversity (often excessive and even capricious). These are not only changes worth considering; they are changes which will exact a price, both literally and metaphorically. On the other hand, this price may well be worth paying – at any rate for some types of accident-causing situations. Thus, in German practice, full litigation of matters of medical malpractice leading to physical harm is avoided through administrative adjudication of such disputes. If the awards made in such cases may strike some – especially American lawyers – as small, they are also achieved with a relatively low level of hassle; and this, too, is worth something!

There is another economic and not legal kind of consideration which must be carefully weighed in transnational litigation, though, hitherto, it has received little attention by academics and even practitioners. This is linked to the different wealth of different nations or, to put it more

---

[9] English courts are very much alive to this problem. In the case of a foreign resident suing in England the court will be required to decide (where it is in issue) where the claimant is likely to reside and what the rates are in that country for the cost of care, housing etc. This can, however, work both ways. If a seriously injured claimant is a patient and is likely to return to his or her native land, the cost of administering the damages may be much higher than in England. That is the case, e.g., in South Africa.

[10] The peculiarities of the national workmen's compensation schemes is another factor which must be taken into account, for the extent to which national schemes exclude recourse to tort law can have a significant bearing on what the successful claimant can receive.

mundanely, the differences in the per capita income and the cost of living of the various nations of the world.

At first blush this may seem an odd consideration to try and factor into any internationally-flavoured class action settlement. After all, victims of defective products – usually pharmaceutical – or those affected by transborder pollution (or other such torts) are suffering similar injuries from the same product, often marketed under similar or identical conditions. Why should the legal consequences of things going wrong lead to a different legal treatment at the compensation phase of the process? After all, humans are the same the world over; and are not 'worth' more in some systems and less in others. But that is where different state wealth, differing annual national incomes and the different purchasing power of some currencies, enter the calculation.[11]

The questions advanced above, so obviously in favour of equal treatment of plaintiffs the world over, are thus seriously weakened when one takes into account national incomes and standards of living. For why should a woman, literally on or below the poverty line in India, or Somalia, or Nigeria, become a millionaire by the standards of her own country for having received a defective heart valve designed in the USA by Shelley-Borg or suffering from an 'imploding' silicon breast implant?[12] And if one were to remark that such examples are exaggerated if applied to the poorest women of some of the world's poorest countries, one can retort that other toxic torts, such as the Bhopal incident in Northern India approximately two decades ago, can raise essentially the same type of questions and objections against equal treatment. And in between, one can envisage a whole host of examples, involving claimants from poor, moderately rich, to rich countries where incomes, earning capacity and a variety of legal rules combine to produce much smaller awards. In such cases, the arguments against equal compensation are less convincing

---

[11] However, it is essential if justice is to be done that the awards should properly compensate the victims. In England, as in the USA, there is a Vaccine Damage Compensation Scheme. The limit of compensation is £30,000 irrespective of the seriousness of the injury. In many cases that is wholly insufficient. Contrast the position in the USA where proper compensation is provided to a successful applicant to the scheme.

[12] The awards made by the Foreign Fracture Panel in the *Shiley Heart Valve* litigation, n. 8 above, took careful account of these differences both in relation to poor nations and those where either earnings and/or the cost of living was higher than in the USA. In order for justice to be done it was necessary to ensure, as far as possible, that the amounts awarded were truly compensatory and neither provided a windfall to the claimant nor left them short of sufficient money to meet their future needs.

than one might think at first instance.[13] The downscaling of American awards in a way that is even moderately appropriate for each of these systems becomes a complex exercise[14] which, it must be admitted, can only attempt to reach an overall 'fair' conclusion.

The necessity to attempt the above task, however distasteful it may be in some of its aspects, will become more obvious as the early attempts in the USA on extending class settlements to overseas (probably)[15] gains momentum. But the exercise at that stage becomes not just potentially unsavoury but also very complex since it involves evidence about how the compensation systems of foreign countries work in practice. Collecting reliable information about law, access to courts, judicial delays, costs, standards of available medical treatment and the like is as difficult as getting a realistic picture of the economic standard of living in many countries of the world. For, generally speaking, the statistical and electronic evidence available in the USA to answer these questions is excellent, as it is good (or fairly good) for most Continental European countries. Such confidence in accessing the relevant data can be extended to countries such as Israel, South Africa, Japan and, of course, Australia, Canada and New Zealand (to give some of the most obvious examples). But the difficulties become increasingly frustrating as one moves to other countries and systems which, for better or worse, are less known to practitioners and academics and for which it is simply impossible to find experts to testify in court, short of augmenting the numbers already called to unworkable limits.

---

[13] See above. True equality is to be found in meeting the needs of the individual, not in the amount of the award. For example, a claimant should be compensated for loss of earnings by an amount equal to what they would, on the balance of probabilities, have been able to earn in the country in which they reside and not by a comparison with what a similar individual might have earned in a different country.

[14] It was attempted in the USA for the first time in *Bowling v. Pfizer, Inc.* 143 F.R.D. 141 (S. D. Ohio 1992); *Bowling v. Pfizer, Inc.* 159 F.R.D. 492 (S. D. Ohio 1994). Two of the authors of this book (Basil Markesinis and Augustus Ullstein) were members of the panel of experts that helped design the formula which is described in detail by Professor Harold Luntz (also a panel member) in his illuminating (and partly critical) article 'Heart Valves, Class Actions and Remedies: Lessons for Australia?' in Nicholas Mullany (ed.), *Torts in the Nineties* (1997), p. 72 ff. The principles were subsequently applied in *In Re Dow Corning Corporation* 255 B.R. 445 (Bankr. E. D. Mich. 2000), a case in which the above-mentioned three lawyers were, again, involved.

[15] Given the cost of defending mass action in the USA, the desire of American companies, faced with class actions, to reach worldwide settlements is not, in our view, to be underestimated. But we have injected a word of caution in our text, above, for in at least one European country – Germany – considerable doubts have been voiced about class actions. The Constitutional Court took this view in its judgment of 25 July 2003, BVerfG NJW 2003, 2598.

It is here that comparative methodology can play a part to alleviate these problems. For comparative methodology can help trace the movement of ideas from one 'parent' (or exporting) system to an 'importer' and then, in a variety of different ways, try to make allowances for local variations. The Korean Civil Code, for instance, can trace its origins to the French which, as is well known, acted as a model for a substantial number of legal systems in the world. If the French codal model, however, is based (as it is) on the notion of fault, the search must then extend to specific statutes (often consumer in nature) which have tried to alleviate the codal harshness. As this shift from primary legislation moves into a more specific regime, other dangers, connected with local social habits, begin to become apparent. True enough, the relevant Korean statute at the time of the *Dow Corning* litigation[16] was said to be used not, as an American strict liability statute would be, to facilitate the case of a plaintiff, but as a spur towards some kind of extra-judicial conciliation given the (known) far-Eastern dislike for litigation.[17] Citing these enactments before an American court could thus easily lead to the erroneous belief that the Korean implantee of a silicon breast was more or less in the same position as the American. But she is not. And that is why so many Korean litigants tried to receive the same treatment as their American counterparts. The different level of damages was not the only reason; the difficulty of bringing a successful action in Korea was also an important factor. The Korean litigants in the *Dow Corning* cases thus had to settle for lower amounts than their American counterparts; and did so not just because of rules of law but also because of a complex evaluation of a wide variety of factors.

'Applied' comparative law thus holds part of the answer to these types of questions and issues which we suspect will increase not decrease with the passage of time. We call it 'applied' for, as one of us explained in a monograph recently published,[18] these kinds of real issues will help revive the comparative study of the legal systems of the world. But this revival

---

[16] Since then, a new (Korean) Product Liability Act (in force since 1 July 2002) has expanded manufacturers' liability by introducing strict liability for defective products. This latest change is reviewed in General Cologne Re, Special Report from Phi5/2001: see www.gcr.com/sharedfile/pdf/PHi20015-KoreanPLA.pdf

[17] The English courts under the CPR have moved towards mediation and ADR. They now have the power to order a stay to enable the parties to mediate. That may be done of the court's own motion: CPR 26.4. Further, the Court of Appeal refused the successful party their costs because they had refused to consider mediation (*Dunnett* v. *Railtrack plc (in railway administration)* [2002] EWCA Civ 303; [2002] 1 WLR 2434).

[18] Basil Markesinis, *Comparative Law in the Courtroom and the Classroom* (Hart Publishing, 2003).

will also mean that comparative law or methodology will have to move away from legal history and Roman law and even trendy subjects such as feminist or critical legal studies and get its teeth into the law in action and its actual functions in practice. Such a re-orientation of the subject should not cause concern to academic purists. For the exercise involved is not just relevant; it is also intellectually stretching and, indeed, very stimulating. In its need also to involve data from other disciplines such as politics, economics, statistics etc., it will also fit in well with the prevailing trend in the leading universities of the Western world to approach law in an interdisciplinary manner.

The above general observations form part of the beliefs which underlie this book. But we have tried to flesh them out by providing solid, legal evidence about the rules which shape the law of damages in three major European legal systems. The aim thus is obvious: to facilitate the theoretical and practical attempts to note and then study the areas of divergence and convergence which can then be put to some kind of applied use. If the method (still, it must be admitted, in its infancy) remains far from perfect, we submit this does not invalidate the basic assumption that the major legal systems must be brought into some sort of logical juxtaposition not for the sake of then grouping them into families, but for the sake of drawing practical conclusions in national reform, harmonisation attempts and, finally, international litigation. The term used earlier on – applied comparative law – captures, we think, this idea neatly.

## More specific conclusions

The preceding general observations, along with the contents of this book, merit the following more specific observations which are mentioned *summarily* under eight headings. We stress 'summarily' since we wish to emphasise that we are here raising these points for the sake of further research and consideration and not advancing them as incontrovertible conclusions.

### 'European' and 'American' law

We mention first the appreciable similarity in the level of awards between the three major European legal systems discussed in this book and also stress the apparent (and often very real) difference with American awards. This statement is, in our view, significant and in need of at least one major qualification. We start with the latter since it is relevant for much of what has been said thus far and will be repeated in this chapter about American law.

The caveat is born of the obvious difficulty already alluded to and associated with the term of 'convenience' we have used, namely, American law. In fact, there is no such thing as American law but a law of fifty states (or fifty-one if we include the federal jurisdiction). One is not being pedantic in reminding the readers of this well-known fact, for the differences in awards between various states (and within various counties of the same state) can be very significant indeed.[19] This divergence may be caused by the presence or absence of particular legal notions or institutions (e.g., no punitive damages in Louisiana law), different rules about the collateral source rule (emanating from statute or case law practice), and different (and highly) complex 'capping' statutes which can lay down highly varying caps for damage flowing from different types of tortious situations (e.g., medical malpractice, car accidents etc.). Statistical information about jury awards also reveals significant local variations which are not, necessarily, attributable to rules of the kind mentioned above but which can often be linked (tenuously?) to a variety of other, non-quantifiable (or even verifiable) factors such as local wealth, jury predilections, political affiliations. The list is both endless and intriguing. The European victim who is contemplating a legal action in the USA must bear these variations in mind. And the American lawyer who might be tempted to describe European awards as pitifully small should be aware of the fact that he must be explicit in what he is comparing.

The wider and, for lack of a better term, 'jurisprudential' observation is the one alluded to at the very beginning of this chapter, namely, that English law is increasingly diverging from American law[20] and converging

---

[19] A glimpse of this can be obtained by looking at Table 11 of 'Litigation-Mania in England, Germany and the United States: Are We So Very Different?' originally published in (1990) CLJ 233 and republished as ch. 20 in Basil Markesinis, *Foreign Law and Comparative Methodology* (Hart Publishing, 1997).

[20] Perhaps the reverse is just as true and American law is, itself, either abandoning original English practice (and case law) or, increasingly true nowadays, refusing even to consider it. An example of the first trend, particularly appropriate to this monograph, is found in the American Wrongful Death Statutes. Originally modelled on Lord Campbell's Act of 1845 (and the subsequent Fatal Accident Acts), the American statutes only compensated economic losses affecting the dependants of persons killed as a result of a tort. Progressively, however, the wording of these statutes was changed to allow *solatium* type claims to cater for (mainly) the death of young children who were not, at the time of their death, supporting parents or relatives (listed by the statutes as 'dependants in law'). We discuss this below along with the more modern tendency to call these claims for loss of 'companionship or consortium'.

with Continental European law. This not being a monograph about substantive law, it is not necessary to labour this point too much. Yet one cannot help but note that in a wide spectrum of subjects – defamation, privacy, patterns of federalism, employment law, protection against sexual discrimination – this estrangement seems to be taking place. If this thesis is arguable, it certainly gains further support by comparing American with European levels of damages.

Yet, it is the misfortune of lawyers – if few other professions – to see (or force themselves to see) 'the other side of the coin' and in this case this means that, once again, European lawyers must approach the issue of size of American awards. For allowances must be made for (a) the absence of social security coverage for medical necessities of all kinds; (b) a significant reduction of the award itself, in order to cover the costs (or combined costs) of litigation; and (c) the other background factors alluded to earlier on in this book. In this context, one must also mention the often ignored fact that the American awards that reach European audiences tend to be the original jury awards which (because of their size) attract considerable publicity. On the other hand, the fact that these awards are subsequently reduced because of settlements, remittiturs,[21] appeals and the like, rarely receive much attention,[22] even by the members of the (European) legal profession. All that one can say is that we Europeans are different from the Americans but, maybe, not that different when all these additional but important elements are factored into our calculations.

## Punitive damages

In terms of specifics, the single greatest difference between American law on the one hand and European law (including English law) is the prominence of the punitive element in American tort awards. Here, the danger lies largely on the American side, who can be tempted to believe that punitive awards are made in systems which theoretically at least

---

[21] In the USA, despite the constitutionally protected status of jury trial, a widespread practice exists which allows a trial judge the discretion to offer a claimant a smaller amount than that offered by an (excessive) jury award. Remittiturs have survived constitutional challenge, whereas the exact reverse – an additur, where the judge offers the defendant a larger amount to that awarded by the jury – has been condemned by the US Supreme Court as long ago as *Dimick* v. *Schiedt*, 293 U.S. 474 (1935).

[22] The famous 'Ford Pinto' case which in *Grimshaw* v. *Ford Motor Company*, 119 Cal. App. 3d 757, 174 Cal. Rptr. 348 (1981) led to one of the highest awards of those times – US $125 million – was remitted to US $3.5 million! As the late Professor John Fleming observed: 'The discrepancy by a factor of more than thirty illustrates the subjectivity of assessing these damages'. John Fleming, *The American Tort Process* (OUP, 1988), p. 136.

seem to sanction them in principle. This issue was hotly debated in the *Dow Corning* litigation, especially as far as Australia is concerned, where it was shown that such awards (though claimed) are very rarely made[23] in product liability cases.

The availability of punitive damages, combined with the contingent fee system, in our view makes (parts) of the American legal profession fairly aggressive in raising and pursuing such claims, arguably even in cases where they may not be truly meritorious. But the 'nuisance effect' that such claims can have on corporate defendants may well 'force' them to settle, thus augmenting the trend (or the image) of large awards.[24]

A growing volume of empirical studies in the USA can substantiate some of these observations while making others more questionable. But here we raise some of these points not simply in order to reinforce observations already made elsewhere, but also to lament the (relative) absence of such empirical studies in the European area. This absence of this different and we submit additional 'tool' may be particularly linked to the more 'dogmatic' study of the law in Continental European universities, though it is less easy to explain in Britain.

This difference is important not only if one compares and contrasts 'American' law on the one hand and 'European' law on the other but also if one is comparing and contrasting English law, German law and Italian law. Here the comparison is easy at a superficial level – England recognises the heading, the other countries do not – but more difficult at a more sophisticated level. For, first, one must decide to what extent the ever-changing dicta of English judges reflect a tendency to restrict or expand the availability of punitive damages. In addition, one must take into account the fact that European systems – German and Italian in particular (but also French) – conceal a punitive element under a different heading. So, if one disregards terminology for a moment, one can see that from the German perspective, the 'deterrent effect' which has been

---

[23] In fact only one case was found making such an award in a product liability setting.
[24] It was the view of many defence lawyers in England that legal aid served to fuel the same aggression. Certainly the absence of legal aid for personal injury cases and the advent of conditional fees have led to a downturn in the number of claims. Defendants are also becoming more aggressive in their approach to litigation. As Michael Spencer QC said on behalf of SmithKline Beecham in the MMR litigation: 'The days of commencing wholly speculative litigation in the hope of forcing defendants to pay off cases through a costs blackmail are, we say, over. The courts will be astute to ensure that only properly viable cases are brought and will be quick to strike down cases which are wholly speculative and brought without any evidentiary foundation': *Sayers v. SmithKline Beecham plc* [2002] EWHC 1280, 1st case management conference, 3 September 1999.

attributed to the '*Schmerzensgeld*' in the yellow-press cases (such as the famous 'Caroline of Monaco' cases) may well be understood as to imply an
element of 'punitive damages'. Moreover, the well-established '*Genugtu-
ungsfunktion*' of the '*Schmerzensgeld*', whether it is translated as satisfaction
or atonement, clearly also conceals a punitive component. Indeed, one of
the earliest cases on this topic, the case of the Professor of Law,[25] is replete
with words and ideas that can be taken to have punishment in mind. The
above observations, important though they are, must not mislead anyone
into thinking that such punitive or deterrent elements can be found in
German and Italian awards in the domain of personal injury. Here, the difference with the common law systems – especially the American common
law – is more marked.

## Variations in awards within national European systems

The regional variations in American awards mentioned above must be
more than simply noteworthy to a foreign litigant who is considering the
possibility of a legal action in the USA. But just as noteworthy and, in geographical terms, unjustified, is the regional variation of damage awards in
European systems such as the Italian.[26] The contrast here with Germany
and, even more so with Britain, is striking; and the degree of variation
is not, in our view, justified by looking at the undoubted difference of
wealth between North and South which, after all, can also be found in
other countries (including Britain). A glance at the tables reproduced in
the Appendix thus shows that these differences of levels do not follow
strictly the pattern: North (rich), South (poor).

The above observation does more than point out a point which directly
affects the level of awards – the primary concern of this book. Indeed, it
goes even further than giving an insight to law reform or, if that sounds
too 'highfaluting' a term, law change. For attempts under foot in Italy to
extend the *national*, medium award for *danno biologico* to instances of (permanent) invalidity exceeding 9 per cent reveal some further differences
between the systems. The idea that this could be fixed by delegated legislation, or simple ministerial decision, largely on the basis of a mathematical
calculation of the average amount of the regional variations, is surprising
to say the least. For in other systems one would envisage a prolonged process of hearings, lobbying and other such ways of trying to fix this crucial

---

[25] BGH 19 September 1961, BGHZ 35, 363 = NJW 1961, 2059; English translation in Basil
Markesinis and Hannes Unberath, *The German Law of Torts: A Comparative Treatise* (4th edn,
2002), p. 420 (henceforth referred to as *GLT*).

[26] And the French which, however, is not the subject of examination in this work.

amount, which insurers would like to see set at lower levels and claimants at higher ones. Prophesying the future is a hazardous activity; but we venture the thought that the chances of some Italian litigant challenging the statute (or the new tables) on the grounds that they are incompatible with articles 2 and 32 of the Italian Constitution (protection of health and personality) cannot be a fanciful possibility. This question of 'levels', by the way, must not be seen as raising issues of tort law or constitutional law. For, as we noted in passing in the Introduction, the question of damages and thus insurance costs is also one in which the government has a strong interest.

But the Italian experience on this point also underscores the point made earlier in the Introduction about local allegiances. For history, not covered in this book for reasons of space, shows how some local courts branched out in their own, individual evaluation of these amounts under the influence of writings for their local law school. Here, then, we not only have an instance of academic/judicial co-operation which is such a hallmark of Continental European law and so absent, until recently, from English law; we also have an excellent example of judicial deference to the academic side of the legal profession. The Genovese and Pisa schools thus deserve to be singled out for praise by us now as they were nearly a decade ago by the Corte Costituzionale.[27] This is mentioned not merely for its historical significance but also because of the impact this tradition has had in the writing of Italian law books. To put it differently, what was contributed in this volume by our Italian colleague is not simply an accurate account of Italian law but also an account recast for an Anglo-Saxon readership. If properly done, this presentation of local law does not betray its substance but merely transforms aspects of its appearance for the purposes of making it accessible to interested foreign observers. How well it was done in this book is not the real question. The question is: did it have to be done? On this question none of us has any doubt that the answer is in the affirmative. Those common lawyers who have happened to have glanced at Italian works on the subject will agree with us that without such adaptations, the presentation of Italian law to a non-Italian readership is extremely difficult, if not impossible.

*Easy access to justice as a prerequisite to obtaining compensation*

The American way of financing litigation largely through the contingency fee system has another effect on the different operation in practice

---

[27] 14 April 1995, no. 4255, 1955, Resp. civ.prev. 519 and note Ponzanelli.

of apparently similar tort law rules. Thus, all systems to a greater or lesser extent realise that modern tort law must take into account the fact that its rules are no longer the only ones that determine compensation for loss. The need to regulate the interrelationship between all these disparate rules of compensation is thus manifest in all of them; and if one were to rely solely on books (or even the majority of judicial decisions), one might easily be led to the conclusion that the systems reason in a very similar manner: the tort victim must be indemnified for his loss but he must not make a profit out of it. This should mean that 'cumulation of benefits' should be avoided wherever possible and, indeed, this is the case in Germany, Italy and, perhaps somewhat less rigidly, in English law.[28] But in the USA, once again, the position – in so far as there is a unified position – is different, since the 'system' there shows greater tolerance towards the possibility of cumulation of different benefits. To European lawyers, the different result may, at first blush, appear confusing since so many of the arguments invoked in this debate are perfectly familiar to them, as well. A simple glance at the leading American tort textbooks confirms this instantly. Yet, arguably, the different result is really justified (or becomes justifiable) by the fact that a substantial part of the award goes towards financing the costs of tort litigation and if this were to be removed from the plaintiff's award, he would not be made whole. Though this 'background' difference may thus seriously affect the operation of tort law in practice, it seems rarely to be openly acknowledged. There does, however, exist the occasional frank judicial admission which makes such an idea plausible and thereby underscores the need to study legal rules within their wider political and socio-legal context in which they operate.[29] Here, therefore, is another example of these 'background factors' which, in practice, transforms the operation of rules which, in the books, are the same in most countries.

---

[28] English law rules in relation to whether collateral benefits fall to be deducted from awards are too long and complicated to explain here. It is right to say, however, that they are not entirely logical and need to be looked at on a case by case basis.

[29] In *Helfend* v. *Southern California Rapid Transit District*, 2 Cal. 3d 1, 465 P.2d 61 (1970), the Supreme Court of California did just that. It thus argued that: 'Generally the jury is not informed that plaintiff's attorney will receive a large portion of the plaintiff's recovery in contingent fees or that personal injury damages are not taxable to the plaintiff and are normally deductible by the defendant. Hence [the plaintiff] rarely actually receives full compensation for his injuries as computed by the jury. The collateral source rule partially serves to compensate for the attorney's share and does not actually render 'double recovery' for the plaintiff'.

*Problems of comparison with non-pecuniary damages*

Another highly significant difference lies in the area of non-pecuniary damages sometimes referred to (rather incorrectly) as damages for pain and suffering or (rather vaguely) as '*dommage morale*'.

We touch upon this issue in the Conclusions not in order to repeat figures given in earlier chapters. Nor do we wish to stress that in the USA this heading can represent the largest[30] and most subjectively determined part of the award. This time the issue is raised in order to stress that such awards are often made in the USA in areas in which they would be unknown in Europe (including England). Additionally, these awards also raise another problem. For not only do they cover items which are not recognised by European law; they also often result in overcompensation of the parents of the deceased foetus or child, who end up as the ultimate beneficiaries of these amounts. It will be clear from the preceding sentence that we are referring to claims for compensation for the death of children and also for claims for foetal injuries which often (but not always) are linked to claims for loss of consortium or companionship. This, again, is an area where English law should be bracketed with Continental European law rather than its American relation.

Deaths of young children or infants can rarely generate in European (including English) law substantial awards under Fatal Accidents Act legislation. This is clearly because none of the systems under comparison is willing to recognise such claims or, if they do, they do little more than provide very modest or conventional sums. If the 'bereavement' or 'loss of companionship' claims receive such short shrift, the possible claim for lost dependency fares even worse. We submit rightly so, not only because it is speculative, particularly where the victim who was killed was very young, but also because such claims, if they were ever to be recognised, should also entail an appropriate reduction for expenses 'saved' by the parent/claimant. A parent should thus not be allowed to make a claim for a possible future dependency *and* not have it adjusted to take into account the fact that, but for the child's death, he would have had to incur (substantial) expenses to maintain, bring up and educate the child which, one day, was to become its supporter.

---

[30] Like all general statements, however, this must be qualified in at least one sense, namely, that in Germany, as well, the largest amount of money – DM1.7 billion – was, according to figures of insurance payments in the context of traffic accidents for the year 1999, reserved for compensating pain and suffering. This must be contrasted with DM300 million being paid for medical treatment. For further details see Hein Kötz and Gerhard Wagner, *Deliktsrecht* (9th edn, 2001), no. 511.

The American courts which do allow such claims are conceptually at any rate on safer grounds when they admit that these are claims for loss of companionship rather than claims for loss of what is often a highly speculative loss of consortium or companionship. Or, in pursuing this line of reasoning, they are making up for a deliberate omission from the original English Fatal Accident Acts which, as already stated, served as models to the late nineteenth century American legislation of all claims for bereavement or *solatium*. Notwithstanding this, such awards can still be very substantial;[31] and coupled with the contingent fee system, enticing enough to give rise to litigation which can fall little short of gold-digging.

Claims arising from foetal injuries (or pre-conception injuries, typically to the mother) are, in our view, even more worrisome, especially in those American jurisdictions which allow them *even* where there is no live birth of the foetus.[32]

The idea that damages can 'compensate' the parents for having being deprived of the opportunity of having the child (and enjoying its company)

---

[31] Some American courts have extended this attempt to do 'justice' to borderline situations. Thus, see *Haumersen* v. *Ford Motor Company*, 257 N.W.2d 7 (Iowa 1977) awarding US $100,000 for the loss of a seven-year-old child 'with a talent as a cartoonist'. A handful of cases, seem, literally, to have gone overboard. See *Andrews* v. *Reynolds Memorial Hospital, Inc.*, 499 S.E.2d 846 (W.Va. 1997) where the court awarded US $1.75 million for loss of future earnings attributable to the death of a one-day-old baby! Note, however, that not all courts have been willing to depart from the original model of the Fatal Accident Acts. Thus, see, *Prather* v. *Lockwood*, 19 Ill.App.3d 146; 310 N.E.2d 815 (1974).

[32] On the 'born alive' requirement, the American courts seem divided. Most take the view that live birth is not necessary for a wrongful death action. Thus *Volk* v. *Baldazo*, 103 Idaho 570, 651 P.2d 11 (1982); *Dunn* v. *Rose Way, Inc.*, 333 N.W.2d 830 (Iowa 1983); *Summerfield* v. *Superior Court*, 144 Ariz. 467, 698 P.2d 712 (1985); *Moen* v. *Hanson*, 85 Wn.2d 597, 537 P. 2d 266 (Wash. 1975). Others, probably under the influence of *Roe* v. *Wade*, 410 U.S. 113, 93 S. Ct. 705 (1973), have held that live birth is a prerequisite of recovery. Thus, see, *State of Missouri ex rel. Hardin* v. Sanders, 538 S.W.2d 336 (1976); *Justus* v. *Atchison*, 19 Cal. 3d 564, 565 P.2d 122 (1977); *Chatelain* v. *Kelley*, 322 Ark. 517, 910 S.W.2d 215 (1995). A number of recent decisions have adopted this position, often reaching this result on the ground that a stillborn foetus is not a 'person' under applicable wrongful death legislation. Thus *Witty* v. *American General Capital Distributors, Inc.*, 727 S.W.2d 503 (Tex. 1987); *Milton* v. *Cary Medical Center*, 538 A.2d 252 (Me. 1988); *Giardina* v. *Bennett*, 111 N.J. 412; 545 A.2d 139 (1988), criticised in (1989) 21 *Rutgers LJ* 227. A final variation to this kaleidoscope of differing solutions can be found in cases that refuse wrongful death actions where foetuses are born dead, but allow the mother to recover for her mental anguish. Thus, see, *Tanner* v. *Hartog*, 696 So. 2d 705 (Fla. 1997); *Giardina* v. *Bennett*, 545 A. 2d 139 (1988); *Krishnan* v. *Sepulveda*, 916 S.W.2d 478 (Tex. 1995). Though these last cases do not come anywhere near representing the majority of jurisdictions, they seem to have much to commend them since, at least, they seem to have grasped the nettle. Simply put, this is that compensating parents under wrongful statute clauses seems inappropriate given that these enactments were always intended to compensate the loss of a provable pecuniary advantage i.e., the lost dependency.

is debatable or, at the very least, the idea of the damages being anything more than a small conventional figure, seems to be unconvincing. The outcome – compensation – becomes even less convincing if we realise that these amounts can, in effect, duplicate the parents own claims for pain and suffering. Yet, this risk is not, apparently, accounted for when determining the award. The fact that little if any judicial guidance seems to be given on this point might also suggest that the augmented size of the award may reflect American realities i.e., that part of it will not end up in the pocket of the parents but of their lawyers. But though there is some evidence to suggest that this kind of 'concealed' calculation takes place in other instances, e.g., the collateral source rule, we found none to support our supposition in those cases which we were able to examine.

The objections against such awards reach a climax when one realises that the viability at the time of the injury (rather than the live birth requirement) can result in the never-born-alive foetus claiming money (through whom? for what?) under one of the Survival Statutes (the American equivalents of the English Law Reform Act 1934). On this possibility we feel no further comment is called for.

Though these illustrations come from the domain of fatal accident litigation, which was not included in the purview of this monograph, they are mentioned because they tie in well with the American claims for pain and suffering and the rather open-ended nature of awards made under this heading. Such tendencies are not to be found in Continental European law – indeed, they are also absent from English law. In this sense, they confirm once again our perception of the English position as being closer philosophically – as well as de lega lata – to that of Continental Europe than to the USA.

The above discussion, however, also shows that the courts may be using this amorphous heading of non-pecuniary damages to perform functions other than compensation. The occasionally very substantial damages awarded by American courts under headings such as loss of companionship may thus owe their origins to the fact that in fatal accident claims parents had no lost dependency that they could plausibly claim from the tortfeasor for the death of their infant child. The feeling that such 'injustice' could not be left without a remedy may lie behind some of the most recent developments described briefly above.

Though European law has nothing comparable to show in the kind of cases discussed above, European judges may also be taking advantage of the amorphous nature of the heading in order to achieve other aims. The discussions in Italian law about danno morale, its availability when no crime was committed, and its extent, likewise seem to conceal judicial preoccupation with Italian factors such as variation of awards depending on the social status of the victim. The frequent reference in Italian academic and judicial literature that the amount of compensation is to be left to the fair or equitable discretion of the judge only helps to facilitate flexibility but, it could be argued, affects the transparency of the judicial process. Still, points such as these can only be put tentatively for the sake of further discussion and nothing more.

*Danno morale* as well as *danno biologico* (and, indeed, the German equivalent of '*Schmerzensgeld*') may also conceal the award of a sum of money which in the common law might appear under a distinct heading. All of which goes to show that an attempt to impose upon other legal systems the taxonomy known to the common law can work up to a point but no further.

### Specificity about the size of awards

Closer to the contents of this book is another observation. It concerns the highly developed and systematic nature of the German law of damages. Overall we find this feature less obvious in Italian law, with the result that one must often admit the considerable difficulty in finding reliable sources of damages awards. On the issue of quantum of damages, in our experience, the position in French law may even be more problematic; but we do no more than touch on this point since French law was not included in the purview of this study.[33]

The English position calls for a different comment. The starting point must be the fact that everything that pertained to damages was within the province of juries. Not surprisingly, therefore, even a cursory glance at books of all kinds of forty or more years ago would reveal paucity – relative at any rate compared to the German scene – of principles, rules and guidelines on all of the issues discussed in this book. Yet the scene has radically changed since the 'revolution' of the mid-1960s mentioned in the Introduction of this book and the entrusting of this topic in the hands of trained judges.

This observation has more than a historical significance. For it shows that some systems have spent more time in thinking about what should be compensated and how it should be classified (in law books) or explained to litigants and practitioners. From a comparative (and transnational

---

[33] One of the most recent and thorough surveys on this elusive topic can be found in Duncan Fairgrieve, *State Liability in Tort* (2003), esp. p. 218 ff.

litigation) point of view the consequence of this difference is that the headings of damages are not always identical. Care must thus be taken when comparing notions which sound similar or, conversely, where they do not sound identical but nonetheless may conceal in them headings of damage which in other systems might be dealt with independently. At the risk of some (minor) repetition we thus note that these distinctions and subdivisions are not always made clear in the German books on the subject; yet they are in the judges' minds when fixing the level of compensation for *Schmerzensgeld* as is seen from the actual decisions and books which contain summaries of awards. Yet, it is in a certain respect narrower than some of its common law counterparts. For an award of *Schmerzensgeld* presupposes that the victim suffered personal injury. In short, the object of an award of *Schmerzensgeld* is to compensate for all kinds of non-material harm suffered as a consequence of personal injury.

The difficulty alluded to in the previous section and connected to the fact that the compensable heading of damage are not identical or coterminous is complicated by the fact that often a court may deal with a heading of damage not by compensating it directly but by augmenting some other recognisable heading. There are many reasons why this may happen; but the way this is brought about may conceal the fact that compensation for a heading (a) has taken place or may, alternatively, (b) give the impression that it has been undercompensated. For transnational litigation purposes this practice has its dangers in so far as it may lead the uninitiated to assume that two systems compensate a particular type of injury in a very different way. An illustration from German law can help make this point.

In a decision delivered on 3 December 1974,[34] the Federal Supreme Court had, inter alia, to decide what compensation if any were to be given to a woman who had suffered a facial scar. The claim included the cost of remedial operation (estimated at that time at DM2,590) to remove a 2.5cm scar next to the claimant's right ear. At the same time, in some extreme cases there may be reasons for rejecting claims for cost of medical treatment for personal injury. As already stated, the final award depends upon the court's appreciation of the reasonableness of the request. While re-affirming the general view that purely cosmetic surgery could be recovered as part of the 'restoration' owed by the defendant under § 249 BGB, the court also stated that the starting point was the ascertainment of the reasonableness of the request. The Federal Court stressed that

---

[34] BGHZ 63, 295. But see OLG München 30 November 1984, VersR 1985, 868 (scar on the face of a beautician) (see p. 70).

reasonableness depends on the circumstances of each case. Accordingly, a balancing operation had to be undertaken. This included the severity of the injury, the scale of the claimed cost and the motives of the plaintiff. The Federal Court accepted the Court of Appeal's finding that awarding compensation would be unreasonable in the present case. It *seems*[35] that this was because the scar was regarded as insignificant and, in any event, hardly visible and likely to disappear over time. Yet, the final result was not as harsh as it may appear at first sight since the court pointed out that the plaintiff was awarded a correspondingly higher amount of money under the heading of damages for pain and suffering. The decision, the correctness of which has never been doubted, would thus suggest that where the cost of reinstatement to the status quo ante appears unreasonable, the plaintiff may obtain some other monetary compensation, e.g., in the form of an increased award of damages for pain and suffering.

## Nature and wealth of the defendant as a determinant of the size of the award

To an English and Italian lawyer this heading is almost meaningless; but to American tort claimants this can be a very relevant factor. For there is ample statistical evidence to show that tort litigation, heard in the states before juries, can produce differing levels of awards depending upon whether the defendant is an individual defendant, a government entity or a corporate defendant. In one of his most original books,[36] the late Professor John Fleming of the University of Berkeley at California demonstrated this to European readers in a vivid manner; and many (less well-known but fascinating) empirical studies of the Rand Corporation have supplied ample, additional and intriguing evidence about this phenomenon.[37]

We mention this 'unusual feature' not because we wish, again, to diverge into American law but because in this instance one finds a 'distant relative' in the German provision of § 829 BGB. This, it will be remembered, allows the judge in some cases to take into account the financial

---

[35] We stress 'it seems' for the facts are not fully and clearly stated – something which marks out German from Anglo-American cases which have to consider facts in detail if they are to perform the distinguishing function which is so central to the common law process of deciding cases.

[36] *The American Tort Process* (OUP, 1988), p. 111 ff.

[37] Chin and Paterson, *Deep Pockets, Empty Pockets: Who Wins in Cook County Jury Trials* (Rand Corp., 1985); Hensler, Vaiana, Kakalik and Peterson, *Trends in Tort Litigation: The Story Behind the Statistics* (Rand Corp., 1987).

means of the defendant[38] (including the availability of insurance) and adjust accordingly the amount of compensation. The desirability of such an option, especially *in the context of personal injury litigation*, may strike many as dubious; and we put the point in that way in order to lead up to our last observation.

## Proposals for reform?

We approach this subheading first from the point of view of a narrow but important topic – that of costs and method of payment of the award – and then from the wider angle of European law reform.

Litigation costs and how the award should be paid to the successful claimant are topics which are currently under review in English law. The reader will have noticed that we did not discuss them beyond what was strictly speaking necessary for our stated aims. But these are topics that could spiral out of control and provide a monograph of their own. Yet, one cannot – and should not – allow the opportunity to be missed and fail to signpost two points. First, to our knowledge there is no similar debate currently taking place in the two other systems discussed in this book. This does not mean that the topic is not important; but it does mean that non-English lawyers reading this book may well wish to glance at these English debates and see what the issues currently occupying their English counterparts are. Secondly, one must note the growing dissatisfaction with the lump sum method of payment of awards and the growing interest in the annuity system. Without going into the drawbacks of this alternative – and there are some – we note, again, the fact that they are not used as often as one might have thought in the two systems (German and Italian) which already have them.

So much, then, for the narrower topic; what about the wider discussion of reform?

While the information contained in this monograph and, perhaps, some of its ideas, may prove of some interest to law reformers, this book was not written with them in mind. It thus contains no express formulations on this subject. For a variety of reasons we refrained from even becoming involved in this task despite the fact that it is quite *en vogue* these days on the European Continent. Here are some.

---

[38] It is disputed, however, whether the *poverty* of the defendant should set a barrier to claims which otherwise would be successful (*Sozialstaatsprinzip*; see MünchKomm-BGB, vor §§ 823 ff BGB no. 77). It is different at the 'procedural level' where rules regulating execution of judgments preserve certain minimum assets of impecunious defendants in order to allow them to survive financially. This, of course, is true of all systems.

First, as the reader of our Preface will recall, this was never one of our stated aims. Nor could it be, given that this study focused on three countries only and, for a variety of technical (not doctrinal or philosophical) reasons, left out many others, including the very important French legal system. Proposals of the kind we have submitted can only be credibly formulated by looking at all the legal systems concerned though, contrary to what might be termed the 'politically correct' view, we do not believe that all of them deserve the same degree of scrutiny.

Secondly, we are aware of course of the fact that many jurists from a number of European countries are clamouring for unification or harmonisation. These ambitions range from the entire domain usually covered by civil codes to the matter here in hand. Two of the countries whose lawyers seem to be in the forefront of this movement – Germany and Italy – are represented in this survey, while the sceptics are headed by England (and the Netherlands, whose law is not included in this study). Yet, in writing this small monograph we experienced at first hand the difficulties of even presenting the three systems in a reasonably coherent and logical juxtaposition and also noted in various parts of this book how awards can be made under different guises, how they can differ, in some cases substantially, and how their real value is actually determined only by taking additional factors into account, such as, e.g., the cost of living and earning levels in each country in question. Moreover, we noted how in Italy the measure of awards, influencing as it does insurance payments and thus insurance premiums, has attracted the attention of the government. Additionally, we also noted in various parts of the book the unusual degree of variation of awards, even for *danno biologico*. If that is the picture that emerges from one country alone, how can one *realistically* talk – *at this stage of the process of European integration* – of a unification movement with a realistic chance of success? For a unification attempt that would try to push awards[39] up towards the highest currently available level in Europe would be costly, just as any attempt to move them downwards towards the lowest figures would be unacceptable to those countries (and their citizens) who would be asked to give up existing rights. A compromise in the middle would, we suspect, leave everyone unhappy while lacking any rational justification. There is a time for everything; and, at present, we suggest that for

---

[39] We are, of course, talking here about awards for non-pecuniary losses, for (a) these are the ones which, logically it could be argued, should be the same across Europe and (b) are less income/earnings related than the pecuniary losses. In our view, unification or harmonisation attempts for this heading of damages are even further away.

those who believe in Europe the first priority is to streamline the European Constitution, more threatened than ever by the enlargement of the Union.

The above should not be taken to suggest that the differences between the European legal systems – certainly the ones we have discussed in this book – overshadow their similarities. On the contrary, we hope we have shown that the similarities are notable and cover both basic general principles and technical quantification rules.

Thus, on the first front we note *indicatively* that all three of our systems accept compensation as the prime aim of the law of torts; make[40] the cardinal distinction between pecuniary and non-pecuniary damages;[41] distinguish, in principle, between (what English law calls) psychiatric injury and mere mental pain or grief (and treat the former more sympathetically than the latter); accept the position that the defendant's characteristics and (on the whole) his financial resources should not affect the measure of the award; treat as unacceptable the *a priori* capping of awards for negligently inflicted harm; and accept the heritability of pecuniary and non-pecuniary loss damages. Many important, practical rules flow from these commonly accepted wide principles, so the coincidence of views is of great significance.

Similarities of great import can also be found at the level of technical rules concerning indemnification for tortiously inflicted harm. Thus, to mention but a few, we note that our systems take the same sympathetic view towards non-sentient victims (even though strict logic might require no compensation); there is a growing convergence in practice on the award of damages for bereavement (where English law made a move towards the Continental solution of awarding damages for bereavement, but Continental systems, on the whole, award small amounts[42] under this heading); all our systems acknowledge that non-pecuniary damages are,

---

[40] Germany, as stated, providing a limited exception for damages which aim to provide satisfaction rather than compensation.

[41] Spain seems to depart from this (important) rule, at any rate in the area of traffic accidents which generate the bulk of tort litigation.

[42] France is not included in the scope of this book but one notes with interest that French law, most generous in its definition of dependants liable to obtain compensation for the death of a third person, makes awards which on average are almost indistinguishable in size from the statutory amount given in English law. We have stressed, in this book and elsewhere, the importance of qualifying the generosity of French substantive law by reference to the low levels of awards made in some types of claims. On the whole, this is true of *individual* awards for *dommage morale*. On the other hand, it is likely – but to our knowledge not yet demonstrated by any survey – that the *total* amount of these awards may be considerable.

essentially, arbitrary in nature, lacking the degree of objectivity one finds in the case of compensation of pecuniary losses; and finally, and surprisingly perhaps, accept fairly similar awards for the most serious kind of injury – quadriplegia.[43] Continuing such a list would be tantamount to summarising in a crass and unqualified way the preceding chapters of this book, though we do refer the reader to a table produced by Dr Fairgrieve[44] which gives levels of damages in England and France for a variety of forms of impairment ranging from the most serious, persistent vegetative state, to amputation of two legs, one leg, total loss of hearing in one ear, total loss of one eye, down to a serious injury to a thumb. This table shows how remarkably similar the awards made in these two systems can be; indeed, the French awards may, in reality, be even higher given the lower cost of living in France than in England.

However, our last observation does need to be elaborated somewhat since it prompts thoughts of its own.

It is, we believe, correct to assert that the awards made for quadriplegia are amazingly similar in the three systems we have discussed in this book,[45] *especially if one tries to factor in the appropriate adjustments for cost of living, earnings and the like.* But this, after all, is one type of permanent injury; and it says little about other (lesser) types of permanent invalidity, not to mention transient forms of injury which represent a considerable proportion of the total number of tort claims. Yet, the figure given for quadriplegia is significant for three reasons. The conclusions of a book are no place to solve these complex issues; but we raise them as being all suitable topics for further comparative study.

First, the amount given for quadriplegia is the top amount and helps set a benchmark for all, lesser, forms of permanent injury. Yet, as we move down the scale, we note that some European systems (e.g., the Italian) do not continue this de facto parallel policy and thus do not compensate the lesser forms of permanent incapacity in an entirely comparable manner. Total blindness, for instance, receives a lesser amount in England than in Italy (though in France, it seems, the parallel approach prevails). Though the difference between English and Italian law is not huge, the reasoning process behind the size may be important in so far as it may suggest not a different 'valuation' but a difference in legal methodology. Thus, in Italy,

---

[43] This is broadly speaking true of English, French, German and Italian law but not so for other (significantly less generous) systems such as the Dutch and the Austrian.

[44] See n. 33 above at p. 222.

[45] For present purposes, and for the reasons given earlier in this chapter, we include France in this statement.

blindness is treated by the tables as tantamount to a 95 per cent incapacity and will thus produce a compensation figure that comes close to the quadriplegia amount. In England, by contrast, where there is no recourse to tables of incapacity but a search for judicial precedents and guidelines, the amount seems to be set at a lower level. Though in both systems there is judicial discretion to correct these 'pre-existing' determinations, the fact of the matter is that the one system approaches compensation from the point of view of how the injury affects the claimant's working ability (in which case the Italian approach may be more commendable) whereas the other approaches the question in a more holistic manner, relying on the guiding value of earlier precedents.

Secondly, most systems need to give more thought to the question of the overcompensation or undercompensation that may result from one-off awards. This is a hugely complex topic which in England recently attracted the attention of the Master of the Rolls.[46] Though the problem need not be so acute in systems which opt for annuities or rents, we have seen that both the German and, even more so the Italian, systems do not always make extensive use of this option which is theoretically available to them. It is at this stage that one must also mention the mechanism of structured settlements and ask the question – one can do no more here – whether other systems would not be well-advised to study more carefully this device.

The third and final issue we raise returns our concluding thoughts to the unification or harmonisation debate. Might it thus not be more pragmatic, realistic and, indeed, necessary for immediate practical needs if this initially took the form of trying to discover and understand comparable headings of compensation? For one of the difficulties experienced in this book and, we submit, in international litigation, is to discover what is compensated and where a particular heading may be 'hidden' if it is obviously missing from a particular system's list of reparable headings of damage. Such an approach would also be truer to the purpose of comparative studies. For comparative methodology is as much the art of overcoming the obscurity generated by packaging as it is of discovering a presentation method which makes a foreign idea or concept recognisable and thus welcome to other lawyers. This modest study of the law of damages of three major legal systems of the world shows that more work still has to be done both on the substance and the art of presentation of the law of compensation for personal injury.

---

[46] Lord Phillips (unpublished) lecture.

# Appendix
# Comparative tables on the evaluation of physical injury (IP) for micro-permanent injuries

*April 2000 (and subsequent updating)*

Arranged in decreasing order in relation to the compensation considered on the basis of the indicative tables applied by the courts of the chief towns of Italian regions.

**PERMANENT INVALIDITY 2%**
**Typology of injury according to current forensic medical doctrine:**
Anatomic loss of the left hand ring finger ungual phalange
Outcome of partial meniscectomy performed in arthroscopy
Scars due to previous laparotomy for every 10 cm of length
Outcome of fracture of the right or left foot II, III, IV metatarsus

| Age | 20 | 40 | 60 |
|---|---|---|---|
| Bologna | 7.544.000 | 6.420.000 | 4.045.000 |
| Bari | 7.544.000 | 6.420.000 | 4.045.000 |
| Triveneto | 5.412.000 | 4.888.000 | 4.138.000 |
| Genova | 5.648.000 | 4.806.000 | 3.029.000 |
| Cagliari | 4.600.000 | 4.180.000 | 3.100.000 |
| **Medium average of the courts** | **3.937.000** | **3.437.000** | **2.613.000** |
| Ancona | 3.600.000 | 3.300.000 | 3.000.000 |
| Torino | 3.200.000 | 3.000.000 | 2.800.000 |
| Aosta | 3.765.000 | 3.204.000 | 2.019.000 |
| Milano | 3.077.000 | 2.737.000 | 2.297.000 |
| Napoli | 3.077.000 | 2.737.000 | 2.297.000 |
| Potenza | 3.077.000 | 2.737.000 | 2.297.000 |
| Perugia | 2.769.000 | 2.463.000 | 2.157.000 |
| **Statute 5.3.2001, n. 57** | **2.508.000** | **2.224.000** | **1.980.000** |
| Firenze | 2.800.000 | 2.240.000 | 1.680.000 |
| Palermo | 2.461.000 | 2.190.000 | 1.918.000 |
| Roma | 2.210.000 | 1.841.000 | 1.350.000 |
| Reggio. C. | 2.210.000 | 1.841.000 | 1.350.000 |

**PERMANENT INVALIDITY 5%**
Typology of injury according to the current forensic medical doctrine:
Loss of olfaction
Loss of taste
Anatomic loss of the two phalanges of the right ring finger
Complete monolaterar nasal stenosis
Articular relaxation of the knee due to non surgically treated ligamental lesions
Outcome of a kneecap breaking without anatomic losses
Outcome of the I metatarsus of the left or right foot fracture

| Age | 20 | 40 | 60 |
|---|---|---|---|
| Bologna | 23.536.000 | 20.027.000 | 12.620.000 |
| Genova | 20.536.000 | 20.027.000 | 12.620.000 |
| Bari | 18.862.000 | 16.050.000 | 10.114.000 |
| Triveneto | 13.875.000 | 12.530.000 | 10.615.000 |
| Aosta | 13.203.000 | 11.235.000 | 7.079.000 |
| Cagliari | 11.500.000 | 10.500.000 | 8.500.000 |
| Medium average of the courts | 12.090.000 | 10.463.000 | 7.849.000 |
| Palermo | 11.500.000 | 9.500.000 | 8.000.000 |
| Ancona | 9.000.000 | 8.250.000 | 7.250.000 |
| Milano | 9.050.000 | 8.050.000 | 7.050.000 |
| Napoli | 9.050.000 | 8.050.000 | 7.050.000 |
| Potenza | 9.050.000 | 8.050.000 | 7.050.000 |
| Torino | 9.080.000 | 8.142.000 | 6.692.000 |
| Statute 5.3.2001, n. 57 | 8.550.000 | 7.650.000 | 6.750.000 |
| Perugia | 8.145.000 | 7.245.000 | 6.345.000 |
| Firenze | 9.000.000 | 7.200.000 | 5.400.000 |
| Roma | 7.533.000 | 6.278.000 | 4.604.000 |
| Reggio. C. | 7.533.000 | 6.278.000 | 4.604.000 |

PERMANENT INVALIDITY 9%
**Typology of injury according to the current forensic medical doctrine:**
Splenectomy (around 9%)
Post traumatic scapulohumeral periarthritis with muscular strength reduction
and slight limitation of the upper limb movements (around 9%)
Ankylosis of the radius-carpus articulation (wrist) in rectilinear extension with
movements of free prono-supination (around 9%)
Tight pseudarthrosis of the right radius (around 9%)
Outcome in exuberant callus of the combined shinbone-peroneal fracture with
slight deflection of the longitudinal axis and functional limitation, between 1/3
and 1/4, of the ankle movements (around 9%)
Occasional but documented fits of convulsions with epileptic
electroencephalographic changes in patient suitable for long-term anti-epilepsy
therapy (around 9%)

| Age | 20 | 40 | 60 |
|---|---|---|---|
| Bologna | 42.365.000 | 36.049.000 | 22.717.000 |
| Genova | 42.365.000 | 36.049.000 | 22.717.000 |
| Bari | 33.951.000 | 28.890.000 | 18.205.000 |
| Triveneto | 27.783.000 | 24.777.000 | 21.870.000 |
| **Medium average of the courts** | **25.958.000** | **22.293.000** | **16.991.000** |
| Aosta | 27.160.000 | 23.112.000 | 14.564.000 |
| **Statute 5.3.2001, n. 57** | **23.598.000** | **21.114.000** | **18.630.000** |
| Cagliari | 25.047.000 | 20.691.000 | 16.879.000 |
| Ancona | 22.806.000 | 20.286.000 | 17.776.000 |
| Milano | 22.806.000 | 20.286.000 | 17.776.000 |
| Napoli | 22.806.000 | 20.286.000 | 17.776.000 |
| Potenza | 22.806.000 | 20.286.000 | 17.776.000 |
| Torino | 21.334.000 | 19.138.000 | 15.723.000 |
| Perugia | 20.525.000 | 18.257.000 | 15.989.000 |
| Palermo | 20.700.000 | 17.100.000 | 14.400.000 |
| Firenze | 21.600.000 | 17.280.000 | 12.960.000 |
| Roma | 20.791.000 | 17.326.000 | 12.706.000 |
| Reggio. C. | 20.791.000 | 17.326.000 | 12.706.000 |

(Elaboration by Luigi Cipriano)

# Index

# CAMBRIDGE STUDIES IN INTERNATIONAL AND COMPARATIVE LAW

*Books in the series*

*Compensation for Personal Injury in English, German and Italian Law*
*A Comparative Outline*
Basil Markesinis, Michael Coester, Guido Alpa, Augustus Ullstein

*Dispute Settlement in the UN Convention on the Law of the Sea*
Natalie Klein

*The International Protection of Internally Displaced Persons*
Catherine Phuong

*Colonialism, Sovereignty and the Making of International Law*
Antony Anghie

*Necessity, Proportionality and the Use of Force by States*
Judith Gardam

*International Legal Argument in the Permanent Court of International Justice*
*The Rise of the International Judiciary*
Ole Spiermann

*Great Powers and Outlaw States*
*Unequal Sovereigns in the International Legal Order*
Gerry Simpson

*Local Remedies in International Law*
C. F. Amerasinghe

*Reading Humanitarian Intervention*
*Human Rights and the Use of Force in International Law*
Anne Orford

*Conflict of Norms in Public International Law*
*How WTO Law Relates to Other Rules of Law*
Joost Pauwelyn

*The Search for Good Governance in Africa*
*Making Constitutions in the States of the Commonwealth*
Peter Slinn and John Hatchard

*Transboundary Damage in International Law*
Hanqin Xue

*European Criminal Procedures*
Edited by Mireille Delmas-Marty and John Spencer

*The Accountability of Armed Opposition Groups in International Law*
Liesbeth Zegveld

*Sharing Transboundary Resources*
*International Law and Optimal Resource Use*
Eyal Benvenisti

236

*International Human Rights and Humanitarian Law*
René Provost

*Remedies Against International Organisations*
*Basic Issues*
Karel Wellens

*Diversity and Self-Determination in International Law*
Karen Knop

*The Law of Internal Armed Conflict*
Lindsay Moir

*International Commercial Arbitration and African States*
Amazu A. Asouzu

*The Enforceability of Promises in European Contract Law*
James Gordley

*International Law in Antiquity*
David J. Bederman

*Money-Laundering*
Guy Stessens

*Good Faith in European Contract Law*
Reinhard Zimmerman and Simon Whittaker

*On Civil Procedure*
J. A. Jolowicz

*Trusts*
*A Comparative Study*
Maurizio Lupoi

*The Right to Property in Commonwealth Constitutions*
Tom Allen

*International Organizations Before National Courts*
August Reinisch

*The Changing International Law of High Seas Fisheries*
Francisco Orrego Vicua

*Trade and the Environment*
Damien Geradin

*Unjust Enrichment*
Hanoch Dagan

*Religious Liberty and International Law in Europe*
Malcolm D. Evans

*Ethics and Authority in International Law*
Alfred P. Rubin